COOKING
from
THE CUPBOARD

COOKING
from
THE CUPBOARD

Meals in Minutes
from Your Pantry

JEANNE JONES

RODALE

Printed in the United States of America
Rodale Inc. makes every effort to use acid-free ∞, recycled paper ♻.

Interior photographs by Mitch Mandel
Photograph (dishes on shelf) © Photodisc/Getty
Photographs © Rodale Inc.

Book design by Carol Angstadt
Front cover recipe (Beef and Vegetable Stew) page 178

Library of Congress Cataloging-in-Publication Data

Jones, Jeanne.
    Cooking from the cupboard : meals in minutes from your pantry / Jeanne Jones.
        p.   cm.
    Includes index.
    ISBN 1–57954–816–4   hardcover
    1. Quick and easy cookery.   I. Title.
TX833.5.J6597   2004
641.5'55—dc21   2003009705

2 4 6 8 10 9 7 5 3 1   hardcover

RODALE

WE INSPIRE AND ENABLE PEOPLE TO IMPROVE
THEIR LIVES AND THE WORLD AROUND THEM

FOR MORE OF OUR PRODUCTS

WWW.RODALESTORE.COM
(800) 848-4735

Notice

This book is intended as a reference volume only, not as a medical manual. The information given here is designed to help you make informed decisions about your diet and health. It is not intended as a substitute for any treatment that may have been prescribed by your doctor. Keep in mind that nutritional needs vary from person to person, depending upon age, sex, health status, and total diet. If you suspect that you have a medical problem, we urge you to seek competent medical help.

Mention of specific companies, organizations, or authorities in this book does not imply endorsement by the publisher, nor does mention of specific companies, organizations, or authorities imply that they endorse this book.

Internet addresses and telephone numbers given in this book were accurate at the time it went to press.

To Vicky Holly, in deep appreciation
for all of the time and talent
you have contributed
to this book.

CONTENTS

ACKNOWLEDGMENTS

In grateful appreciation to all of the people who helped make this book possible:

Carol Angstadt
Thomas Beek
Laurie Block
Donald Breitenberg
Anne Egan
Kathy Everleth
Donna DeGutis
Kathryn Fishback
Jennifer Giandomenico
Margret McBride, my agent
Connie Mneinme
Eric Nutt, Jr.
Jennifer Reich
Jean Rogers
Renee Vincent

INTRODUCTION

Some years ago, I wrote a pantry cookbook, and it was very popular. My objective was to create tasty, low-fat recipes that could be prepared entirely from items that keep for a long time and are easy to have on hand. It was perfect for camping and boating trips as well as a time-saver for busy days. And it provided real stress relief when unexpected guests arrived for dinner.

Today, more than ever, the idea has great appeal. We've become even busier, despite the wealth of laborsaving devices around us. And years of newscasts have made us mindful of snow storms, hurricanes, earthquakes, and other events that can impede quick trips to the store.

With even more healthy choices now abundant in pantry products, I felt it was time for a new take on the subject. The fat-free and low-fat mayonnaise, ice cream, sour cream, chips, soups, and more in supermarkets today are a vast improvement over what was available even a few years ago. Water-packed tuna and chicken outsell their oil-packed counterparts. Fruits packed in water and juice maintain their fresh taste. And thanks to current labeling laws, we really know what is inside the can, bottle, or box we are buying.

Using these products, I focused on maximizing flavor and simplicity, with an eye toward convenience and economy rather than showmanship. I was happy with the results, but I wanted to make sure you would be, too.

To do the final testing on the recipes in this book, my husband and I packed all of the necessary pantry products and went out on a houseboat on Lake Mojave for 10 days. Out on the lake, what we didn't have we couldn't get, making it an ideal testing site for this kind of menu planning. I am happy to report that we were both amazed and delighted by the quality and variety of our meals.

When we returned home, I started serving some of my new pantry menus for dinner parties, purposely not telling my guests that they were dining on dishes prepared out of cans, bottles, and sealed boxes. Our guests not only raved about the food but almost always asked for the recipes.

A few words about the nutritional information provided with the recipes: It is based on software highly regarded by nutritionists and dietitians. However, this information should be used as a guideline for planning healthier meals, not as a basis for designing menus for people with strict dietary requirements. Ingredients listed as optional are not included in the nutritional data. And when alternate choices of ingredients are given, the first item listed was the one used to compute the nutritional figures.

I urge you to stock your cupboards, dig out your can opener, and start cooking from your own pantry!

Planning Your Pantry

The goal of a well-stocked pantry is to have enough food stored to prepare delicious and satisfying meals at a moment's notice. Ideally, you should keep about 2 weeks' worth of food on hand. That covers you for an extra-busy work schedule, unexpected houseguests, bad weather, sudden illness, and all those other occurrences that hinder trips to the store and preclude long sessions at the stove.

When I speak of the "pantry," I include the kitchen cupboards, the refrigerator, the freezer, and other areas—including storerooms and the garage—where you can safely store food. Each person's pantry planning will be different based on personal tastes and the amount of storage space available.

Keep in mind, however, that if we lose electric power for any length of time, we also lose our cold storage. For this reason, I place more emphasis on dry storage items, both for pantry planning and in most of the recipes in this book, than on ingredients requiring constant refrigeration. I would also urge you to keep cans of propane or Sterno on hand for heating your food if you live in an area where loss of power is a problem.

On the following pages, I detail many items used in my recipes, as well as other long-keeping foods. Use the lists as a guideline for stocking your own pantry. You certainly don't have to rush right out and buy everything shown in order to have a well-stocked kitchen. Start by buying the things you know you like and use most frequently, while slowly adding to your herb and spice inventory.

Remember that this is only a guide to help you use pantry ingredients, not a blueprint that you must follow exactly. If you don't have the exact pasta, rice, or beans called for in a recipe, substitute another type. If you don't have canned chicken, use tuna and vice versa. If you don't have the particular herb or spice mentioned, have fun experimenting with what's on hand.

"Par" for the Course

In restaurant kitchens, they have a pantry-control system called "par" stock. Par is the number they never drop below. For example, if par on tomato sauce is one case, they order another case when only one case is left. This is also a good system for running your home pantry. Let's say you frequently use canned water-packed tuna and it would be frustrating to run out of it. You would make two cans your par on tuna, and when you had only two cans left, you would put tuna on your shopping list and buy two more cans.

If you have enough storage space, you can save a great deal of money buying the items you use most frequently at warehouse-type stores that offer huge discounts on cases. Also take advantage of weekend and seasonal specials to stock up on price-reduced staples. And don't forget to watch for sales on the nonfood pantry supplies you need: cleaning products, foil, plastic bags, paper products, and the like.

Pantry Pride

Most of what you keep on hand will qualify as "dry pantry" items. They're the canned, bottled, boxed, and other packaged foods that keep for a long time without refrigeration. If there's not room for them in your kitchen, any cool, dry place will do.

Although the majority of my recipes use up a whole container of most pantry items, you will occasionally have leftovers. Read labels carefully to determine storage requirements. Many dried foods will need to be repackaged and refrigerated. I've marked them with an asterisk (*). All canned foods, of course, would need refrigeration after opening. Other things—like flour, grains, and pasta—should at least be put into plastic bags or other airtight containers to keep them fresh.

As you look over the lists, you might notice a few obvious omissions. They are not oversights. I purposely did not include dried parsley, cilantro, or lemon grass because I think they all taste more like dried alfalfa than their uniquely flavorful fresh counterparts. When a recipe calls for fresh parsley or cilantro and you don't have it, just omit it. If you don't have fresh lemon grass, substitute grated lemon peel to taste.

I omitted bouillon cubes of all types because I don't like their taste. I think canned broths are a much more appealing alternative. And they come in a wide variety of fat-free, reduced-sodium flavors.

Do lay in a good supply of bottled water. You never know when circumstances will dictate its use.

DRY PANTRY BASICS

Note: Items and categories marked with an asterisk (*) should be refrigerated after opening.

BAKING STAPLES

Baking powder
Baking soda
Biscuit and pancake mix
Cocoa powder
Coffee, instant and regular
Cornbread mix
Cornstarch
Flour, unbleached all-purpose and whole wheat
Gelatin, unflavored
Graham cracker crumbs
Graham cracker pie crust, ready-made
Milk, fat-free instant powdered
Potato Buds
Powdered egg whites
Salt
Sugar, white, brown, and confectioners'
Tea

EXTRACTS

Almond
Coconut
Rum
Vanilla
Vanilla butter and nut

OILS

Canola
Dark sesame*
Olive, extra-virgin
Walnut*

VINEGARS

Balsamic
Cider
Raspberry
Red wine

Rice
Sherry
White

CONDIMENTS AND DRESSINGS

Angostura bitters
Barbecue sauce*
Capers*
Chili sauce*
Hoisin sauce*
Horseradish*
Hot-pepper sauce
Ketchup*
Liquid smoke
Mayonnaise, low-fat or fat-free*
Mustard, Dijon and brown*
Olives*
Peppers, roasted red*
Pickle relish*
Pickles*
Pimientos*
Salad dressing, low-fat or fat-free*
Salsa*
Sauce, pasta, pizza, and pesto*
Soy sauce, reduced-sodium*
Teriyaki sauce, reduced-sodium
Worcestershire sauce*

SYRUPS AND JAMS

All-fruit jams and jellies*
Corn syrup
Honey
Maple syrup*

COLD CEREALS

All-Bran
Granola, low-fat

(continued)

Dry Pantry Basics—cont.

Grape-Nuts
Kashi, puffed
Puffed rice, wheat, and corn
Shredded wheat

GRAINS AND HOT CEREALS

Bran, wheat and oat
Bulgur (cracked wheat)
Cornmeal
Grits, corn
Kashi, mixed-grain
Millet
Oats, rolled
Quinoa
Rye berries

RICE

Arborio
Brown, quick-cooking and regular
Jasmine
White, quick-cooking and regular
Wild, quick-cooking and regular

PASTAS

Bow ties and other shapes
Couscous
Linguine
Rigatoni
Rotelli
Shells
Spaghetti

DRY BEANS

Black
Black-eyed peas
Cannellini
Chickpeas (garbanzo beans)
Kidney
Lentils
Pinto

Split peas
White, small

DRIED FRUITS AND VEGETABLES

Apples, unsulfured*
Apricots*
Dates*
Figs*
Mushrooms
Prunes*
Raisins*
Tomatoes, oil-free sun-dried

FRESH VEGETABLES

Garlic*
Onions*
Potatoes

WINES*

Madeira
Port
Red, dry
Sherry
Vermouth
White, dry

LIQUORS AND LIQUEURS

Amaretto
Brandy
Grand Marnier or other orange liqueur
Kahlúa
Mirin (rice wine)
Pernod
Rum
Sake

NUTS

Almonds*
Peanuts*
Pecans*

Pine nuts*
Walnuts*

CANNED BROTH*

Beef, fat-free, reduced-sodium
Chicken, fat-free, reduced-sodium
Vegetable

CANNED SOUPS*

Chili, vegetarian
Cream of celery, reduced-fat, reduced-sodium
Cream of chicken, reduced-fat, reduced-sodium
Cream of mushroom, reduced-fat, reduced-sodium
Onion
Pea
Potato
Tomato, reduced-sodium

CANNED JUICES*

Apple
Pineapple
Tomato
V8

CANNED FRUIT*

Litchi nuts, in syrup
Mandarin oranges, in juice
Peaches, sliced, in water
Pears, in juice
Pineapple, crushed and chunks, in juice

CANNED VEGETABLES*

Artichoke hearts, in water
Bamboo shoots
Beans, green
Caponata
Carrots
Corn, whole kernels and creamed
Green chile peppers, diced and whole
Hearts of palm, in water
Mushrooms

Onions
Peas
Potatoes and new potatoes
Pumpkin, solid-pack
Tomatoes, whole, chopped, and seasoned
Tomato paste
Tomato sauce
Water chestnuts, in water

CANNED BEANS*

Black
Cannellini
Chickpeas (garbanzo beans)
Kidney
Pinto
Refried, fat-free and vegetarian

CANNED SEAFOOD*

Clam juice
Clams, chopped and minced
Crab, white
Oysters
Salmon
Shrimp
Tuna, in water

CANNED POULTRY*

Chicken, in water
Turkey, in water

CANNED MEATS*

Beef, corned
Beef, roast, in gravy
Ham, chunk

OTHER

Bacon, imitation bits
Milk, fat-free evaporated and fat-free condensed*
Peanut butter, old-fashioned (unhomogenized)*
Tofu, shelf-stable*
Water, sparkling and still

The Indoor Herb Garden

Herbs are the leaves of aromatic plants. Spices come primarily from the buds, bark, stems, fruit, roots, and seeds of plants and trees. Both herbs and spices make everything taste better. When you use herbs and spices in your cooking, your reputation as a creative cook will skyrocket.

These aromatics contain practically no calories and, when used liberally, can compensate for salt if you're trying to cut back on your sodium intake. Besides individual seasonings, there are lots of salt-free herb and spice blends.

You can change the whole character of a recipe simply by using different seasonings. For example, you can take a basic chicken recipe and change the flavor to Italian by adding oregano, to Indian with curry powder, to French with a little thyme or tarragon, to Scandinavian with dill, to Asian with ginger, or to Southwestern with cumin and chili powder.

When you're cooking from your cupboard, you'll rely heavily on dried herbs and spices. They're quick and convenient to use, and they'll help you add new flair to a dish with a mere flick of the wrist. Many of the recipes in this book include a "Quick Switch." These are quick and easy flavor swaps you can use to instantly give the recipe a different flavor twist by changing just one ingredient, usually an herb or spice. Here's how to get the most out of dried herbs and spices.

- When possible, buy them whole and grind or crush them as needed.

- If you do buy ready-ground varieties, get small quantities and label them with the purchase date. They lose much of their aroma and flavor after 6 months.

- A mortar and pestle are efficient for crushing spices. So is a small coffee mill. (Reserve one just for spices so your spices don't taste like coffee.)

- Rub whole herbs and herb flakes between your hands to bring out their flavor.

- Look for freeze-dried herbs (and some aromatic vegetables). They have better flavor and color than regular dried herbs.

- Store herbs and spices in a cool, dry place where they are not exposed to sunlight or heat. (Above the stove is not a good choice.)

- Alphabetize herbs and spices for easy access. It may sound fussy, but as you acquire more herbs and spices, it will save you both time and frustration.

A well-stocked pantry would contain the following seasonings. You should start with a few basics that you use often and expand your collection as you see fit.

SEASONINGS

HERBS AND SPICES

Allspice, whole and ground
Anise, seeds and ground
Basil
Bay leaves
Caraway seeds
Cardamom, ground
Cayenne
Celery, seeds and ground
Chervil
Chili powder
Cinnamon, sticks and ground
Cloves, whole and ground
Coriander, ground
Cumin, seeds and ground
Curry powder
Dill seeds
Dill weed
Fennel, seeds and ground
Garlic powder and flakes
Ginger, ground
Juniper berries
Mace
Marjoram
Mint
Mustard, seeds and powdered
Nutmeg, whole and ground
Onion flakes
Oregano
Paprika
Peppercorns, black and white
Poppy seeds
Red-pepper flakes
Rosemary
Saffron
Sage
Savory
Sesame seeds
Star anise
Tarragon
Thyme
Turmeric

BLENDS

Cajun blend
Chinese five-spice powder
Italian blend
Southwestern blend
Thai blend

SPLENDID HERB BLENDS

The right combination of herbs and spices can transform simple foods into culinary treats, as if by magic. Herb blends are easy to prepare, and making them ahead prevents last-minute fumbling with half a dozen (or more) bottles. Try the following combos or invent your own. Store them in dark, airtight containers in a cool, dark, dry place. Heat, light, and exposure to air destroy the flavor of dried herbs and spices.

Beef seasoning. Combine 2 teaspoons **each** dried parsley, garlic powder, onion powder, and ground black pepper. Beef has strong flavors of its own, and this simple blend enhances those natural flavors without overpowering them. Add this seasoning to almost any beef dish during cooking.

Cajun spice. Combine 2 teaspoons **each** paprika and ground black pepper; 1½ teaspoons garlic powder; 1 teaspoon **each** crushed red-pepper flakes, dried thyme, dried oregano, and onion powder; and ¼ teaspoon dry mustard. Lend a bit of zip to any Creole or Cajun dish with this Louisiana seasoning. Or rub it into catfish or red snapper fillets as a "blackening" seasoning before cooking.

Chili powder. Combine 1 tablespoon ground cumin; 1 teaspoon **each** dried oregano, garlic powder, and onion powder; ½ teaspoon **each** cayenne and paprika; and ¼ teaspoon ground allspice. Commercial chili powders often contain salt. This spicy salt-free recipe is great in chili, Sloppy Joes, bean dishes, soups, stews, and savory sauces. For a milder mix, cut back on the cayenne.

Italian herb seasoning. Combine 1 tablespoon **each** dried oregano and dried basil and 1 teaspoon dried thyme. (For a zestier blend, add ½ teaspoon onion powder and ¼ teaspoon **each** garlic powder and crushed red-pepper flakes.) This all-purpose blend perks up soups, stews, gravy, tomato sauce, meat loaf, lasagna, chicken cacciatore, and pot roast. Or sprinkle it on baked potatoes and pizza.

Poultry seasoning. Combine 2 teaspoons **each** dried marjoram and onion powder; 1 teaspoon **each** dried thyme, dried sage, and dried savory; and ½ teaspoon ground black pepper. This blend brings out the best flavors of chicken and turkey as well as soups, stews, casseroles, stuffings, and dumplings.

Pumpkin pie spice. Combine 2 teaspoons **each** ground cinnamon and ground nutmeg, 1 teaspoon ground ginger, and ½ teaspoon **each** ground cloves and ground mace. Try it in spice cakes, cookies, and sweet breads as well as pumpkin and sweet potato pies.

Vegetable seasoning. Combine 1 teaspoon **each** dried basil, dried chervil, dried chives, dried marjoram, and dried parsley and ¼ teaspoon **each** dried savory and dried thyme. A few shakes of this salt-free blend enhance vegetables, soups, and casseroles. ∎

Cool, Calm, and Collected

With some long-keeping staples in the fridge, you can whip up pantry meals that taste delightfully fresh. A little parsley, cilantro, lemon juice, or lemon grass does wonders for so many dishes. Apples and citrus fruits have lengthy storage lives. Aged Parmesan, Romano, and Cheddar cheeses last for months in the refrigerator and also keep for at least 2 weeks without refrigeration. A little freshly grated Parmigiano-Reggiano, Pecorino Romano, or high-quality aged Cheddar can make a simple pantry dish seem truly gourmet. (But a bit of the grated boxed stuff can ruin the taste of an otherwise excellent, totally fresh culinary creation.)

If the broth you buy isn't fat-free, store the unopened cans in the refrigerator. The fat in them will congeal on top for easy removal. If onions always bring tears to your eyes when you chop them, you can store them in the refrigerator, too. The cold inhibits the tear-causing chemicals in them.

This list includes items that should always be stored in the refrigerator, opened or not. Remember that the dry pantry items on pages 3 to 5 marked with an asterisk (*) should be refrigerated after opening.

REFRIGERATOR BASICS

Apples
Bread
Butter
Buttermilk
Cabbage mix
Cheese, fresh and aged
Cilantro
Citrus fruits
Coleslaw mix

Dough, bread, biscuit, and pizza
Eggs and liquid egg substitute
Lemon grass (if you don't use it often, freeze it)
Milk, fat-free or 1%
Parsley
Sour cream, fat-free or reduced-fat
Tofu, fresh
Yogurt, fat-free or reduced-fat

Frozen Assets

You don't need a walk-in freezer to keep a decent supply of ready-to-use or quick-thawing foods on hand. Just a few frozen foods can form the basis of many easy, delicious meals. Plus frozen foods can be quick and easy to use. Frozen chopped onions can go right into the pan without thawing. Loose-pack berries, peas, and corn easily pour from the bag. (Always opt for unsweetened fruit.) Juice concentrates can be spooned from the container when you need just a tablespoon or two. When freezing meat, package it in small amounts and thin layers for quick defrosting.

If you keep the following foods on ice, you'll always be assured of a meal in mere minutes.

FREEZER BASICS

MEAT AND POULTRY

Beef, lean ground and cubed
Chicken, skinned and boned breasts
Turkey, ground

SEAFOOD

Crab
Lobster
Shrimp

VEGETABLES

Broccoli
Corn
Onions, chopped
Peas
Spinach, chopped and leaf
Stew mixes
Stir-fry mixes

FRUIT

Blueberries
Cherries, pitted
Cranberries
Peaches, sliced
Raspberries
Strawberries

OTHER

Bread dough
Frozen yogurt, fat-free or reduced-fat
Ice cream, fat-free or reduced-fat
Juice concentrates, orange and apple
Phyllo dough
Pizza dough
Whipped topping, fat-free or reduced-fat

Shop Talk

The grocery industry is doing everything possible to make shopping more fun. In many suburban areas, the supermarket is the social gathering place where people meet after work for coffee or a glass of wine and do their shopping together. No matter how large or small your favorite market may be, there are things you can do to make shopping easier.

Keep a shopping list in your kitchen. That may sound elementary, but you'd be surprised how many people don't. Every time you run out of something or are down to your par quantity, put it on the list. I like to divide my shopping list into the basic categories that reflect the shopping areas in the market. In this way I don't have to run back and forth looking for the items on my list.

Before going to the market, plan your weekly menu and add all of the necessary ingredients to your list. Never go to the market without your list—you'll fall into the impulse-buying trap.

Even with the expanding inventory of most supermarkets, one-stop shopping is not always possible. You may have to go to a health food store or an ethnic market for some items. Consider it time well spent in the pursuit of quick future meals.

Read the labels! Pay close attention to the nutritional information given and be sure to check how many servings are in the container. Sometimes the calories and fat seem low until you realize that the servings are unreasonably small. Note, too, the percentage figure that follows fat and saturated fat. It tells you how much of your daily "allowance" is in a serving of the food.

Try to avoid preservatives. They're usually

BUT I CAN'T FIND A 12-OUNCE CAN!

What happens when you can't find the exact size can called for in a recipe? If you automatically look for another recipe, rethink your approach to cooking. For practically anything but fussy, fancy baked goods, it doesn't matter whether you improvise a little. A 14- or 15-ounce can of beans works as well as 16 ounces. Six ounces of clams are as good as 6½ ounces.

Manufacturers are notorious for changing can sizes. (It's common for them to shrink the can rather than increase the cost.) And quantities can vary from brand to brand. Keep this in mind as you use the recipes in this book. Reach for a near approximation and enjoy the results. ∎

a sign of overly processed foods. A good rule of thumb is to bypass products with too many ingredients that you can't pronounce.

As for whether it's better to buy brand-name products or generic (store-brand) ones, there's just no hard and fast rule. What I recommend is that you try a single package of a generic before you commit to a whole case and find you don't like the product. There's no point in filling your pantry with foods you will ultimately not use. Besides wasting money, it takes up valuable storage space.

A Recipe for Success

The recipes in this book are designed for healthy, quick, easy, and economical meals. When possible, I have used only one cooking method in each recipe. Rather than starting on top of the stove and then transferring to the oven, most dishes start and finish in the same pot or pan. This saves both time and energy, and it makes cleanup easier.

If a recipe calls for fresh milk and you don't have any, just make the amount you need using milk powder and water. You can also buy powdered buttermilk to avoid keeping fresh buttermilk on hand.

If you have fresh herbs and prefer to use them instead of dried, a good rule of thumb is to use three times as much. The only exception is rosemary, because the flavor of the fresh herb is just as intense as the dried; so use the same amount.

Dried beans and peas are more economical than canned, but they take much longer to prepare and therefore are not as convenient. For this reason, I used canned beans in the recipes. I have had readers tell me that when the first thing they read in a recipe is "soak the beans overnight," they turn the page. They want a meal on the table in 30 minutes instead of tomorrow. If you are cooking for a large family and don't want to spend the extra money for canned beans, here is a time-saving tip: Soak lots of beans overnight, drain, and store in bags

LABEL RECIPES: WORTH A TRY?

They're generally a safe bet. Recipes printed on product labels are thoroughly tested. They're meant to entice you into using the product—and hopefully you'll like it so much that you will buy more of it. Some label recipes have become so popular that they are the standard for judging all other recipes in the same category. Good examples are Toll House Cookies and German Chocolate Cake. ∎

in the freezer. Although they'll still need to be cooked for an hour later, they're at least ready to put on the stove.

If you've got fresh or frozen seafood, poultry, and meat, don't hesitate to use it in place of the canned products called for. And by all means, freeze leftover cooked meat and poultry in 1-cup amounts for just such use.

The highest-quality canned poultry product is chunk white chicken packed in water. It is also the most expensive. Therefore, unless you are limited to canned ingredients, I recommend keeping boneless, skinless chicken breasts in the freezer.

The only way you can buy canned beef is to get roast beef in gravy. I don't happen to like the way it tastes. That is why I always rinse, drain, and shred it in my recipes. If you've got a large canned ham on hand, chop about three-quarters of a cup of it for each can called for in a recipe.

Pantry recipes tend to be higher in sodium than strictly fresh foods. Wherever practical, I've called for reduced-sodium products. By mixing and matching the recipes in this book, you can usually stay within the American Heart Association's guidelines for daily sodium intake. Also, with each recipe, I've provided complete nutritional information, including Carb Choices for those who wish to track their intake of carbohydrates.

Breakfasts and Baked Goods

If you're like most of us, you know time is of the essence at breakfast. That's where pantry products really shine. There are many excellent low-fat mixes that get pancakes, muffins, and breads on the table fast. Cereal is, of course, the quintessential pantry food, whether it's eaten hot or cold. Here are some of my favorite foods for fast morning meals. Some you can toss together on the spot; others are prepared ahead for a quick reheat. (If you practically faint at the idea of baking bread, the fast focaccia is your kind of recipe!)

14

in this chapter ...

Rye and Raisin Cereal

This is my favorite hot cereal. I freeze single servings in zip-top plastic bags. In the morning, I just pop the bag into the microwave for 1 minute, and I have a truly satisfying breakfast. I like this cereal with a spoonful of low-fat ricotta cheese on top.

4½ cups water

1½ cups uncooked rye berries

1 tablespoon ground cinnamon

1 tablespoon vanilla extract

1½ teaspoons caraway seeds

¾ cup raisins

Low-fat ricotta cheese (optional)

1. In a large saucepan, combine the water, rye berries, cinnamon, vanilla, and caraway seeds. Bring to a boil over medium heat. Reduce the heat to low, cover, and cook, stirring occasionally, for 45 minutes. (Add a little more water if the mixture becomes too dry.) Stir in the raisins and cover. Cook for 15 minutes. Serve warm with a spoonful of ricotta cheese on top (if using).

Makes 4 cups

Per ½-cup serving: 61 calories, 1 g protein, 15 g carbohydrates, 0 g fat, 0 mg cholesterol, 1 g dietary fiber, 3 mg sodium

1 Carb Choice

QUICK
SWITCH • Replace the caraway seeds with ground ginger.
• Or replace the raisins with mixed dried fruit bits.

Oatmeal Crème Brûlée

Here's a delightfully different way to serve your morning cereal. In fact,
I like it so much I included it on menus I created for Windstar Cruises,
and it was a big hit. It also makes a good dessert, served warm or cold.

1. Preheat the broiler.

2. In a medium saucepan, mix the milk, oats, salt, and 2 tablespoons of the brown sugar. Bring to a boil over medium heat. Reduce the heat to low and simmer, stirring constantly, for 1 minute, or until thickened. Stir in the raspberries.

3. Divide the mixture between 2 ovenproof bowls. Divide the ice cream between the bowls and sprinkle evenly with the remaining 2 tablespoons brown sugar. Place under the broiler for 1 to 2 minutes, or until the sugar starts to bubble.

Makes 2 servings

Per serving: 389 calories, 14 g protein, 75 g carbohydrates, 5 g fat, 13 mg cholesterol, 3 g dietary fiber, 246 mg sodium

6 Carb Choices

1 **can (12 ounces) fat-free evaporated milk**

½ **cup quick-cooking rolled oats**

⅛ **teaspoon salt**

4 **tablespoons packed dark brown sugar**

½ **cup frozen unsweetened raspberries**

½ **cup reduced-fat vanilla ice cream**

QUICK
SWITCH • Add ¼ teaspoon ground cinnamon to the oats.
• Or replace the raspberries with frozen blueberries or blackberries.

Oatmeal Pancakes

These unusual pancakes are worth getting up for! I always make more
than I need and freeze the rest in individual plastic bags. I reheat
the frozen pancakes in the toaster when I'm really in a hurry.

1½ **cups old-fashioned rolled oats**

1 **tablespoon sugar**

1 **tablespoon ground cinnamon**

½ **teaspoon baking powder**

½ **teaspoon baking soda**

¼ **teaspoon salt**

3 **egg whites**

1 **can (12 ounces) fat-free
   evaporated milk**

1 **teaspoon vanilla extract**

1. In a blender or food processor, process the oats to the consistency of coarse flour. Transfer to a large bowl and stir in the sugar, cinnamon, baking powder, baking soda, and salt.

2. In a medium bowl, whisk together the egg whites, milk, and vanilla. Pour over the dry ingredients and stir until completely moistened.

3. Coat a large nonstick skillet with cooking spray and warm over medium-low heat for 3 minutes, or until water drops sprinkled in the skillet "dance" on the surface. Spoon in 3 tablespoons of batter for each pancake and cook until the top of each pancake is covered with tiny bubbles and the bottom is brown. Turn and brown the other side.

Makes 12 pancakes

Per 2-pancake serving: 216 calories, 13 g protein, 36 g carbohydrates, 3 g fat, 2 mg cholesterol, 1 g dietary fiber, 318 mg sodium

2 Carb Choices

QUICK
SWITCH • Replace the cinnamon with 1 teaspoon nutmeg or ginger.

Jeanne's **TOP 10** Pantry Picks

Paring down this list wasn't easy, but these are the foods I consider absolutely indispensable for a well-stocked cupboard. They're convenient, versatile, and long lasting. With these in the house, you've always got a delicious meal at your fingertips. (Be sure to buy products that are low in fat and sodium. And remember that quick-cooking grains and canned beans are a real plus.)

1. **Chicken broth, condensed cream soups, and boxed soups**

2. **Evaporated milk and milk powder**

3. **Diced tomatoes and tomato paste**

4. **Canned tuna, chicken, and clams; clam juice**

5. **Pasta (including couscous), rice, beans, and nuts**

6. **Herbs, spices, and extracts**

7. **Dried mushrooms, sun-dried tomatoes, and assorted dried fruit**

8. **Extra-virgin olive oil and canola oil**

9. **Assorted vinegars**

10. **Unflavored gelatin**

Gingerbread Pancakes

[Photograph on page 115]

Gingerbread has always been one of my favorite desserts, so the idea of gingerbread pancakes really appealed to me. In fact, these unusual pancakes have become my favorite special-occasion breakfast. I like to serve them with light sour cream and apple butter or apple slices. For a higher-protein, lower-fat topping, process low-fat ricotta cheese until it is satin smooth and use it in place of sour cream.

1 cup whole wheat flour

¾ teaspoon baking soda

½ teaspoon ground ginger

½ teaspoon ground cinnamon

¼ teaspoon ground cloves

¼ teaspoon salt

2 teaspoons instant decaffeinated coffee powder

¼ cup hot tap water

6 ounces frozen unsweetened apple juice concentrate, thawed

2 tablespoons butter, melted

1 egg

1. In a large bowl, mix the flour, baking soda, ginger, cinnamon, cloves, and salt.

2. In a medium bowl, dissolve the coffee powder in the hot water. Whisk in the juice concentrate, butter, and egg. Pour over the dry ingredients and stir until completely moistened; the mixture will be lumpy.

3. Coat a large nonstick skillet with cooking spray and warm over medium-low heat for 3 minutes, or until water drops sprinkled in the skillet "dance" on the surface. Spoon in ¼ cup of batter for each pancake and cook until the top of each pancake is covered with tiny bubbles and the bottom is brown. Turn and brown the other side.

Makes 8 pancakes

Per 2-pancake serving: 245 calories, 6 g protein, 40 g carbohydrates, 8 g fat, 68 mg cholesterol, 4 g dietary fiber, 456 mg sodium

2½ Carb Choices

Cinnamon Waffles

Most waffle recipes call for beaten egg whites to be folded into the batter as the last step. These easy cinnamon waffles skip that time-consuming step. In fact, they can be made in minutes, and they freeze well.

1. In a large bowl, combine the whole wheat flour, all-purpose flour, milk powder, cinnamon, baking powder, baking soda, and salt. Stir well.

2. In a medium bowl, combine the egg whites, egg, oil, and vanilla. Pour over the flour mixture. Add the buttermilk and stir well.

3. Heat a nonstick waffle iron coated with cooking spray according to the manufacturer's directions. Pour ½ cup of the batter into the center of the hot waffle iron and cook for 6 minutes, or until the batter stops steaming. (Cooking time will vary greatly depending on the type of waffle iron you are using.) Repeat to make 7 more waffles, coating the waffle iron lightly with spray between waffles.

Makes 8 waffles

Per waffle: 214 calories, 9 g protein, 30 g carbohydrates, 7 g fat, 30 mg cholesterol, 2 g dietary fiber, 462 mg sodium

1½ Carb Choices

1 **cup whole wheat flour**

1 **cup unbleached all-purpose flour**

⅓ **cup fat-free milk powder**

1 **tablespoon ground cinnamon**

1 **tablespoon baking powder**

½ **teaspoon baking soda**

½ **teaspoon salt**

2 **egg whites**

1 **egg**

3 **tablespoons canola oil**

2 **teaspoons vanilla extract**

2 **cups buttermilk**

Make-Ahead Florida French Toast

This is a terrific breakfast to prepare for house guests. You can do almost all the work
the night before and put a sensational meal on the table in just minutes.

12 slices (¾" thick) French bread

1 cup fat-free liquid egg substitute

1 can (12 ounces) fat-free evaporated milk

1 teaspoon grated orange peel (optional)

¼ cup orange juice

1 tablespoon granulated sugar

1 teaspoon vanilla extract

¼ teaspoon canola oil

Confectioners' sugar

1. Place the bread in a shallow baking dish large enough so that the slices do not overlap.

2. In a medium bowl, mix the egg substitute, milk, orange peel (if using), orange juice, granulated sugar, vanilla, and oil. Pour over the bread and turn the slices to coat evenly. Cover and refrigerate overnight.

3. Coat a large nonstick skillet with cooking spray and warm over medium-low heat for 3 minutes, or until water drops sprinkled in the skillet "dance" on the surface. Working in small batches, cook the bread for 5 minutes per side, or until golden. Serve sprinkled with confectioners' sugar.

Makes 12 servings

Per serving: 116 calories, 7 g protein, 18 g carbohydrates, 2 g fat, 0 mg cholesterol, 1 g dietary fiber, 222 mg sodium

1 Carb Choice

FRESH BREAD IN A JIFFY

Large supermarkets usually have in-store bakeries where you can buy anything from dense pumpernickels to crusty French loaves. Most breads freeze well, so you can purchase several loaves at once and put them in the freezer when you get home. Slice them first to make it easier to thaw the amount you need at a moment's notice. Voilà—instant fresh bread! ∎

Sourdough Milk Toast with Honeyed Peaches

[Photograph on page 117]

This proves that you can make wonderful French toast without using eggs.
Although I specify peaches here, you may use any fresh, canned, or frozen fruit you
happen to have on hand. In fact, this is an excellent way to use up overripe fruit.

1. Place the bread in a shallow baking dish large enough so that the slices do not overlap.

2. In a small bowl, stir the milk powder into the water until completely dissolved. Stir in the cinnamon, vanilla, and salt. Pour over the bread and allow to stand for 5 minutes. Turn the bread and allow to soak until most of the liquid has been absorbed.

3. Coat a large nonstick skillet with cooking spray and warm over medium-low heat for 3 minutes, or until water drops sprinkled in the skillet "dance" on the surface. Add the bread and pour any remaining liquid over it. Cook for 5 minutes per side, or until golden. Transfer to a serving plate and keep warm.

4. Add the peaches and honey to the hot skillet. Cook, stirring frequently, for 4 minutes. Spoon over the bread. If desired, sprinkle lightly with more cinnamon.

Makes 4 servings

Per serving: 179 calories, 9 g protein, 35 g carbohydrates, 1 g fat, 3 mg cholesterol, 2 g dietary fiber, 315 mg sodium

2 Carb Choices

4 slices sourdough bread

½ cup fat-free milk powder

½ cup water

½ teaspoon ground cinnamon

½ teaspoon vanilla extract

  Pinch of salt

1 can (16 ounces) sliced peaches packed in water, drained

1 tablespoon honey

QUICK
SWITCH • Replace the cinnamon with pumpkin pie spice.
• Or replace the vanilla with ¼ teaspoon almond extract.

Cinnamon Quick Bread

[Photograph on page 116]

Now you can have cinnamon bread whenever you want it. It's great fresh from
the oven, but you can also toast it or freeze slices for instant gratification later.
If you prefer a sweeter, more coffeecake-like breakfast bread, double or
even triple the amount of streusel you stir into the batter.

BATTER

- **2 cups unbleached all-purpose flour**
- **¾ cup sugar**
- **4 teaspoons baking powder**
- **2 teaspoons ground cinnamon**
- **¾ teaspoon salt**
- **1 cup fat-free or 1% milk**
- **1 egg**
- **2 egg whites**
- **¼ cup canola oil**
- **2 teaspoons vanilla extract**

STREUSEL

- **2 tablespoons sugar**
- **1 teaspoon ground cinnamon**
- **2 teaspoons butter, softened**

1. Preheat the oven to 350°F. Coat a 9" × 5" loaf pan with cooking spray.

2. *To make the batter:* In a large bowl, mix the flour, sugar, baking powder, cinnamon, and salt. In a medium bowl, whisk together the milk, egg, egg whites, oil, and vanilla. Pour into the dry ingredients and stir until just moistened. Do not overmix; the batter will be lumpy. Pour into the prepared loaf pan.

3. *To make the streusel:* In a small bowl, mix the sugar, cinnamon, and butter. Sprinkle over the batter and swirl slightly with a knife to marble the streusel into the batter.

4. Bake for 55 minutes, or until a sharp knife inserted in the center comes out clean. Cool on a wire rack for 10 minutes, then remove from the pan and cool on the rack.

Makes 1 loaf; 12 slices

Per slice: 197 calories, 4 g protein, 33 g carbohydrates, 6 g fat, 20 mg cholesterol, 0 g dietary fiber, 286 mg sodium

2 Carb Choices

QUICK
SWITCH • Replace the cinnamon in both the batter and streusel with half the amount of ground nutmeg.

Blueberry Muffins

Blueberry muffins are quick to throw together. Frozen berries, which
plump up during baking, taste and look better than either thawed or fresh.
In fact, I always freeze fresh blueberries before using them in baked goods.

1. Preheat the oven to 400°F. Coat 12 standard-size muffin cups with cooking spray.

2. In a medium bowl, combine the sugar, butter, and applesauce. Stir in the egg.

3. In a small bowl, combine the flour, baking powder, and salt. Add to the sugar mixture, alternating with the milk, stirring just until blended. Do not overmix.

4. Fold the blueberries into the batter. Fill the muffin cups two-thirds full. Bake for 25 minutes, or until a wooden pick inserted in the center of a muffin comes out clean. Cool in the pan on a rack for 5 minutes. Remove from the pan and cool completely.

Makes 12 muffins

Per muffin: 134 calories, 4 g protein, 24 g carbohydrates, 3 g fat, 23 mg cholesterol, 1 g dietary fiber, 1,721 mg sodium

1½ Carb Choices

¼ **cup sugar**

2 **tablespoons butter, softened**

2 **tablespoons unsweetened applesauce**

1 **egg, lightly beaten**

2 **cups unbleached all-purpose flour**

1 **tablespoon baking powder**

¼ **teaspoon salt**

1 **cup 1% or fat-free milk**

1½ **cups frozen blueberries**

Bread Pudding Muffins

These easy muffins freeze extremely well. For a fast and healthy breakfast, simply pop one into the microwave. You can use most any kind of dried fruit—including apricots, cherries, cranberries, figs, peaches, and pears—for infinite variety.

1 can (12 ounces) fat-free evaporated milk

4 egg whites

¼ cup sugar

1 tablespoon butter, melted

1 tablespoon ground cinnamon

1 tablespoon vanilla extract

12 slices whole wheat bread, cut into ½" cubes

⅔ cup dark raisins

1. Preheat the oven to 350°F. Coat 12 standard-size muffin cups with cooking spray.

2. In a large bowl, mix the milk, egg whites, sugar, butter, cinnamon, and vanilla. Stir in the bread and raisins; allow to soak for 5 minutes. Spoon into the prepared muffin cups. Bake for 30 to 35 minutes, or until firm and browned. Cool on a wire rack for at least 10 minutes before removing from the muffin cups.

Makes 12 muffins

Per muffin: 169 calories, 6 g protein, 32 g carbohydrates, 3 g fat, 3 mg cholesterol, 4 g dietary fiber, 264 mg sodium

2 Carb Choices

QUICK
SWITCH • Replace the vanilla with coffee liqueur or strong coffee. • Or replace the cinnamon with ½ teaspoon ground cardamom.

THE SPICE RACK **A HINT OF CINNAMON**
Most everybody likes sweet, fragrant cinnamon. From a sprinkling on buttered toast to a cinnamon stick swirled in cider, the possibilities for using this spice are practically limitless. Ground cinnamon adds wonderful flavor to pilaf, baked goods, rice pudding, pumpkin pie, winter squash, and much more. It's also a great addition to traditional poultry rubs. Use cinnamon sticks as stirrers or garnishes or toss them into a pot of simmering apple cider to infuse it with an irresistible flavor. Just remember to always remove cinnamon sticks when you use them for cooking.

Apricot-Pecan Scones

These tasty breakfast pastries are also good served in place of rolls or bread with a variety of dishes. They're wonderful plain or with a little dab of butter.

1. Preheat the oven to 400°F. Coat a baking sheet with cooking spray.

2. In a large bowl, combine the flour, 3 tablespoons of the sugar, the baking powder, baking soda, and salt. Using a pastry blender or a fork, cut the butter into the flour mixture until evenly dispersed. Add the apricots and pecans. Stir to mix.

3. In a medium bowl, combine the buttermilk or yogurt and egg white. Beat with a fork to mix. Add to the flour mixture. Stir with a fork until the dough comes together.

4. Spoon onto the prepared baking sheet in 12 equal portions. In a small bowl, combine the remaining 2 teaspoons sugar and the cinnamon. Sprinkle over the scones.

5. Bake for 15 minutes, or until lightly browned. Remove to a rack to cool for 5 minutes.

Makes 12 scones

Per scone: 178 calories, 4 g protein, 32 g carbohydrates, 4 g fat, 1 mg cholesterol, 2 g dietary fiber, 228 mg sodium

2 Carb Choices

QUICK
SWITCH • Substitute dried sour cherries for the apricots and semisweet chocolate chips for the nuts.

2 cups unbleached all-purpose flour

3 tablespoons + 2 teaspoons sugar

2 teaspoons baking powder

½ teaspoon baking soda

¼ teaspoon salt

2 tablespoons cold butter, cut into small pieces

1¼ cups chopped dried apricots

¼ cup chopped toasted pecans

¾ cup buttermilk or low-fat plain yogurt

1 egg white

¼ teaspoon ground cinnamon

Baking Powder Biscuits

Whether you eat them plain or with jam or butter, these light
and tender biscuits are perfect for a cozy breakfast.

**2 cups unbleached all-purpose
flour**

¾ teaspoon salt

1 tablespoon baking powder

**3 tablespoons cold butter, cut
into small chunks**

¾ cup 1% or fat-free milk

1. Preheat the oven to 450°F.

2. Sift the flour, salt, and baking powder into a medium
   bowl. Scatter the butter pieces over the flour mixture.
   Using a pastry blender or a fork, cut the butter into the
   flour mixture until it resembles the texture of cornmeal. Add the milk. Stir quickly just to bind into a light,
   soft dough.

3. Turn the dough onto a lightly floured work surface.
   Knead it gently for no more than 30 seconds. Pat to a
   ½" thickness. With a floured 2" cookie cutter or rim of
   a juice glass, cut out 12 biscuits. Place them several
   inches apart on an ungreased baking sheet.

4. Bake for 10 minutes, or until lightly browned. Serve
   warm.

Makes 12 biscuits

Per biscuit: 107 calories, 3 g protein, 17 g carbohydrates, 3 g fat,
8 mg cholesterol, 0 g dietary fiber, 261 mg sodium

1 Carb Choice

Popovers

A popover is a muffin-shaped bread with a crispy brown crust and
a nearly hollow interior. The thin batter creates so much steam during baking
that the popovers literally pop over the sides of the pan as they bake.

1. Preheat the oven to 450°F. Coat 8 custard cups (8 ounces each) with cooking spray.

2. Beat the eggs in a medium bowl with a fork. Add the milk and butter. Stir to mix. Add the flour and salt. With an electric mixer on high speed, beat for 2 minutes.

3. Pour the batter into the prepared custard cups, each half-full. Bake for 15 minutes. Reduce the heat to 350°F. Bake for 15 minutes longer. Pierce the side of each popover with a sharp knife. Bake for 5 minutes to dry out the interiors. Serve warm.

Makes 8 popovers

Per popover: 99 calories, 4 g protein, 14 g carbohydrates, 3 g fat, 58 mg cholesterol, 0 g dietary fiber, 113 mg sodium

½ **Carb Choice**

2 **eggs**

1 **cup 1% or fat-free milk**

1 **tablespoon butter, melted**

1 **cup unbleached all-purpose flour**

¼ **teaspoon salt**

FREEZE 'EM FOR LATER

These treats freeze well. To freeze, cool the popovers to room temperature and wrap them in airtight plastic wrap followed by foil. To reheat, completely unwrap them and place on a baking sheet. Bake at 350°F for 15 minutes, or until thoroughly heated. ∎

Spoon Bread

Southern to its core, this delicate casserole dish is more like a soufflé
than a bread. Best eaten warm, it's often served as a side dish. In the South,
spoon bread is traditionally made with white cornmeal; however, the taste
and texture are just the same when made with yellow cornmeal.

⅔ **cup cornmeal**

1 **teaspoon salt**

1 **teaspoon baking powder**

1 **teaspoon sugar**

2 **cups 1% or fat-free milk**

1 **tablespoon butter**

3 **eggs, separated**

1. Preheat the oven to 350°F. Coat a 2-quart baking dish
   with cooking spray.

2. In a small bowl, combine the cornmeal, salt, baking
   powder, and sugar.

3. Bring the milk almost to a boil in a medium saucepan
   over high heat. Gradually add the cornmeal mixture,
   stirring constantly. Cook, stirring constantly, for 3 minutes, or until the mixture just comes to a boil. Remove
   from the heat. Stir in the butter.

4. Whisk the egg yolks in another small bowl for 1
   minute, or until creamy. Add one-quarter of the cornmeal mixture and stir well. Pour the yolk mixture back
   into the saucepan and stir well.

5. In a large bowl, beat the egg whites with an electric
   mixer on high speed until stiff peaks form. Fold into
   the cornmeal mixture. Place in the prepared baking
   dish. Bake for 25 to 30 minutes, or until puffed and
   lightly browned.

Makes 6 servings

Per serving: 142 calories, 7 g protein, 17 g carbohydrates, 5 g
fat, 113 mg cholesterol, 1 g dietary fiber, 509 mg sodium

1 Carb Choice

Breakfast Pizza

Children love this easy treat for after-school snacks as well as for breakfast.

1. Preheat the broiler.

2. Cut the muffin in half and use a rolling pin to make each half much flatter and larger in diameter. Place on a baking sheet, cut side up, and broil until lightly browned. Spread with the jam and sprinkle with the cheese. Broil for another 2 minutes, or until the cheese is melted and very lightly browned.

Makes 2 servings

Per serving: 243 calories, 11 g protein, 40 g carbohydrates, 6 g fat, 15 mg cholesterol, 3 g dietary fiber, 376 mg sodium

2½ Carb Choices

1 **whole wheat English muffin**

¼ **cup all-fruit jam**

½ **cup shredded reduced-fat mozzarella cheese**

Southern Bacon Cornbread

I find that the cornbread turns out moister if I don't thaw the frozen corn
before mixing it in. For a perfect portable snack, line the pan with foil, allowing
at least 6" to overhang on all four sides. When the cornbread is cool,
just wrap it up in the foil and you're ready to go.

1 **cup cornmeal**

1 **cup unbleached all-purpose flour**

¼ **cup imitation bacon bits**

1 **tablespoon baking powder**

½ **teaspoon salt**

¼ **teaspoon ground black pepper**

1 **cup fat-free or 1% milk**

1 **egg**

3 **tablespoons honey**

2 **tablespoons canola oil**

1 **package (10 ounces) frozen corn kernels, unthawed**

1. Preheat the oven to 375°F. Coat an 8" × 8" baking dish with cooking spray.

2. In a large bowl, mix the cornmeal, flour, bacon bits, baking powder, salt, and pepper.

3. In a medium bowl, whisk together the milk, egg, honey, and oil. Stir in the corn. Pour over the dry ingredients and stir until completely moistened; do not overmix. Pour into the prepared baking dish and bake for 25 minutes, or until golden brown. Cool on a wire rack for at least 10 minutes before unmolding the bread.

Makes 8 servings

Per serving: 243 calories, 8 g protein, 42 g carbohydrates, 6 g fat, 27 mg cholesterol, 2 g dietary fiber, 448 mg sodium

2½ Carb Choices

QUICK
SWITCH • Replace the honey with maple syrup.

Fast Focaccia

[Photograph on page 125]

This homemade "pizza bread" takes less than 20 minutes to make.
It's a fantastic brunch item.

1. Preheat the oven to 400°F.

2. Unroll the dough onto a large baking sheet, stretching it to fit over the entire surface. Push your fingertips lightly into the dough, creating depressions all over the surface. Bake for 7 minutes.

3. Brush the top with the oil and sprinkle evenly with the cheese. Bake for 6 minutes, or until the cheese melts and starts to brown lightly.

Makes 12 servings

Per serving: 72 calories, 2 g protein, 11 g carbohydrates, 2 g fat, 1 mg cholesterol, 0 g dietary fiber, 32 mg sodium

½ **Carb Choice**

1 package (10½ ounces) unbaked pizza dough

1 tablespoon extra-virgin olive oil

¼ cup shredded Parmesan cheese

QUICK
SWITCH • Sprinkle the top with hot-pepper flakes, Italian herb blend, or crushed rosemary before baking. • Or turn the focaccia into a full-blown pizza with your favorite toppings. For something out of the ordinary, try drained and flaked ham, well-drained crushed pineapple, and shredded mozzarella—with or without tomato sauce.

EASY CHEESY FLAVOR

When you need just a touch of a hard cheese like Parmesan or Cheddar to liven up a dish, try shaving some off with a citrus zester instead of a grater. This will give you exactly the amount you need, and you won't have to clean a large grater. ∎

Soups

Making soup needn't be an all-day affair. The soups in this chapter come together quickly, thanks to pantry products like canned tomatoes, beans, evaporated milk, or fruit. Many get a burst of flavor from reduced-sodium broth and build on it with herbs and other aromatics. Some even start with canned soup as an ingredient and embellish it until the end result is something very different. That's a perfectly valid—and smart—way to get dinner on the table fast. Many of the soups are one-dish meals; some can double as sauces for other dishes. All are mmmmm good.

in this chapter…

Gazpacho

This cold Mexican soup is even better if made the day before you plan
to serve it, and it will keep for several days in the refrigerator.
It can also serve as a salsa for any Southwestern dish.

2 **cans (11½ ounces each) V8
vegetable juice**

1 **can (14½ ounces) chopped
tomatoes, undrained**

1 **jar (7 ounces) roasted red
peppers, drained and
chopped**

1 **medium onion, finely
chopped, or 1½ cups frozen
chopped onions**

3 **tablespoons lemon juice**

1 **clove garlic, minced**

½ **teaspoon Worcestershire
sauce**

¼ **teaspoon hot-pepper sauce**

¼ **teaspoon ground black
pepper**

⅛ **teaspoon ground cumin**

1. In a large bowl, mix the vegetable juice, tomatoes, red peppers, onion, lemon juice, garlic, Worcestershire sauce, hot-pepper sauce, black pepper, and cumin.

2. Cover and refrigerate for at least 2 hours.

Makes 8 servings

Per serving: 31 calories, 1 g protein, 9 g carbohydrates, 0 g fat, 0 mg cholesterol, 1 g dietary fiber, 389 mg sodium

½ **Carb Choice**

QUICK
SWITCH • Replace the lemon juice with lime juice.

Cold Spiced Peach Soup

This refreshing cold soup works equally well as an appetizer or a dessert.
It even makes a nice sauce for angel food cake or ice cream.

1. In a blender or food processor, combine the peaches, yogurt, sugar, cinnamon, vanilla, allspice, and cloves. Blend until smooth.

2. Pour into a large bowl, cover, and chill for at least 2 hours.

   Makes 4 servings

   Per serving: 44 calories, 1 g protein, 11 g carbohydrates, 0 g fat, 0 mg cholesterol, 1 g dietary fiber, 13 mg sodium

   ½ **Carb Choice**

1 **can (16 ounces) sliced peaches packed in water, undrained**

¼ **cup fat-free or reduced-fat plain yogurt**

2 **teaspoons sugar**

½ **teaspoon ground cinnamon**

½ **teaspoon vanilla extract**

¼ **teaspoon ground allspice**

   Pinch of ground cloves

QUICK
SWITCH • Replace the peaches with apricots or pears.

Pear and Roquefort Soup

What makes this unusual soup so special is the distinctive taste
of Roquefort cheese combined with the sweetness of pears. (If you can't find
Roquefort, use another blue cheese.) Both Monterey Jack and cottage cheese
contribute texture to the soup. If you have any soup left over, serve it cold
as a salad dressing or warm it as a sauce for poached or grilled chicken.

1 **medium onion, chopped, or
1½ cups frozen chopped
onions**

1 **can (16 ounces) Bartlett pear
halves packed in juice,
undrained**

1 **can (14½ ounces) fat-free,
reduced-sodium chicken
broth**

½ **cup shredded reduced-fat
Monterey Jack cheese**

½ **cup crumbled Roquefort
cheese**

½ **cup fat-free or 1% cottage
cheese**

1. Place the onion in a medium saucepan, cover, and cook
   over medium-low heat for 10 minutes, or until soft and
   translucent. (Add a little water, if necessary, to prevent
   scorching.)

2. Drain the juice from the pears into the saucepan; dice
   the pears and set aside. Add the broth to the saucepan
   and bring to a boil. Simmer, uncovered, over medium
   heat for 10 minutes, or until reduced by one-third. Let
   cool for 5 minutes.

3. Transfer the juice and onions to a blender or food
   processor and blend until smooth. Pour the puree back
   into the saucepan through a fine-mesh sieve, pressing
   all liquid through with the back of a spoon.

4. Add the Monterey Jack cheese and stir over low heat
   until melted; do not allow the soup to boil. Remove
   from the heat and stir in the pears, Roquefort cheese,
   and cottage cheese. Serve at room temperature or
   cover and refrigerate until cold.

Makes 8 servings

Per serving: 85 calories, 6 g protein, 8 g carbohydrates, 3 g fat,
11 mg cholesterol, 0 g dietary fiber, 219 mg sodium

½ **Carb Choice**

Curried Pumpkin Soup

[Photograph on page 118]

Canned solid-pack pumpkin is good for more than just pie and is the foundation for an excellent soup. This spicy curried soup is based on one of my favorite African recipes. You can serve it hot or cold, but I like it best just a little warmer than room temperature.

1. Place the onion in a large saucepan, cover, and cook over medium-low heat for 10 minutes, or until soft and translucent. (Add a little water, if necessary, to prevent scorching.)

2. Stir in the applesauce, brown sugar, curry powder, cumin, ginger, salt, cardamom, and pepper. Cook over medium heat, stirring frequently, for 5 minutes. Stir in the pumpkin and broth; bring to a boil. Reduce the heat to low, cover, and cook for 20 minutes.

3. Remove from the heat and stir in the milk. Let cool for 5 minutes.

4. Working in batches, transfer to a blender or food processor and blend until smooth. Serve topped with a spoonful of sour cream and a sprinkling of pumpkin seeds (if using).

Makes 8 servings

Per serving: 79 calories, 4 g protein, 15 g carbohydrates, 0 g fat, 2 mg cholesterol, 3 g dietary fiber, 189 mg sodium

1 Carb Choice

1 **medium onion, chopped, or 1½ cups frozen chopped onions**

1 **cup unsweetened applesauce**

1 **tablespoon packed dark brown sugar**

1 **teaspoon curry powder**

1 **teaspoon ground cumin**

½ **teaspoon ground ginger**

½ **teaspoon salt**

¼ **teaspoon ground cardamom**

¼ **teaspoon ground black pepper**

1 **can (16 ounces) solid-pack pumpkin**

1 **can (14½ ounces) fat-free, reduced-sodium chicken broth**

1 **can (12 ounces) fat-free evaporated milk**

Fat-free or reduced-fat sour cream (optional)

Toasted pumpkin seeds (optional)

THE SPICE RACK | **CUMIN: THE SPICE USED 'ROUND THE WORLD** Cumin is the dried fruit of a plant in the parsley family and has an earthy, rustic flavor. It's available in whole and ground forms, and it's a key ingredient in both curry and chili powder. Cumin is a worldwide favorite and shows up in dishes from the Mediterranean, the Middle East, Asia, Mexico, and the Southwest.

Curried Chicken Bisque

This mildly flavored curry soup can double as an entrée served over
cooked rice or pasta. (If reheating this soup, be careful not to boil it or it might
scorch.) It is also good cold. When serving it cold, I add 3 tablespoons of mango
chutney, puree the soup after adding the chicken—so it resembles
vichyssoise—and serve it with cinnamon rice cakes.

2 **cans (10¾ ounces each) low-
sodium, low-fat condensed
cream of chicken soup**

1 **can (10¾ ounces) low-
sodium, low-fat condensed
cream of mushroom soup**

1 **can (12 ounces) fat-free
evaporated milk**

1 **teaspoon curry powder**

½ **teaspoon turmeric**

¼ **teaspoon ground ginger**

1 **can (4½ ounces) chunk white
chicken packed in water,
drained and broken into
bite-size pieces**

1. Spoon the chicken soup and mushroom soup into a
   blender or food processor and blend until smooth.

2. Transfer to a medium saucepan. Stir in the milk, curry
   powder, turmeric, and ginger. Bring to a simmer over
   medium heat, stirring often to prevent scorching. Stir
   in the chicken.

Makes 4 servings

Per serving: 192 calories, 14 g protein, 26 g carbohydrates, 4 g
fat, 31 mg cholesterol, 0 g dietary fiber, 830 mg sodium

1½ Carb Choices

CREAM OF THE CROP

Many cream soups come in reduced-sodium and -fat versions, making them a healthier choice. They're also fuss-free toppings for pasta, rice, beans, potatoes, vegetables, fish, poultry, and meat. Here are a few quick—and delicious!—new ways to use your favorite cream soups.

Cream of broccoli. Add ½ teaspoon dried oregano and chopped leftover vegetables. Use as a pasta sauce. Sprinkle with shredded Parmesan.

Cream of chicken. Add ½ cup unsweetened applesauce, ¾ teaspoon curry powder, and ¼ teaspoon ground ginger. Use as a curry sauce.

Cream of mushroom. Add 2 ounces dried wild mushrooms (rehydrated) and 1 tablespoon sherry. Turn plain broiled chicken breast into a gourmet treat.

Cream of potato. Add ⅓ cup sour cream and 3 tablespoons chopped chives. Serve cold like vichyssoise.

For something different, you can easily jell any of these soups for aspics and salads.

Simply soften 1 envelope unflavored gelatin in 2 tablespoons cool water for a few minutes. Stir in ¼ cup boiling water until dissolved. Add to a blender with the soup and process until smooth. Pour into a decorative mold or a loaf pan and refrigerate for several hours, or until firm enough to unmold. Slice or cube and serve as a relish for meat, fish, or poultry.

One envelope of unflavored gelatin will jell 2 cups of liquid. However, when I want a really firm mixture, I use 1 envelope to 1 cup liquid. ∎

Sherried Pea Soup

This quick soup is equally good hot or cold.

1 can (10¾ ounces) condensed green pea soup

1 can (14½ ounces) fat-free, reduced-sodium chicken broth

2 tablespoons sherry or 1 teaspoon sherry extract

Grated lemon peel (optional)

1. In a medium saucepan, mix the soup and broth. Bring to a simmer over medium-low heat. Stir in the sherry or sherry extract. Serve sprinkled with the lemon peel (if using).

Makes 4 servings

Per serving: 64 calories, 3 g protein, 8 g carbohydrates, 1 g fat, 0 mg cholesterol, 1 g dietary fiber, 306 mg sodium

½ **Carb Choice**

QUICK **SWITCH** • Replace the broth with a 12-ounce can of fat-free evaporated milk.

Peanut Soup

It's amazing how much rich peanut flavor you can get from just ¼ cup of peanut butter. Serve this soup with whole grain rolls and a vegetable side dish.

1. Warm the oil in a medium saucepan over medium-low heat. Add the onion and cook, stirring frequently, for 5 minutes, or until translucent. Stir in the flour, curry powder, and salt. Cook, stirring constantly, for 3 minutes.

2. Place the broth in a small saucepan and bring to a boil over high heat. Pour into the onion mixture and whisk until completely incorporated and the liquid is smooth. Whisk in the peanut butter and cook over medium heat for 5 minutes, or until slightly thickened. Slowly whisk in the milk and warm through; do not allow to boil.

Makes 8 servings

Per serving: 108 calories, 6 g protein, 10 g carbohydrates, 5 g fat, 2 mg cholesterol, 1 g dietary fiber, 157 mg sodium

½ Carb Choice

QUICK **SWITCH** • Replace the curry powder with Thai spice blend.

- **2 teaspoons canola oil**
- **1 small onion, finely chopped, or 1 cup frozen chopped onions**
- **2½ tablespoons unbleached all-purpose flour**
- **1 teaspoon curry powder**
- **¼ teaspoon salt**
- **1 can (14½ ounces) fat-free, reduced-sodium chicken broth**
- **¼ cup creamy peanut butter**
- **1 can (12 ounces) fat-free evaporated milk**

Black Bean Soup

The Cubans claim to have created this robust soup, and they serve
it over rice as a main dish. It is also excellent as a first course,
with a small spoonful of light sour cream and chopped scallions.

**1 small onion, chopped, or
1 cup frozen chopped
onions**

**1 can (4 ounces) diced green
chile peppers**

1 clove garlic, minced

**2 cans (15 ounces each) black
beans, undrained**

**1 can (14½ ounces) fat-free,
reduced-sodium chicken
broth**

1 tablespoon red wine vinegar

1 teaspoon ground cumin

**¼ teaspoon ground black
pepper**

**¼ cup sherry or 2 teaspoons
sherry extract**

1. In a large saucepan, combine the onion, chile peppers,
and garlic. Cover and cook over low heat for 10 minutes, or until the onion is translucent.

2. Spoon 1 can of black beans into a blender or food
processor. Add the broth and blend until smooth. Pour
into the saucepan with the onions.

3. Stir the vinegar, cumin, black pepper, and the remaining beans into the saucepan. Bring to a boil over
medium-high heat. Reduce the heat to low and simmer
for 15 minutes. Stir in the sherry or sherry extract and
simmer for 5 minutes.

Makes 8 servings

Per serving: 79 calories, 4 g protein, 15 g carbohydrates, 0 g fat,
0 mg cholesterol, 5 g dietary fiber, 415 mg sodium

1 Carb Choice

QUICK
SWITCH • Replace the cumin with ½ teaspoon chili powder.

SOUP'S ON HOLD

Most soups freeze so well that it just makes good sense to prepare double batches. For the same amount of time, you get a bonus batch to enjoy another day. And as an added reward, some seasonings mellow in the freezer, making soups taste even better when reheated. If freezing softens the stronger spices in chili, chowder, or stew, simply add a pinch more before serving.

Since bacteria develop most rapidly in the temperature zone of 45° to 140°F, it's critical to cool hot soup quickly. Pour the soup into a large, shallow bowl and place it on a low shelf toward the back of the refrigerator, which is the coldest spot. Refrigerate, uncovered, for several hours, until very cold.

Store soup in the freezer in plastic freezer containers. If you don't have many containers, here's a way to keep them from being tied up in the freezer.

Line plastic freezer containers with freezer bags, pressing the bags tightly against the sides of the containers. Ladle the cooled soup into the bags, leaving 1" of headspace for ex-pansion. Place the containers in the freezer for several hours, or until the soup is frozen solid. Remove each bag from its container, seal tightly, and label with the name, amount, and date. Most soups freeze well for up to 6 months.

Keep in mind that cream soups made with milk may separate when they are thawed. To avoid that, prepare the soup according to the recipe without adding the milk. Stir in the milk after you thaw and reheat the soup.

For "free" soup anytime, freeze small amounts of leftover cooked meat, vegetables, grains, beans, and even grated cheese in one large, plastic container. When they add up to a full container, throw them into a pot, cover with broth, and simmer until the flavors blend. You don't even have to thaw the ingredients. Serve as a chunky soup or puree in a blender or food processor with a little low-fat milk, low-fat plain yogurt, or reduced-fat sour cream.

You'll never be hungry again with soup in the freezer. It adds nutrition and variety to your meals for just pennies. ∎

Minestrone

[Photograph on page 118]

This hearty Italian soup makes a wonderful vegetarian entrée served
with either crusty bread or Fast Focaccia (page 33). If desired,
serve the soup with a sprinkle of extra Parmesan on top.

**1 medium onion, chopped, or
1½ cups frozen chopped
onions**

2 cloves garlic, minced

**1 can (14½ ounces) fat-free,
reduced-sodium chicken or
vegetable broth**

**1 can (15 ounces) dark red
kidney beans, undrained**

**1 can (14½ ounces) chopped
tomatoes, undrained**

**1 can (8 ounces) Italian green
beans, drained**

**1 cup shredded cabbage or
coleslaw mix**

¼ cup dry white wine

1 teaspoon chili powder

**¾ teaspoon dried rosemary,
crushed**

**¼ teaspoon ground black
pepper**

**½ cup dry elbow macaroni or
ditalini**

**½ cup shredded Parmesan
cheese**

1. Place the onion and garlic in a large saucepan, cover,
and cook over low heat for 10 minutes, or until soft
and translucent. (Add a little water, if necessary, to prevent scorching.)

2. Add the broth, kidney beans, tomatoes, green beans,
cabbage or coleslaw mix, wine, chili powder, rosemary,
and pepper. Bring to a boil over high heat. Stir in the
macaroni or ditalini and cook over medium heat for 12
minutes, or until the pasta is just tender. Remove from
the heat, add the cheese, and stir until melted.

Makes 7 servings

Per serving: 140 calories, 8 g protein, 22 g carbohydrates, 2 g
fat, 5 mg cholesterol, 5 g dietary fiber, 538 mg sodium

1 Carb Choice

Spinach Soup

Surprise your guests at your next dinner party by adding an 8-ounce can
of oysters to this recipe and calling it Oysters Rockefeller Soup!

1. In a medium saucepan, combine the broth, spinach, and onion flakes. Bring to a boil over medium heat and cook for about 5 minutes, or until the spinach is completely thawed. Let cool for 5 minutes.

2. Transfer to a blender or food processor. Add the sour cream and blend until smooth. To serve cold, pour into a bowl, cover, and refrigerate for at least 2 hours. To serve hot, return to the saucepan and warm briefly; do not boil. Serve sprinkled with the chives (if using).

Makes 6 servings

Per serving: 54 calories, 4 g protein, 9 g carbohydrates, 0 g fat, 0 mg cholesterol, 2 g dietary fiber, 107 mg sodium

½ **Carb Choice**

1 **can (14½ ounces) fat-free, reduced-sodium chicken broth**

1 **package (10 ounces) frozen chopped spinach**

1 **tablespoon dehydrated onion flakes**

1 **cup fat-free or reduced-fat sour cream**

Chopped chives (optional)

QUICK
   SWITCH • Add ½ teaspoon dried dill weed and a pinch of ground nutmeg. • Or replace the spinach with frozen broccoli.

Cheddar Cheese Soup

[Photograph on page 119]

Low-fat products make this classic favorite a pleasure you can enjoy often.

2 cans (10¾ ounces each) low-sodium, low-fat condensed cream of celery soup

1 can (14½ ounces) fat-free, reduced-sodium chicken broth

1 can (12 ounces) fat-free evaporated milk

2 tablespoons dehydrated onion flakes

1 cup shredded reduced-fat sharp Cheddar cheese

1. In a large saucepan, whisk together the soup, broth, milk, and onion flakes until smooth. Bring just to a boil over medium heat, whisking often. Reduce the heat to low. Add the cheese and stir until melted; do not boil.

Makes 6 servings

Per serving: 142 calories, 9 g protein, 13 g carbohydrates, 5 g fat, 11 mg cholesterol, 0 g dietary fiber, 541 mg sodium

½ **Carb Choice**

QUICK
SWITCH • Replace the cream of celery soup with cream of mushroom and add 1 tablespoon sherry or ½ teaspoon sherry extract.

Crab Bisque

This soup is so surprisingly good that you will want to make it
for dinner parties even when you aren't in a hurry. It can also be served cold
and is a great addition to summer brunch and picnic menus.

1. In a medium saucepan, whisk together the tomato soup, pea soup, milk, and crab. Bring just to a boil over medium heat, whisking often. Reduce the heat to low. Whisk in the butter until melted. Remove from the heat and whisk in the sherry or sherry extract.

Makes 6 servings

Per serving: 169 calories, 10 g protein, 21 g carbohydrates, 4 g fat, 23 mg cholesterol, 2 g dietary fiber, 694 mg sodium

1 Carb Choice

1 can (10¾ ounces) reduced-sodium tomato soup

1 can (10¾ ounces) condensed green pea soup

1 can (12 ounces) fat-free evaporated milk

1 can (6½ ounces) crab, rinsed and drained

1 tablespoon butter

¼ cup sherry or 2 teaspoons sherry extract

Oyster Stew

You can replace the oysters with other types of seafood in this basic recipe.

½ **cup water**

⅓ **cup dry Potato Buds**

1 **can (12 ounces) fat-free evaporated milk**

1 **bottle (8 ounces) clam juice**

¼ **teaspoon ground celery seeds**

¼ **teaspoon ground black pepper**

1 **can (8 ounces) oysters, undrained**

1. Bring the water to a boil in a medium saucepan over high heat. Pour into a small bowl and stir in the potatoes until smooth.

2. In the same saucepan, mix the milk, clam juice, celery seeds, and pepper. Bring to a boil over medium-low heat. Remove from the heat and stir in the potatoes. Stir in the oysters. Cover and let stand for 3 minutes.

Makes 4 servings

Per serving: 81 calories, 7 g protein, 9 g carbohydrates, 2 g fat, 32 mg cholesterol, 0 g dietary fiber, 126 mg sodium

½ **Carb Choice**

THE SPICE RACK **PICKING PEPPER**
The world's most popular spice comes in shades of black, white, and green. Regardless of their color, all peppercorns are from the same plant. They're harvested while still green, then processed to yield the differences in color and flavor. Pink peppercorns aren't really peppercorns at all but the berry of an unrelated tree. Pepper adds zip to just about anything!

Clam Chowder

[Photograph on page 118]

This soup has the taste of a long-simmered New England
chowder without the fuss or the fatty bacon.

1. Warm the oil in a large saucepan over low heat. Add
   the onion and garlic. Cover and cook for 10 minutes, or
   until soft and translucent. Uncover and continue to
   cook, stirring frequently, until browned.

2. Add the corn, milk, soup, clams, water, pimientos,
   basil, pepper, liquid smoke, and parsley (if using).
   Cover and simmer for 10 minutes.

Makes 6 servings

Per serving: 161 calories, 7 g protein, 28 g carbohydrates, 4 g
fat, 6 mg cholesterol, 2 g dietary fiber, 827 mg sodium

1½ Carb Choices

1 tablespoon canola oil

1 medium onion, chopped, or
1½ cups frozen chopped
onions

1 clove garlic, minced

1 can (16½ ounces) cream-style
corn

1 can (12 ounces) fat-free
evaporated milk

1 can (10¾ ounces) low-
sodium, low-fat condensed
cream of potato soup

2 cans (6½ ounces each)
chopped or minced clams,
undrained

1 cup water

1 jar (2 ounces) sliced
pimientos, undrained

½ teaspoon dried basil, crushed

¼ teaspoon ground black
pepper

¼ teaspoon liquid smoke

2 tablespoons chopped fresh
parsley (optional)

Seafood Soup

This hearty, satisfying soup is a wonderfully easy one-dish meal.
All you need to add is some crusty whole grain or sourdough bread.

1 tablespoon extra-virgin olive oil

1 medium onion, chopped, or 1½ cups frozen chopped onions

2 cloves garlic, minced

1 can (10¾ ounces) reduced-sodium tomato soup

2 cans (6½ ounces each) chopped or minced clams, undrained

1 can (6½ ounces) crab, rinsed and drained

1 can (6 ounces) shrimp, rinsed and drained

1 jar (2 ounces) sliced pimientos, undrained

1⅓ cups water

¼ cup chopped fresh parsley (optional)

¼ teaspoon dried basil, crushed

¼ teaspoon dried oregano, crushed

¼ teaspoon salt

¼ teaspoon ground black pepper

⅛ teaspoon red-pepper flakes

1. Warm the oil in a large saucepan over low heat. Add the onion and garlic. Cover and cook for 15 minutes, or until soft and translucent.

2. Stir in the soup, clams, crab, shrimp, pimientos, water, parsley (if using), basil, oregano, salt, pepper, and pepper flakes. Cover and cook for 10 minutes.

Makes 4 servings

Per serving: 167 calories, 20 g protein, 9 g carbohydrates, 5 g fat, 114 mg cholesterol, 1 g dietary fiber, 687 mg sodium

½ **Carb Choice**

Senegalese Soup

This is a really quick version of the famous West African curried chicken soup. It's quicker and lower in fat but retains all of the taste appeal of the original.

1. Put the almonds in a small skillet and stir over medium heat for 5 minutes, or until toasted. Remove from the heat. Set aside.

2. In a blender or food processor, combine the milk, soup, applesauce, and curry powder. Blend until smooth. Pour into a medium saucepan and bring to a boil over medium-low heat, stirring constantly. Stir in the liquid from the chicken.

3. Remove from the heat. Break the chicken into bite-size pieces and stir into the soup. Serve sprinkled with the almonds.

Makes 6 servings

Per serving: 135 calories, 13 g protein, 13 g carbohydrates, 4 g fat, 27 mg cholesterol, 0 g dietary fiber, 480 mg sodium

½ Carb Choice

6 teaspoons chopped raw almonds

1 can (12 ounces) fat-free evaporated milk

1 can (10¾ ounces) low-sodium, low-fat condensed cream of chicken soup

½ cup unsweetened applesauce

½ teaspoon curry powder

1 can (9¾ ounces) chunk white chicken packed in water, undrained

BOXED SOUPS

Ready-made boxed soups come in aseptic packages and are shelf-stable. There are lots of flavors to choose from, and they're extremely versatile. Most of them are just as good cold as they are heated. In the summer, one of my favorite first courses is chilled butternut squash soup. I add ½ teaspoon curry powder and ⅛ teaspoon ground ginger to 2 cups creamy butternut soup and stir in 2 tablespoons mango chutney. ∎

Southwestern Corn and Chicken Soup

If you'd like, you can crush some baked tortilla chips
and sprinkle them over the soup.

1 tablespoon canola oil

1 small onion, finely chopped,
or 1 cup frozen chopped
onions

3 tablespoons unbleached all-
purpose flour

¾ teaspoon ground cumin

½ teaspoon chili powder

1 can (14½ ounces) fat-free,
reduced-sodium chicken
broth

1 can (14½ ounces) chopped
tomatoes, undrained

1 package (10 ounces) frozen
corn kernels

1 can (12 ounces) fat-free
evaporated milk

1 can (9¾ ounces) chunk white
chicken packed in water,
undrained

1. Warm the oil in a large saucepan over medium-low heat. Add the onion and cook, stirring frequently, for 5 minutes, or until translucent. Add the flour, cumin, and chili powder. Cook, stirring constantly, for 3 minutes.

2. Meanwhile, bring the broth to a boil in a small saucepan. Add to the onion mixture and whisk until completely incorporated and the liquid is smooth. Stir in the tomatoes and corn. Slowly stir in the milk and the liquid from the chicken. Bring to a simmer; do not boil. Break the chicken into bite-size pieces and stir into the soup.

Makes 8 servings

Per serving: 140 calories, 18 g protein, 18 g carbohydrates, 3 g fat, 17 mg cholesterol, 2 g dietary fiber, 305 mg sodium

1 Carb Choice

QUICK
SWITCH • Replace the cumin and chili powder with 1 teaspoon Italian herb seasoning.

Thai Chicken and Water Chestnut Soup

Look for fish sauce and chili paste in the international section of your supermarket. These high-flavor ingredients enhance many Asian dishes and keep for a long time.

1. In a large saucepan, mix the water, broth, fish sauce, brown sugar, vinegar, chili paste, cilantro, and the liquid from the chicken. Bring to a boil over medium-high heat. Reduce the heat to medium-low and simmer for 10 minutes. Add the water chestnuts. Break the chicken into bite-size pieces and stir into the soup. Heat through.

Makes 6 servings

Per serving: 88 calories, 10 g protein, 20 g carbohydrates, 2 g fat, 22 mg cholesterol, 1 g dietary fiber, 232 mg sodium

½ **Carb Choice**

2 cups water

1 can (14½ ounces) fat-free, reduced-sodium chicken broth

3 tablespoons fish sauce

1 tablespoon packed light brown sugar

1 tablespoon rice vinegar

1 teaspoon chili paste

½ teaspoon dried cilantro, crushed

1 can (9¾ ounces) chunk white chicken packed in water, undrained

1 can (8 ounces) sliced water chestnuts, drained

Chicken and Rice Soup

For a more economical soup, use half the amount of dried mushrooms
or replace them with two 4-ounce cans of sliced mushrooms (drained).
If you prefer not to use the wine, simply omit it.

2 ounces dried mushrooms

2 cans (14½ ounces each) fat-free, reduced-sodium chicken broth

1 can (9¾ ounces) chunk chicken packed in water, undrained

½ cup uncooked quick-cooking brown rice

¼ teaspoon ground celery seeds

2 tablespoons Madeira wine

1. Place the mushrooms in a heatproof bowl. Pour enough boiling water over them to cover them completely. Allow to stand for 20 minutes.

2. In a large saucepan, bring the broth and the liquid from the chicken to a boil over medium heat. Add the rice and celery seeds, cover, and cook for 5 minutes. Remove from the heat and allow to stand, covered, for 5 minutes.

3. Drain the mushrooms and discard the liquid or save for another use. Rinse the mushrooms well, picking over them to remove any grit. Cut off and discard the stems. Slice the caps into ¼" strips and add to the saucepan. Break the chicken into bite-size pieces and add to the saucepan.

4. Bring to a boil over medium heat. Reduce the heat to low, cover, and simmer for 5 minutes. Remove from the heat and stir in the wine.

Makes 6 servings

Per serving: 141 calories, 10 g protein, 20 g carbohydrates, 1 g fat, 21 mg cholesterol, 1 g dietary fiber, 232 mg sodium

1 Carb Choice

QUICK
SWITCH • Replace the celery seeds with 1 teaspoon dried thyme.

DRIED MUSHROOMS:
BIG FLAVOR IN A SMALL PACKAGE

How many times have you bought a bag of fresh mushrooms only to have most of them go bad in the produce bin? You won't have that problem with dried mushrooms. They last virtually forever, and it takes very few to jazz up soups, casseroles, and stir-fries. Store them in the freezer for up to 1 year.

To rehydrate dried mushrooms, place them in a bowl and add enough hot water to cover by about an inch. Let them soak for at least 30 minutes, or until soft. Drain. (You can strain the soaking liquid through cheesecloth to remove any grit and use it in soups or sauces.) Trim away tough stems, thinly slice the caps, and use as though fresh.

Another way to use dried mushrooms—minus the soaking—is to grind them into a powder that can be added to a recipe as a seasoning. No worries about grit this way, either; any grit in the mushrooms will be ground so finely that it will be unnoticeable.

To make dried mushroom powder, coarsely chop a few dried mushrooms, place them in a mini food processor or other small-size food processor, and process in pulses until finely chopped. (You can also use a clean propeller-blade coffee grinder.) Process continuously until the mushrooms turn into powder. Store in a tightly closed container indefinitely.

Dried mushroom powder can be sprinkled into a sauce, a stew, or a soup. It will swiftly season a breading for fried chicken as well as the gravy that is served with it. Dried mushroom powder can be added to salad dressing or pasta dough or sprinkled into simmering rice. ∎

Salads

When I first started working on this book, I felt that really wonderful "pantry" salads would be the greatest challenge. Was I ever surprised! I found a wealth of ingredients for deliciously different salads. Many are designed as entrées, while others are better suited as appetizers or side dishes. Either way, you can coax even more versatility from them by mixing and matching with fresh products you may have on hand. Leftover bits of fish, poultry, meat, and vegetables get new life in a salad. And don't overlook your grocery's salad bar as a source of ready-prepped vegetables and fruits.

in this chapter …

Pear Party Salad

This delightfully different pear salad could also be called
Way-Out Waldorf. Just like the original Waldorf salad, it is a crunchy
combination of a tree fruit, raisins, and nuts. The advantage of this recipe
is that the ingredients can be stored in your cupboard and the salad
put together in minutes for a spur-of-the-moment side dish.

¼ **cup raisins**

½ **cup raw walnuts, chopped**

¼ **cup fat-free or reduced-fat mayonnaise**

¼ **teaspoon curry powder**

¼ **teaspoon ground cinnamon**

2 **cans (16 ounces each) Bartlett pear halves packed in juice, drained and diced**

1 **can (8 ounces) water chestnuts, drained and chopped**

1. Place the raisins in a small bowl and cover with very hot tap water. Set aside for 5 minutes to plump. Drain.

2. Place the walnuts in a medium skillet. Stir over medium heat for 5 minutes, or until lightly toasted. Set aside.

3. In a medium bowl, mix the mayonnaise, curry powder, and cinnamon. Stir in the pears, water chestnuts, and raisins. Cover and refrigerate for at least 1 hour. Stir in the walnuts just before serving.

Makes 4 servings

Per serving: 261 calories, 4 g protein, 43 g carbohydrates, 10 g fat, 0 mg cholesterol, 9 dietary fiber, 127 mg sodium

2½ **Carb Choices**

QUICK
SWITCH • Replace the walnuts with almonds or pecans. • Or replace the raisins with dried cherries or dried apple bits. • Or replace the curry powder with celery seeds.

Tropical Fruit Salad

Here's a refreshing combination of tropical fruits. Serve it with
cottage cheese for a vegetarian lunch. It also makes a nice light dessert.

1. In a large bowl, mix the pineapple, litchi nuts, and oranges. Add the liqueur and stir well. Cover and refrigerate for at least 1 hour.

2. Just before serving, fold in the sour cream. Serve sprinkled with the macadamia nuts (if using).

Makes 6 servings

Per serving: 169 calories, 2 g protein, 35 g carbohydrates, 0 g fat, 0 mg cholesterol, 1 g dietary fiber, 56 mg sodium

2 Carb Choices

QUICK
SWITCH • Replace the orange liqueur with raspberry liqueur. • Or add canned chicken or tuna.

1 **can (20 ounces) pineapple chunks packed in juice, drained**

1 **can (11 ounces) litchi nuts, rinsed and drained**

1 **can (10½ ounces) mandarin orange sections packed in juice, drained**

¼ **cup orange liqueur or frozen orange juice concentrate, thawed**

½ **cup fat-free or reduced-fat sour cream**

2 **tablespoons crushed macadamia nuts (optional)**

Potato Salad

If you're putting together an impromptu picnic and want a really quick potato salad,
this is it. From start to finish, it takes about 7 minutes.

⅓ cup fat-free or reduced-fat
mayonnaise

1 tablespoon brown mustard

1 teaspoon cider vinegar

½ teaspoon celery seeds

¼ teaspoon salt

¼ teaspoon ground black
pepper

2 cans (15 ounces each) new
potatoes, drained and diced

1 jar (4 ounces) sliced
pimientos, drained

1 small onion, chopped, or
1 cup chopped frozen onions

1. In a large bowl, mix the mayonnaise, mustard, vinegar,
celery seeds, salt, and pepper. Add the potatoes,
pimientos, and onion. Mix well.

2. If desired, cover and refrigerate for at least 1 hour.

Makes 8 servings

Per serving: 59 calories, 2 g protein, 12 g carbohydrates, 0 g fat,
0 mg cholesterol, 2 g dietary fiber, 495 mg sodium

½ **Carb Choice**

QUICK
SWITCH • Replace the brown mustard with
honey mustard.

Christmas Cabbage Salad

Because the ingredients in this recipe mirror the traditional holiday colors of green, red, and white, I call it a Christmas salad. But it's good any time of the year. It's also great for entertaining because it can be made ahead of time and works well on buffets.

1. In a large bowl, mix the cabbage, peas, dressing, and chervil.

2. Cover and refrigerate for at least 2 hours.

Makes 6 servings

Per serving: 63 calories, 2 g protein, 12 g carbohydrates, 0 g fat, 0 mg cholesterol, 2 g dietary fiber, 443 mg sodium

½ **Carb Choice**

3 cups finely chopped red cabbage

1 package (10 ounces) frozen peas, thawed, or 1 can (8½ ounces) peas, drained

¾ cup fat-free or reduced-fat ranch dressing

½ teaspoon dried chervil, crushed

QUICK **SWITCH** • Replace the ranch dressing with peppercorn Parmesan or Italian.

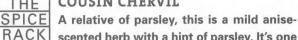 **COUSIN CHERVIL**
A relative of parsley, this is a mild anise-scented herb with a hint of parsley. It's one of the main elements in *fines herbes*, a classic mixture of very finely chopped herbs, the others being chives, tarragon, and parsley. The leaves are the most commonly used part of the herb, but the root is also edible. Though the flavor of fresh is far superior, dried chervil is also available. Use the same way you'd use parsley, but avoid boiling chervil, as the flavor will suffer.

Hearts of Palm
and Mandarin Orange Salad

Although it sounds exotic, this salad uses readily available ingredients.
The honey-mustard dressing is very versatile and is wonderful
on greens or other fruits and vegetables.

¼ cup fat-free or reduced-fat mayonnaise

2 tablespoons honey mustard

1 teaspoon grated lime peel

2 tablespoons lime juice

2 teaspoons extra-virgin olive oil

1 can (18 ounces) hearts of palm, drained and cut lengthwise into thin strips

1 can (10½ ounces) mandarin orange sections packed in juice, drained

1. In a small bowl, whisk together the mayonnaise, mustard, lime peel, and lime juice. Whisk in the oil.

2. Arrange the hearts of palm and oranges on individual plates. Drizzle with the mayonnaise mixture.

Makes 4 servings

Per serving: 88 calories, 1 g protein, 16 g carbohydrates, 3 g fat, 0 mg cholesterol, 2 g dietary fiber, 361 mg sodium

1 Carb Choice

Curried Tomato and Tofu Salad

For best flavor, make this salad several hours before serving.
It is also a perfect filling for vegetarian pita sandwiches.

1. In a large bowl, mix the mayonnaise, soy sauce, curry powder, turmeric, pepper, ginger, and pepper flakes (if using). Add the tomatoes, tofu, and onion. Mix well.

2. Cover and refrigerate for at least 2 hours. Serve sprinkled with the cilantro (if using).

Makes 6 servings

Per serving: 43 calories, 4 g protein, 6 g carbohydrates, 1 g fat, 0 mg cholesterol, 1 g dietary fiber, 265 mg sodium

½ **Carb Choice**

2 **tablespoons fat-free or reduced-fat mayonnaise**

1 **tablespoon reduced-sodium soy sauce**

1 **teaspoon curry powder**

½ **teaspoon turmeric**

¼ **teaspoon ground black pepper**

¼ **teaspoon ground ginger**

⅛ **teaspoon red-pepper flakes (optional)**

1 **can (14½ ounces) chopped tomatoes, drained**

1 **package (10½ ounces) low-fat silken firm tofu, drained and diced**

1 **small onion, chopped, or ½ cup frozen chopped onions**

Fresh cilantro leaves (optional)

Jelled Borscht Salad

This unusual salad is quite beautiful. You can also serve the partially
jelled borscht as a cold soup (refrigerate it for only about an hour, until thick
but still spoonable) and use the beets in other salads or in hot dishes.

1 **jar (16 ounces) borscht with beets**

½ **teaspoon dried dill weed**

2 **envelopes unflavored gelatin**

¼ **cup reduced-fat sour cream**

1. Pour the borscht through a strainer into a medium bowl. Transfer the beets from the strainer to a small container, add the dill, cover, and refrigerate until needed.

2. Pour ¼ cup of the beet liquid into a small bowl and sprinkle with the gelatin. Let stand for 5 minutes to soften. Bring ¾ cup of the remaining liquid to a boil in a small saucepan. Pour over the softened gelatin and stir until completely dissolved. Add to the remaining liquid and mix well. Pour into an 8" × 8" baking dish and refrigerate for 3 hours, or until firm.

3. To serve, divide the reserved beets among individual soup bowls or plates. Cut the jelled borscht into small cubes and spoon over the beets. Top each serving with a spoonful of sour cream.

Makes 4 servings

Per serving: 60 calories, 4 g protein, 10 g carbohydrates, 0 g fat, 1 mg cholesterol, 1 g dietary fiber, 264 mg sodium

½ **Carb Choice**

THE SPICE RACK

DISTINCTIVE DILL

Dill is an annual herb that has refined feathery green strands with a distinctive lemony caraway flavor. Although dried dill weed doesn't really hold a candle to fresh, it's still an acceptable addition to chicken and fish sauces, fish chowder, cucumber salad, and yogurt dips. Dill seeds also have a caraway flavor, but they're much stronger. They are enhanced by heating, so add them early in the cooking process.

Lemon Chicken Noodle Aspic

This unlikely combination of ingredients is amazingly tasty
and a perfect "ladies luncheon" entrée. Serve on a bed of wilted spinach
and sprinkle with toasted sliced almonds.

1. Place the gelatin in a large bowl. Add the water and stir until the gelatin is completely dissolved. Transfer to a blender. Add the cream cheese, mayonnaise, and tarragon. Blend until smooth. Pour back into the bowl. Stir in the soup and mix well.

2. Fold in the water chestnuts, scallions (if using), and chicken. Spoon into an 11" × 7" baking dish or individual molds. Refrigerate for several hours, or until firm. Unmold.

Makes 4 servings

Per serving: 228 calories, 16 g protein, 34 g carbohydrates, 3 g fat, 39 mg cholesterol, 2 g dietary fiber, 954 mg sodium

2 Carb Choices

QUICK
SWITCH • Replace the chicken with canned tuna, crab, or shrimp or a combination of chopped leftovers.

1 **box (4-serving-size) lemon gelatin**

¾ **cup boiling water**

1 **package (8 ounces) fat-free or reduced-fat cream cheese**

½ **cup fat-free or reduced-fat mayonnaise**

1 **teaspoon dried tarragon, crushed**

1 **can (10¾ ounces) low-sodium, low-fat chicken noodle soup**

1 **can (8 ounces) water chestnuts, drained and finely chopped**

6 **scallions, chopped (optional)**

1 **can (9¾ ounces) chunk white chicken packed in water, drained and broken into bite-size pieces**

Three-Bean Salad

[Photograph on page 127]

Three-bean salad is a classic for good reason. It's easy to prepare,
and people like it. It's ideal for picnics and casual lunches. If you want
a little "zippier" taste, add about ½ cup of chopped onion.

¾ **cup fat-free or reduced-fat Italian dressing**

¼ **cup sugar**

1 **can (16 ounces) cut green beans, drained**

1 **can (16 ounces) cut wax beans, drained**

1 **can (15 ounces) dark red kidney beans, rinsed and drained**

1. In a large bowl, combine the dressing and sugar. Whisk until the sugar dissolves. Stir in the green beans, wax beans, and kidney beans.

2. Cover and refrigerate for several hours or overnight.

Makes 7 servings

Per serving: 124 calories, 4 g protein, 26 g carbohydrates, 0 g fat, 0 mg cholesterol, 5 g dietary fiber, 791 mg sodium

1½ **Carb Choices**

Black Bean Salad

Invite this spicy salad to picnics and tailgate parties. It's good warm or at room temperature. You can also turn it into a dip for baked tortilla chips just by pureeing the beans before combining them with the other ingredients.

1. Place the onion and garlic in a large saucepan, cover, and cook over low heat for 10 minutes, or until soft and translucent. (Add a little water, if necessary, to prevent scorching.)

2. Stir in the chile peppers, chili powder, black pepper, cumin, and salt. Cook, stirring often, for 3 minutes. Add the beans and mix well.

Makes 8 servings

Per serving: 75 calories, 4 g protein, 16 g carbohydrates, 0 g fat, 0 mg cholesterol, 6 g dietary fiber, 491 mg sodium

1 Carb Choice

QUICK
SWITCH • Replace the chili powder with ½ teaspoon Cajun spice blend.

1 **medium onion, chopped, or 1½ cups frozen chopped onions**

1 **clove garlic, minced**

1 **can (4 ounces) diced green chile peppers**

1½ **teaspoons chili powder**

½ **teaspoon ground black pepper**

½ **teaspoon ground cumin**

¼ **teaspoon salt**

2 **cans (15 ounces each) black beans, rinsed and drained**

Roasted Sweet Pepper and Pinto Bean Salad

Cooking the ingredients for this salad really intensifies their flavor. To turn this into a hot or cold entrée, stir in canned tuna or chicken.

1 tablespoon extra-virgin olive oil

1 clove garlic, minced

1 medium onion, chopped, or 1½ cups frozen chopped onions

¾ teaspoon dried oregano, crushed

¾ teaspoon dried basil, crushed

¼ teaspoon ground black pepper

⅛ teaspoon red-pepper flakes (optional)

2 jars (7 ounces each) roasted red peppers, drained and sliced

1 can (15 ounces) pinto beans, rinsed and drained

1. Warm the oil in a large nonstick skillet over medium heat. Add the garlic and cook for 1 minute. Stir in the onion, oregano, basil, black pepper, and pepper flakes (if using). Cook, stirring frequently, for 5 minutes, or until the onion is translucent. Stir in the red peppers and beans. Cook for 2 minutes. Serve at room temperature or refrigerate until cold.

Makes 4 servings

Per serving: 148 calories, 6 g protein, 23 g carbohydrates, 4 g fat, 0 mg cholesterol, 4 g dietary fiber, 457 mg sodium

1½ Carb Choices

QUICK **SWITCH** • Replace the basil with ground cumin.

Cannellini Bean Salad

Here's a terrific salad for picnics and tailgate parties because it contains
no animal protein and is therefore safe to leave unrefrigerated for several hours.
Also, it tastes better at room temperature than cold.

1. In a large bowl, mix the oil, lemon juice, oregano, pepper, pepper flakes (if using), and garlic. Add the tomatoes, beans, onion, and parsley (if using). Toss to mix well.

Makes 4 servings

Per serving: 178 calories, 9 g protein, 28 g carbohydrates, 4 g fat, 0 mg cholesterol, 7 g dietary fiber, 172 mg sodium

1½ Carb Choices

QUICK SWITCH • Replace the lemon juice with white wine vinegar.

1 tablespoon extra-virgin olive oil

1 tablespoon lemon juice

½ teaspoon dried oregano, crushed

¼ teaspoon ground black pepper

⅛ teaspoon red-pepper flakes (optional)

1 clove garlic, minced

1 can (14½ ounces) chopped tomatoes, drained

1 can (15 ounces) cannellini beans, rinsed and drained

¼ cup chopped onion

2 tablespoons chopped fresh parsley (optional)

Green Bean Caesar Salad

This egg-free pantry version of a Caesar salad is made with thawed green
beans rather than romaine lettuce. Try adding leftover poultry or meat for
a main course and serve with whole grain bread, pasta, rice, or beans.

**2 tablespoons extra-virgin
olive oil**

1 clove garlic, minced

**1 bag (16 ounces) frozen
french-cut green beans,
thawed**

2 tablespoons lemon juice

**1 tablespoon Worcestershire
sauce**

1 tablespoon red wine vinegar

1½ teaspoons anchovy paste

**¼ teaspoon ground black
pepper**

**½ cup shredded Parmesan
cheese**

**1½ cups Homemade Croutons
(page 85)**

1. Combine the oil and garlic in a large nonstick skillet.
   Stir over medium heat for 1 minute, or just until the
   garlic sizzles. Add the beans and cook, stirring constantly, for 3 minutes.

2. Remove from the heat and stir in the lemon juice,
   Worcestershire sauce, vinegar, anchovy paste, and
   pepper. Sprinkle with the cheese and toss to combine.
   Serve warm or refrigerate until cold. Sprinkle with the
   croutons.

Makes 6 servings

Per serving: 120 calories, 6 g protein, 8 g carbohydrates, 8 g fat,
7 mg cholesterol, 2 g dietary fiber, 215 mg sodium

½ Carb Choice

QUICK
SWITCH • Replace the red wine vinegar with balsamic
vinegar.

VINEGAR VARIETIES

Confused by all the choices? Here's what makes each one special.

Balsamic. An aged, low-acid vinegar, its deep color and rich flavor lend a sophisticated touch to salads.

Champagne. This smooth, mildly flavored vinegar has a hint of champagne.

Cider. This is a fruity, tart vinegar with a strong apple presence.

Flavored. Steeped with ingredients ranging from raspberries and herbs to garlic and chile peppers, this is often used in conjunction with "neutral" vinegars to add just a hint of extra taste.

Red wine. This vinegar has a mellow tartness and a medium body that work well with vinaigrettes. It can be combined with balsamic vinegar for a flavorful nuance.

Rice. This has a mild, almost sweet flavor and is often used in Asian salads.

Sherry. A mild vinegar, it has an undertone of dry sherry.

White wine. This mildly flavored vinegar has a hint of white wine. ∎

Mediterranean Tuna Salad

This light salad is delightful served
on fresh greens or mixed with pasta, rice, or beans.

1 **can (12 ounces) solid white
tuna packed in water, drained
and flaked**

12 **kalamata olives, pitted and
thinly sliced**

2 **tablespoons capers**

½ **teaspoon grated lemon peel
(optional)**

¼ **cup lemon juice**

1. In a large bowl, mix the tuna, olives, capers, lemon peel
(if using), and lemon juice.

Makes 4 servings

Per serving: 135 calories, 23 g protein, 2 g carbohydrates, 4 g
fat, 36 mg cholesterol, 0 g dietary fiber, 487 mg sodium

0 Carb Choices

QUICK
SWITCH • Add ½ teaspoon crushed dried herbes de
Provence or basil.

Dilled Tuna and Pasta Shell Salad

[Photograph on page 120]

You can make this recipe with any type of pasta, but the shells create
a great-looking salad for parties. The pimientos add beautiful color,
so I suggest you keep several jars in the pantry for just such use.

1. In a large bowl, mix the mayonnaise, yogurt, vinegar,
dill, tarragon, salt, and pepper. Add the pasta, tuna,
pimientos, and peas. Mix well.

Makes 4 servings

Per serving: 195 calories, 17 g protein, 27 g carbohydrates, 2 g
fat, 18 mg cholesterol, 2 g dietary fiber, 385 mg sodium

1½ Carb Choices

¼ **cup fat-free or reduced-fat
mayonnaise**

¼ **cup fat-free or reduced-fat
plain yogurt**

1 **tablespoon rice vinegar**

½ **teaspoon dried dill weed,
crushed**

¼ **teaspoon dried tarragon,
crushed**

⅛ **teaspoon salt**

⅛ **teaspoon ground black
pepper**

2 **cups cooked pasta shells**

1 **can (6 ounces) solid white
tuna packed in water, drained
and flaked**

1 **jar (2 ounces) sliced
pimientos, drained (optional)**

½ **cup frozen peas, thawed**

DON'T BOIL OVER!

To prevent pasta from boiling over and making a mess,
dab a little oil on your index finger and run it around the
rim before the pot gets hot. The oil will coat rising bubbles,
causing them to burst before they can climb out of the pot. ∎

Tuscan Tuna Salad

This salad is better served at room temperature than cold. To take it along on a
picnic, bring a can opener and add the tuna just before serving. Serve the salad with
crisp vegetables. Leftover salad is good warmed and served over pasta.

2 **cans (16 ounces each)
cannellini beans, rinsed and
drained**

1 **tablespoon extra-virgin
olive oil**

1 **can (12 ounces) solid white
tuna packed in water, drained
and flaked**

1 **small onion, thinly sliced**

2 **teaspoons dried basil,
crushed**

1½ **tablespoons lemon juice**

½ **teaspoon ground black
pepper**

1. Mix the beans and oil in a large bowl. Add the tuna,
onion, basil, lemon juice, and pepper; mix well.

Makes 4 servings

Per serving: 407 calories, 39 g protein, 53 g carbohydrates, 5 g
fat, 26 mg cholesterol, 12 g dietary fiber, 300 mg sodium

3½ Carb Choices

Curried Tropical Chicken Salad

For variety, replace the chicken with tuna or even canned shrimp. I like serving this salad with fat-free cinnamon rice cakes, which are a perfect taste accompaniment.

1. Place the almonds in a small skillet. Stir over medium heat for 5 minutes, or until lightly toasted. Remove from the heat. Set aside.

2. In a large bowl, mix the mayonnaise, chutney, curry powder, ginger, and pepper flakes (if using). Add the chicken, pineapple, and bamboo shoots. Mix well.

3. Cover and refrigerate for at least 1 hour. Serve sprinkled with the almonds.

Makes 4 servings

Per serving: 197 calories, 14 g protein, 22 g carbohydrates, 6 g fat, 31 mg cholesterol, 4 g dietary fiber, 532 mg sodium

1 Carb Choice

QUICK **SWITCH** • Replace the bamboo shoots with water chestnuts.

¼ **cup raw almonds, chopped**

⅓ **cup fat-free or reduced-fat mayonnaise**

3 **tablespoons mango chutney**

1¼ **teaspoons curry powder**

¼ **teaspoon ground ginger**

⅛ **teaspoon red-pepper flakes (optional)**

1 **can (9¾ ounces) chunk white chicken packed in water, drained and broken into bite-size pieces**

1 **can (8 ounces) pineapple chunks packed in juice, drained**

1 **can (8 ounces) sliced bamboo shoots, drained**

Chinese Chicken and Pineapple Salad

This salad uses gelatin to thicken the dressing and give it the slightly creamy
texture usually associated with higher-fat dressings. When possible,
make this type of dressing the day before you plan to use it.

2 **tablespoons cool water**

½ **teaspoon unflavored gelatin**

¼ **cup boiling water**

¼ **cup rice vinegar**

1 **tablespoon packed dark brown sugar**

2 **teaspoons reduced-sodium soy sauce**

½ **teaspoon Chinese five-spice blend**

1 **clove garlic, minced**

2 **teaspoons toasted sesame oil**

¼ **cup chopped raw almonds**

1 **package (8 ounces) coleslaw mix**

2 **cans (9¾ ounces each) chunk white chicken packed in water, drained and broken into bite-size pieces**

1 **can (20 ounces) pineapple chunks packed in juice, drained**

1. Place the cool water in a medium bowl. Sprinkle with the gelatin and let stand for 5 minutes, or until the gelatin is softened. Add the boiling water and stir until the gelatin is completely dissolved. Stir in the vinegar, brown sugar, soy sauce, spice blend, and garlic. Slowly whisk in the oil.

2. Pour into a bottle with a tight-fitting lid. Refrigerate for at least 2 hours. Shake well before using.

3. Put the almonds in a small skillet and cook over medium heat, stirring frequently, for 3 minutes, or until toasted. Remove from the heat. Set aside.

4. Place the coleslaw mix in a large bowl. Add the dressing and toss until all the leaves glisten. Add the chicken and pineapple; toss thoroughly. Serve topped with the almonds.

Makes 4 servings

Per serving: 247 calories, 25 g protein, 12 g carbohydrates, 11 g fat, 65 mg cholesterol, 1 g dietary fiber, 746 mg sodium

½ **Carb Choice**

THE SPICE RACK

FIVE PARTS FLAVOR
Chinese five-spice powder is a pungent mixture of five ground spices: cloves, cinnamon, star anise, fennel seeds, and Szechuan peppercorns. It is used mainly in Chinese cooking and is available in Asian markets and most supermarkets.

Taco Salad

[Photograph on page 121]

Be sure to drain the salsa well to keep the chips from getting soggy
and also to remove excess sodium.

1. In a large bowl, mix the salsa and cumin. Stir in the
corn, chicken, and ¼ cup of the cheese. Divide among
individual plates. Sprinkle evenly with the remaining
¼ cup cheese, top with the sour cream, and surround
with the tortilla chips.

Makes 4 servings

Per serving: 281 calories, 21 g protein, 32 g carbohydrates, 8 g
fat, 40 mg cholesterol, 3 g dietary fiber, 683 mg sodium

2 Carb Choices

QUICK
SWITCH • Replace the tortilla chips with warmed corn
tortillas and fill them with salad.

1½ **cups chunky salsa, drained
well**

⅛ **teaspoon ground cumin**

1 **box (10 ounces) frozen corn
kernels, thawed**

1 **can (9¾ ounces) chunk white
chicken packed in water,
drained and broken into bite-
size pieces**

½ **cup shredded reduced-fat
sharp Cheddar cheese**

¼ **cup reduced-fat sour cream**

4 **cups fat-free or reduced-fat
tortilla chips**

Caraway-Ham Coleslaw

[Photograph on page 122]

This is a super coleslaw with or without the ham.

¼ cup fat-free or reduced-fat mayonnaise

2 tablespoons Dijon mustard

1 tablespoon herb vinegar

1 teaspoon sugar

½ teaspoon caraway seeds

⅛ teaspoon salt

⅛ teaspoon ground black pepper

1 bag (8 ounces) coleslaw mix

1 can (5 ounces) extra-lean chunk ham, drained and flaked

1. In a large bowl, mix the mayonnaise, mustard, vinegar, sugar, caraway seeds, salt, and pepper. Stir in the coleslaw and ham.

Makes 6 servings

Per serving: 52 calories, 5 g protein, 5 g carbohydrates, 1 g fat, 9 mg cholesterol, 0 g dietary fiber, 490 mg sodium

0 Carb Choices

QUICK
SWITCH • Replace the ham with corned beef. • Or replace the Dijon mustard with coarse-grain mustard. • Or replace the caraway seeds with crushed dill seeds or fennel seeds.

Reuben Salad

Here you'll find the fabulous flavors of the famous sandwich for which this salad is named. If you are making this salad ahead of time, cover and refrigerate it without adding the crumbs. If you are serving it immediately, you might want to toss the salad instead of layering it and then top each serving with 2 tablespoons of crumbs.

1. In a small bowl, mix the sour cream, chili sauce, onion flakes, and honey.

2. Line the bottom of a large bowl with half of the coleslaw. Top with the sauerkraut and sprinkle with the parsley (if using). Spread the corned beef evenly over the sauerkraut. Sprinkle with the cheese and top with the remaining coleslaw.

3. Spread the sour cream mixture over the top and sprinkle with the caraway seeds. Sprinkle with the breadcrumbs just before serving.

Makes 10 servings

Per serving: 172 calories, 16 g protein, 11 g carbohydrates, 6 g fat, 35 mg cholesterol, 0 g dietary fiber, 792 mg sodium

½ **Carb Choice**

1 **container (8 ounces) fat-free or reduced-fat sour cream**

¼ **cup chili sauce**

2 **tablespoons dehydrated onion flakes**

1 **tablespoon honey**

1 **bag (18 ounces) coleslaw mix**

1 **can (14½ ounces) sauerkraut, rinsed and drained**

¼ **cup chopped fresh parsley (optional)**

1 **can (12 ounces) lean corned beef, crumbled**

1½ **cups diced reduced-fat Swiss cheese**

½ **teaspoon caraway seeds**

1 **cup toasted breadcrumbs**

Light Aïoli

Aïoli is a French garlic mayonnaise from the region of Provence. It is classically
made with egg yolks and a fair amount of olive oil. In this version, I used tofu
as the base and just enough good extra-virgin olive oil to add flavor and smooth out
the texture. I am delighted with my cholesterol-free, lower-calorie aïoli, and I hope
you will be, too. Use it on meats, fish, vegetables, and sandwiches.

1 package (10½ ounces) low-fat
silken firm tofu, drained

2 tablespoons lemon juice

2 tablespoons extra-virgin
olive oil

3 cloves garlic, halved

½ teaspoon salt

⅛ teaspoon ground black
pepper

1. In a blender or food processor, combine the tofu,
lemon juice, oil, garlic, salt, and pepper. Blend until
smooth. Spoon into a container with a tight-fitting lid
and store in the refrigerator.

Makes 1¼ cups

Per 2-tablespoon serving: 37 calories, 2 g protein, 1 g carbohydrates, 3 g fat, 0 mg cholesterol, 0 g dietary fiber, 126 mg
sodium

0 Carb Choices

QUICK
SWITCH • Add 1 teaspoon anchovy paste or 1 teaspoon
chopped capers.

Oil-Free Salad Dressing

This is the easiest dressing you could hope for, and it keeps a long time.
It's also **very versatile. Modify it to your heart's content.**

1. In a medium bowl, whisk together the lemon juice, sugar, and salt until the sugar and salt dissolve. Whisk in the water, vinegar, mustard, garlic, Worcestershire sauce, and pepper. Use immediately or pour into a container with a tight-fitting lid and store in the refrigerator. Shake well before using.

Makes 2 cups

Per 2-tablespoon serving: 6 calories, 0 g protein, 2 g carbohydrates, 0 g fat, 0 mg cholesterol, 0 g dietary fiber, 86 mg sodium

0 Carb Choices

QUICK
SWITCH • *For Italian dressing:* Add 1 teaspoon *each* crushed dried tarragon, oregano, and basil. • *For Southwestern dressing:* Add ½ teaspoon ground cumin. • *For East Indian dressing:* Add 1 teaspoon curry powder and ¼ teaspoon ground ginger. • *For French dressing:* Add 1 tablespoon crushed dried tarragon. • *For creamy dressing:* Add ¼ cup fat-free or reduced-fat plain yogurt or sour cream.

2 **tablespoons lemon juice**

1 **tablespoon sugar**

½ **teaspoon salt**

1 **cup water**

½ **cup red wine vinegar**

1 **tablespoon Dijon mustard**

2 **cloves garlic, finely chopped**

2 **teaspoons Worcestershire sauce**

¼ **teaspoon ground black pepper**

Sun-Dried Tomato Dressing

This simple dressing gets its lovely color from the tomatoes.
The flavor complements just about any tossed salad.

1 cup water

¼ cup oil-free sun-dried tomatoes

½ cup red wine vinegar

2 tablespoons lemon juice

1 tablespoon sugar

1 tablespoon Dijon mustard

2 cloves garlic, chopped

2 teaspoons Worcestershire sauce

½ teaspoon dried basil

½ teaspoon salt

¼ teaspoon ground black pepper

1. In a small saucepan, bring ½ cup of the water to a boil. Add the tomatoes, cover, and remove from the heat. Let stand for 10 minutes. Transfer to a blender and add the remaining ½ cup water. Blend until smooth.

2. Add the vinegar, lemon juice, sugar, mustard, garlic, Worcestershire sauce, basil, salt, and pepper. Blend until the garlic is finely chopped. Use immediately or pour into a container with a tight-fitting lid and store in the refrigerator. Shake well before using.

Makes 2 cups

Per 2-tablespoon serving: 9 calories, 0 g protein, 2 g carbohydrates, 0 g fat, 0 mg cholesterol, 0 g dietary fiber, 104 mg sodium

0 Carb Choices

ROBUST TOMATO FLAVOR

Dried tomatoes are incredibly convenient and provide a concentrated burst of flavor. Stored in an airtight container out of direct light or in the refrigerator, they'll keep for up to a year. Best of all, they're never out of season!

To rehydrate dried tomatoes, cover them with boiling water and let stand about 2 minutes. Drain, reserving the liquid for soups or sauces.

Dried tomatoes that have been packed in oil don't need to be soaked. Simply remove them from the container and blot them dry. ■

Garlic Croutons

[Photograph on page 119]

Packaged croutons are on my list of unacceptable convenience products.
They taste terrible no matter how fresh they are and cost a lot more than homemade
ones. See "Homemade Croutons" below to make your own, or, for something
a little more elaborate, try these garlic-flavored croutons.

2 **tablespoons extra-virgin olive oil**

1 **clove garlic, minced**

4 **slices bread, cut into ½" cubes**

1. Preheat the oven to 300°F.

2. Warm the oil and garlic in a large nonstick skillet over medium-low heat for 2 minutes, or until the garlic starts to sizzle. Remove from the heat and stir in the bread. Continue stirring until all the oil has been absorbed. Spread in an even layer on a baking sheet. Bake, stirring occasionally, for 25 minutes, or until golden brown. Let cool before storing in an airtight container.

Makes 2 cups

Per ¼-cup serving: 64 calories, 1 g protein, 6 g carbohydrates, 4 g fat, 0 mg cholesterol, 0 g dietary fiber, 67 mg sodium

½ **Carb Choice**

QUICK
SWITCH • Add 1 teaspoon of the crushed dried herb of your choice.

HOMEMADE CROUTONS

Here's how to make fabulous plain croutons—it couldn't be easier! Cut bread slices into ½" cubes, spread them on a cookie sheet, and bake at 300°F until golden brown.

Meatless Meals

If you're like I am, you're eating more and more meat-free meals. And you're doing it because you just plain love them. Whether they're built on a base of beans, pasta, grains, or eggs, they're full of flavor and very satisfying. They draw on worldwide cuisines from Asian and Middle Eastern to Mexican and Italian. Every culture has its signature no-meat dishes that can be whipped up from pantry items in no time at all. Here's a nice cross section of them. Believe me, no one will ask "where's the beef?" (For those who want truly vegetarian dishes, vegetable broth can easily replace the chicken broth called for.)

in this chapter ...

Quesadillas

Think of them as Mexican melted cheese sandwiches.
Serve your favorite salsa on the side.

4 fat-free flour tortillas (8" diameter)

1½ cups shredded reduced-fat Monterey Jack cheese

1 can (4 ounces) diced green chile peppers

1. Coat a large nonstick skillet with cooking spray and warm over medium-low heat. Place a tortilla in the skillet. Sprinkle ¼ cup plus 2 tablespoons (a total of 6 tablespoons) of the cheese evenly over the top.

2. Cook for 3 minutes, or until the cheese melts. Sprinkle 2 tablespoons of the peppers over the cheese. Fold the tortilla in half and cut into pie-shape wedges. Repeat to use the remaining tortillas, cheese, and peppers.

Makes 4 servings

Per serving: 285 calories, 17 g protein, 37 g carbohydrates, 8 g fat, 22 mg cholesterol, 3 g dietary fiber, 735 mg sodium

2 Carb Choices

QUICK
SWITCH • Replace the Monterey Jack cheese with sharp Cheddar. • Or add a little fish, poultry, or meat to the filling.

Bean Burritos

You can embellish this basic recipe by adding sautéed onions
or leftover cooked vegetables, meat, or chicken to the beans.
Serve the burritos with salsa and low-fat sour cream.

1. Preheat the oven to 350°F.

2. Wrap the tortillas in foil and place them in the oven for 10 minutes, or until warm and pliable.

3. In a medium saucepan, mix the beans and peppers. Cook over medium heat, stirring frequently, until hot.

4. Spoon ⅓ cup of the bean mixture onto the lower half of each tortilla. Sprinkle with 2 tablespoons of the cheese (if using). Fold the tortilla, envelope style, around the filling.

Makes 10 servings

Per serving: 278 calories, 15 g protein, 47 g carbohydrates, 4 g fat, 8 mg cholesterol, 7 g dietary fiber, 966 mg sodium

3 Carb Choices

10 **fat-free flour tortillas (8" diameter)**

2 **cans (16 ounces each) vegetarian refried beans**

1 **can (4 ounces) diced green chile peppers**

1¼ **cups shredded reduced-fat sharp Cheddar cheese (optional)**

Black Bean and Pea Pasta with Dried-Tomato Sauce

Be sure to use the dry-pack sun-dried tomatoes to avoid the excess fat
of oil-soaked ones. If you don't have the ready-cut ones, simply chop the dried halves.
For a richer sauce, use milk in place of the water.

8 ounces dry rigatoni

1 can (10¾ ounces) low-sodium, low-fat condensed cream of mushroom soup

⅔ cup sun-dried tomato bits

2 cloves garlic, minced, or ¼ teaspoon garlic powder

1½ teaspoons Italian herb blend, crushed

½ teaspoon liquid smoke

¼ teaspoon ground black pepper

1 can (16 ounces) black beans, rinsed and drained

1 package (10 ounces) frozen peas, thawed

½ cup shredded Parmesan cheese (optional)

1. Cook the rigatoni in a large pot of boiling water according to the package directions until just tender. Drain and return to the pot; set aside.

2. In a large saucepan, mix the soup and 1 soup can of water. Stir in the tomatoes, garlic, herb blend, liquid smoke, and pepper. Bring to a boil over medium heat. Reduce the heat to low and simmer, stirring frequently, for 5 minutes.

3. Stir in the beans and peas; heat through. Remove from the heat and stir in the pasta. Serve sprinkled with the cheese (if using).

Makes 4 servings

Per serving: 447 calories, 22 g protein, 80 g carbohydrates, 6 g fat, 8 mg cholesterol, 11 g dietary fiber, 1,193 mg sodium

5 Carb Choices

NEXT-DAY NOODLES

Few leftovers are as easy to prepare as pasta. To reheat leftover noodles, put them in a strainer or colander and immerse them in boiling water for 1 minute. Remove from the water and drain. All that's left is to whip up a quick sauce, and you're on your way! ∎

Eggs Foo Yung

If you don't have any fresh scallion tops to add to these little Chinese omelets,
replace them with a tablespoon of dehydrated onions.

1. In a small saucepan, mix the water and cornstarch until the cornstarch is completely dissolved. Stir in the soy sauce, vinegar, sugar, and salt. Cook over medium-low heat, stirring constantly, for 5 minutes, or until thickened. Keep warm over low heat.

2. In a medium bowl, mix the egg substitute, bean sprouts, shrimp, and scallions (if using).

3. Coat a large nonstick skillet with cooking spray and warm over medium heat for 2 minutes, or until water drops sprinkled in the skillet dance on the surface. Working in batches, if necessary, spoon rounded ¼ cupfuls of the egg mixture into the pan. Cook for 5 minutes, or until browned on the bottom. Flip the eggs, reduce the heat to low, and cook for 5 minutes, or until cooked through. Serve topped with the soy sauce mixture.

Makes 6 servings

Per serving: 143 calories, 23 g protein, 5 g carbohydrates, 3 g fat, 107 mg cholesterol, 0 g dietary fiber, 492 mg sodium

0 Carb Choices

- ½ **cup water**
- 2 **teaspoons cornstarch**
- 2 **tablespoons reduced-sodium soy sauce**
- 1½ **teaspoons cider vinegar**
- 1 **teaspoon sugar**
- ¼ **teaspoon salt**
- 1½ **cups fat-free liquid egg substitute**
- 1 **can (16 ounces) bean sprouts, drained**
- 2 **cans (6 ounces each) shrimp, rinsed and drained**
- ½ **cup finely chopped scallion tops (optional)**

Chile Relleno Casserole

This recipe takes the prize when you want a real Southwestern treat that can be assembled in minutes. Serve it with hot corn tortillas and lots of salsa.

2 cans (4 ounces each) whole green chile peppers, drained

1 cup shredded reduced-fat sharp Cheddar cheese

3 eggs

2 cups fat-free or 1% milk

½ cup unbleached all-purpose flour

¼ teaspoon salt

1. Preheat the oven to 350°F.

2. Coat an 11" × 7" baking dish with cooking spray. Line the bottom with the peppers in a single layer. Sprinkle evenly with the cheese.

3. In a medium bowl, whisk together the eggs, milk, flour, and salt until smooth. Pour over the peppers. Bake for 45 minutes, or until set and lightly browned.

Makes 4 servings

Per serving: 256 calories, 20 g protein, 18 g carbohydrates, 8 g fat, 176 mg cholesterol, 0 g dietary fiber, 444 mg sodium

1 Carb Choice

Fettuccine with Shiitake Mushrooms

[Photograph on page 123]

You'd be well advised to keep dried mushrooms in the pantry because
they are so versatile and add panache to otherwise plain recipes.

1. Place the mushrooms in a heatproof bowl. Pour enough boiling water over them to cover completely. Allow to stand for 20 minutes. Drain; discard the liquid or save for another use. Rinse the mushrooms well, picking over them to remove any grit. Cut off and discard the stems. Slice the caps into ½" strips.

2. Warm the oil in a large nonstick skillet. Add the shallot or onion and garlic. Cook over medium heat, stirring frequently, for 3 minutes, or until soft and translucent. Reduce the heat to low and add the mushrooms. Cook, stirring frequently, for 15 minutes.

3. In a small bowl, mix the water and milk powder until the milk is completely dissolved. Add to the mushrooms. Stir in the sherry or sherry extract, soy sauce, and pepper. Simmer for 10 minutes.

4. Cook the fettuccine in a large pot of boiling water according to the package directions until just tender. Drain and place in a warm bowl. Spoon the mushroom mixture over the top and sprinkle with the parsley (if using).

Makes 3 servings

Per serving: 456 calories, 16 g protein, 85 g carbohydrates, 5 g fat, 2 mg cholesterol, 5 g dietary fiber, 120 mg sodium

5½ Carb Choices

3 **ounces dried shiitake mushrooms**

2 **teaspoons extra-virgin olive oil**

2 **tablespoons minced shallot or onion**

2 **cloves garlic, minced**

½ **cup water**

¼ **cup fat-free milk powder**

¼ **cup sherry or 2 teaspoons sherry extract**

1 **teaspoon reduced-sodium soy sauce**

⅛ **teaspoon ground black pepper**

8 **ounces dry fettuccine**

Finely chopped fresh parsley (optional)

Creamy Butternut Squash Pasta

You can use any type of pasta in this dish. My favorite is pappardelle noodles,
but since they're sometimes hard to find, I substituted lasagna noodles here.

8 ounces dry lasagna noodles

2 teaspoons extra-virgin
olive oil

1 medium onion, finely
chopped

1 clove garlic, minced

1½ teaspoons dried marjoram,
crushed

¼ teaspoon salt

¼ teaspoon ground black
pepper

⅛ teaspoon red-pepper flakes
(optional)

1 box (15 ounces) creamy
butternut squash soup

¼ cup shredded Parmesan
cheese

1. Cook the lasagna noodles in a large pot of boiling
water according to the package directions until just
tender. Drain and set aside.

2. Warm the oil in a large nonstick skillet over medium
heat. Add the onion and garlic and cook, stirring frequently, for 10 minutes, or until soft and translucent.
Stir in the marjoram, salt, pepper, and pepper flakes.
Stir in the soup and bring to a simmer.

3. Divide the noodles among large plates or pasta bowls
and top with the sauce. Sprinkle with the cheese.

Makes 4 servings

Per serving: 294 calories, 11 g protein, 51 g carbohydrates, 5g
fat, 6 mg cholesterol, 2 g dietary fiber, 363 mg sodium

4½ Carb Choices

QUICK
SWITCH • Replace the marjoram with basil or oregano.

PERFECT PESTO

Pesto originated in Genoa as an easy, no-cook basil sauce for pasta. But the basic method lends itself to many variations—and you can keep most of the ingredients on hand for quick preparation.

To use the following pestos as pasta sauce, cook 16 ounces of pasta according to the package directions. Reserve ¼ cup of the cooking water. Place the pasta in a serving bowl. Add the pesto and about 2 tablespoons of the reserved cooking water. Toss and add up to 2 tablespoons more water to make the pesto cling nicely to the pasta.

Asian pesto. In a blender or food processor, combine 1 can (16 ounces) rinsed and drained water chestnuts, ½ cup soy sauce, ⅓ cup rice wine vinegar or white wine vinegar, ¼ cup honey, 1 tablespoon peanut butter, 1 tablespoon toasted sesame oil, and 1½ teaspoons minced garlic. Process until smooth.

Olive pesto. In a blender or food processor, combine ½ cup chopped canned tomatoes, ¼ cup chicken broth, 3 tablespoons pitted olives, 2 tablespoons balsamic vinegar, 1 tablespoon olive oil, 1 tablespoon dried basil, 1 teaspoon minced garlic, and a pinch of salt and pepper. Process until smooth.

Roasted red pepper pesto. In a blender or food processor, combine 1 jar (7 ounces) drained roasted red peppers, ¾ cup chopped parsley, ⅓ cup toasted pine nuts, 1 tablespoon wine vinegar, 1 tablespoon grated Parmesan cheese, 1 teaspoon minced garlic, and a pinch of salt and pepper. Process until smooth. ■

Macaroni and Cheese

Macaroni and cheese equals creamy spoonfuls of comfort. I have added
sour cream to this version to make the sauce even more velvety.

2 cups elbow macaroni

**1½ tablespoons unbleached
all-purpose flour**

½ teaspoon salt

½ teaspoon paprika

**¼ teaspoon ground black
pepper**

⅛ teaspoon cayenne pepper

2 tablespoons butter

1 onion, finely chopped

1 clove garlic, minced

2 cups 2% milk

**2 cups shredded reduced-fat
sharp Cheddar cheese**

8 ounces fat-free sour cream

**1 large slice rye bread,
crumbled**

1. Preheat the oven to 350°F. Coat a 2-quart baking dish
   with cooking spray.

2. Prepare the macaroni according to package directions.
   Drain and place in a large bowl.

3. Meanwhile, in a small bowl, combine the flour, salt,
   paprika, black pepper, and cayenne.

4. Melt the butter in a medium saucepan over low heat.
   Add the onion and garlic and cook, stirring occasionally, for 8 minutes, or until the onion is soft and
   translucent. Add the flour mixture. Cook, stirring constantly, for 3 minutes. Gradually add the milk. Cook,
   stirring constantly, for 8 minutes, or until smooth and
   slightly thickened. Remove from the heat and add the
   cheese. Stir until melted.

5. Add the sour cream to the pasta and mix well. Pour the
   cheese sauce over the macaroni and stir to combine.
   Spoon into the prepared baking dish. Sprinkle with the
   bread. Coat lightly with cooking spray.

6. Bake for 20 minutes, or until hot and bubbly.

Makes 8 servings

Per serving: 318 calories, 18 g protein, 39 g carbohydrates, 9 g
fat, 25 mg cholesterol, 1 g dietary fiber, 525 mg sodium

2½ Carb Choices

Fusilli with Green Beans

[Photograph on page 124]

This easy pasta dish can be made with other canned or leftover cooked vegetables. It is also good with canned fish, poultry, or meat added to it.

1. Cook the fusilli in a large pot of boiling water according to the package directions until just tender. Drain, transfer to a large bowl, and keep warm.

2. In a large nonstick skillet, combine the oil, garlic, black pepper, and pepper flakes. Stir over medium heat for 1 minute, or until the garlic starts to sizzle. Stir in the beans and heat through. Add to the pasta. Sprinkle with the cheese and toss to mix well.

Makes 4 servings

Per serving: 310 calories, 13 g protein, 48 g carbohydrates, 7 g fat, 8 mg cholesterol, 3 g dietary fiber, 192 mg sodium

3 Carb Choices

QUICK SWITCH • Replace the red-pepper flakes with 2 tablespoons sun-dried tomato bits.

- **8 ounces dry fusilli**
- **1 tablespoon extra-virgin olive oil**
- **1 clove garlic, minced**
- **⅛ teaspoon ground black pepper**
- **⅛ teaspoon red-pepper flakes**
- **1 package (10 ounces) french-cut green beans, thawed**
- **½ cup shredded Parmesan cheese**

Spinach and Pasta in a Hurry

I came up with this quick and easy pasta dish one rainy evening when my husband told me that we didn't have anything in the house to eat. I didn't feel like going out in the rain so I decided to get creative with what we did have. Interestingly enough, he has frequently asked me to make "that spinach and pasta thing" again!

1½ **tablespoons extra-virgin olive oil**

¼ **teaspoon salt**

¼ **teaspoon ground black pepper**

⅛ **teaspoon crushed red-pepper flakes**

4 **ounces whole wheat pasta**

2 **bags (6 ounces each) prewashed baby spinach leaves**

¼ **cup shredded Parmesan cheese**

1. In a small bowl, combine the oil, salt, black pepper, and pepper flakes.

2. Prepare the pasta according to package directions. Drain thoroughly and return to the pot. Add the oil mixture and mix well.

3. Poke a hole in each of the unopened bags of spinach and microwave on high power for 90 seconds. Empty each bag of cooked spinach into a separate pasta bowl. Top each bowl of spinach with half of the pasta mixture. Top each with 2 tablespoons of the cheese.

Make 2 servings

Per serving: 371 calories, 17 g protein, 49 g carbohydrates, 15 g fat, 8 mg cholesterol, 5 g dietary fiber, 592 mg sodium

3 Carb Choices

Stir-Fried Ginger Noodles

These spicy noodles are delicious by themselves or combined with tofu, fish, poultry, or meat. If you've got fresh ginger on hand, chop ¼ cup and cook it with the garlic.

1. Cook the pasta in a large pot of boiling water according to the package directions until just tender. Drain, return to the pot, and keep warm.

2. Meanwhile, warm the canola oil in a small saucepan over medium heat. Add the garlic and stir for 1 minute. Stir in the soy sauce, mirin or apple juice, sesame oil, and ginger. Pour over the pasta and toss to coat well.

Makes 6 servings

Per serving: 177 calories, 5 g protein, 30 g carbohydrates, 4 g fat, 0 mg cholesterol, 1 g dietary fiber, 165 mg sodium

2 Carb Choices

QUICK
SWITCH • Replace the soy sauce and mirin or apple juice with ¼ cup teriyaki sauce.

8 **ounces dry angel hair pasta**

1 **tablespoon canola oil**

5 **cloves garlic, minced**

2 **tablespoons reduced-sodium soy sauce**

2 **tablespoons mirin (rice wine) or apple juice**

1 **teaspoon toasted sesame oil**

1 **teaspoon ground ginger**

Moroccan Chickpeas and Couscous

Serve this exotically spiced mixture hot, cold, or at room temperature.
I prefer it surrounded by either fresh orange slices or juice-packed
mandarin orange sections. For a dramatic presentation, press the couscous
into a decorative mold and turn it out onto a serving plate.

1 **medium onion, chopped, or 1½ cups frozen chopped onions**

1 **can (14½ ounces) fat-free, reduced-sodium chicken broth**

¾ **cup water**

1 **can (14½ ounces) chopped tomatoes, undrained**

1 **can (16 ounces) chickpeas, rinsed and drained**

1¼ **teaspoons ground coriander**

1 **teaspoon ground cumin**

1 **box (10 ounces) dry quick-cooking couscous**

1. In a large saucepan, combine the onion and ¼ cup of the broth. Cook over medium-low heat until soft and translucent. Stir in the water, tomatoes, chickpeas, coriander, cumin, and the remaining broth. Bring to a boil. Reduce the heat to low, cover, and simmer for 10 minutes.

2. Add the couscous and mix well. Cover tightly and remove from the heat. Allow to stand for 5 minutes, or until the liquid has all been absorbed. Fluff with a fork before serving.

Makes 8 servings

Per serving: 358 calories, 16 g protein, 65 g carbohydrates, 4 g fat, 0 mg cholesterol, 12 g dietary fiber, 105 mg sodium

4 Carb Choices

THE SPICE RACK

A TASTE FOR CORIANDER (AND CILANTRO)
Coriander seeds are the dried ripe fruit of the cilantro plant. The dark green, lacy leaves are what's known as cilantro or Chinese parsley. There is no similarity at all between the flavor of the seeds and that of the leaves. The seeds have a mild, fragrant flavor similar to a blend of caraway, sage, and lemon. The whole seeds are used in pickling and in drinks such as mulled wine. Ground seeds are used in Scandinavian baked goods and also in Thai and Indian curries. Fresh cilantro keeps for about a week if you wash, dry, and store it in a plastic bag in the fridge. It's far superior to the dried leaves and worth making a point to keep on hand.

Lemon Couscous
with Portobello Mushroom Sauce

Here's a good example of how a few pantry products can produce
a truly memorable dinner in no time flat. I used couscous in this recipe because
it absorbs the sauce so well. However, you can just as easily serve the sauce over any
type of pasta. Feel free to toss any leftovers you may have in your refrigerator—
such as chicken, turkey, or even other vegetables—into the sauce.

1. *To make the sauce:* In a small saucepan, combine the mushrooms and water. Bring to a boil over high heat. Reduce the heat to low and simmer for 20 minutes.

2. Stir in the soup, sherry or sherry extract, and pepper. Bring to a boil over medium heat, then reduce the heat to medium-low and simmer for 5 minutes.

3. *To make the couscous:* In a medium saucepan, combine the broth, lemon peel, lemon juice, oil, and pepper. Bring to a boil over high heat. Remove from the heat and stir in the couscous. Cover tightly and allow to stand for 5 minutes. Fluff with a fork.

4. Divide the couscous among dinner bowls or plates. Top with the sauce and cheese.

Makes 4 servings

Per serving: 265 calories, 12 g protein, 40 g carbohydrates, 7 g fat, 8 mg cholesterol, 2 g dietary fiber, 275 mg sodium

2½ **Carb Choices**

SAUCE

½ **ounce dried portobello mushrooms**

1 **cup water**

1 **box (15 ounces) creamy portobello mushroom soup**

2 **tablespoons sherry or 2 teaspoons sherry extract**

¼ **teaspoon ground black pepper**

COUSCOUS

2 **cups fat-free, reduced-sodium chicken broth**

1 **teaspoon grated lemon peel**

2 **tablespoons lemon juice**

2 **teaspoons extra-virgin olive oil**

¼ **teaspoon ground black pepper**

1 **cup dry quick-cooking couscous**

½ **cup shredded Parmesan cheese**

Herbed Spinach Frittata

I prefer to use prewashed baby spinach in this dish. One 6-ounce bag, steamed
and chopped, equals 1 cup. However, you may use a thawed and drained
10-ounce package of frozen chopped spinach if that's what you have.

1 tablespoon extra-virgin olive oil

1 tablespoon minced onion

1 cup fat-free liquid egg substitute

1 cup chopped cooked spinach, very well drained

½ teaspoon dried oregano, crushed

¼ teaspoon ground black pepper

4 tablespoons shredded Parmesan cheese

1. Preheat the broiler.

2. Warm the oil in a medium skillet or omelet pan over medium-low heat. Add the onion and cook for 5 minutes, or until soft and translucent.

3. In a small bowl, mix the egg substitute, spinach, oregano, pepper, and 2 tablespoons of the cheese. Pour into the skillet and cook over low heat for 5 minutes, or until the edges are lightly browned.

4. Sprinkle the remaining 2 tablespoons cheese over the top and place under the broiler until the cheese is lightly browned.

Makes 4 servings

Per serving: 89 calories, 7 g protein, 5 g carbohydrates, 5 g fat, 4 mg cholesterol, 1 g dietary fiber, 212 mg sodium

0 Carb Choices

THE SPICE RACK

THE JOY OF OREGANO

Oregano, which translates to "joy of the mountain," has a mild resin flavor similar to marjoram. It's used readily in Italian cooking, and many people enjoy it sprinkled on everything from pizza to subs. There's also a Mexican variety that's used in many spicy dishes from that region. Powdered and crumbled oregano keep for about 6 months. Look for the Mexican-style oregano in Latin markets. For a well-balanced and fragrant herb blend, combine oregano with basil, parsley, and thyme.

Overnight Cheddar Cheese Strata

This dish is perfect for Sunday brunch. You can assemble it on Saturday
and refrigerate it until Sunday morning. Then you can put it into a cold oven,
set the timer to turn on the oven an hour before you want to eat,
go to church, and have brunch as soon as you return.

1. Coat an 11" × 7" baking dish with cooking spray.

2. Evenly distribute half of the bread in the baking dish. Sprinkle with half of the cheese. Repeat to use the remaining bread and cheese.

3. In a medium bowl, combine the milk, egg substitute, chives or scallion tops, salt, mustard, Worcestershire sauce, celery salt, and pepper. Pour over the bread mixture. Cover and refrigerate overnight.

4. Remove from the refrigerator 2 hours before baking. Place the baking dish in a larger pan. Add cold water to come about halfway up the sides of the strata dish. Heat the oven to 300°F and bake for 1 hour, or until puffy and lightly browned. Serve with the oranges (if using).

Makes 4 servings

Per serving: 267 calories, 26 g protein, 29 g carbohydrates, 5 g fat, 18 mg cholesterol, 3 g dietary fiber, 665 mg sodium

1½ Carb Choices

- **4 slices whole wheat bread, cut into ¼" squares**
- **4 ounces reduced-fat sharp Cheddar cheese, shredded**
- **1 can (12 ounces) fat-free evaporated milk**
- **1 cup fat-free liquid egg substitute**
- **2 tablespoons chopped chives or scallion tops**
- **¼ teaspoon salt**
- **¼ teaspoon dry mustard**
- **¼ teaspoon Worcestershire sauce**
- **⅛ teaspoon celery salt**
- **⅛ teaspoon ground black pepper**
- **4 medium oranges, peeled and sliced (optional)**

Mexican Pizza

Kids love this "pizza," and they can easily prepare it themselves. It can be served hot or cold, making it perfect for meals at home or for brown bag lunches. I call for unthawed corn kernels because they retain their moisture better during baking and stay plump, creating a much more attractive dish.

4 large whole wheat tortillas (12" diameter)

1 can (16 ounces) vegetarian refried beans

1 cup salsa, drained well

1 cup frozen corn kernels, unthawed

½ cup chopped fresh cilantro (optional)

¾ cup shredded reduced-fat Monterey Jack cheese

¾ cup shredded reduced-fat sharp Cheddar cheese

1. Preheat the oven to 375°F.

2. Place the tortillas on a large baking sheet and mist with cooking spray. Spread evenly with the beans.

3. Top with the salsa, corn, and cilantro (if using). Sprinkle with the Monterey Jack and Cheddar cheeses. Bake for 12 to 15 minutes, or until the cheese is melted and starting to brown. Cool for a few minutes before serving.

Makes 4 servings

Per serving: 484 calories, 31 g protein, 53 g carbohydrates, 17 g fat, 34 mg cholesterol, 7 g dietary fiber, 1,159 mg sodium

3½ Carb Choices

PIZZA SUPREME!

Pizza has long been appreciated as the ultimate in convenience foods. But you don't have to order out to get great taste with no effort. You can find it all right in your own kitchen if you've got a ready-to-bake pizza crust in the freezer. Add your own topping or one of these.

Chicken pizza. Spread the crust with your favorite pizza sauce. Sprinkle with shredded mozzarella cheese and chopped cooked chicken.

Fruit pizza. Spread the crust with low-fat plain or vanilla-flavored yogurt. Top with thawed frozen strawberries, juice-packed pineapple chunks, and thawed frozen blueberries.

Greek pizza. Top the crust with rehydrated dried tomatoes (or fresh, if you have them on hand), crumbled feta cheese, dried oregano, and jarred chile peppers, roasted red peppers, and kalamata olives.

Hawaiian pizza. Spread the crust with your favorite pizza sauce. Sprinkle with shredded mozzarella cheese. Top with pineapple chunks and extra-lean chunk ham.

Mexican pizza. Spread the crust with well-drained salsa and top with shredded Monterey Jack cheese.

Provençal pizza. Top the crust with rehydrated dried tomatoes, onions, drained canned anchovies, olives, and dried fennel.

Raisin-walnut pizza. Spread the crust with reduced-fat cream cheese. Sprinkle with raisins, chopped walnuts, and ground cinnamon.

Tomato and red pepper pizza. Sprinkle jarred minced garlic over the crust. Top with your favorite tomato sauce, dried oregano, and shredded mozzarella cheese. Finish it off with strips of jarred roasted red peppers. ▪

Pear and Gorgonzola Pizza with Walnuts

Serve this when you want to wow guests with a totally different kind of pizza.
If desired, arrange fresh pear slices over the pear sauce.

6 ounces dried pears

⅔ cup water

⅔ cup white wine or apple juice

¼ teaspoon ground black pepper

¼ teaspoon balsamic vinegar

1 tube (10 ounces) ready-to-bake pizza dough

1 teaspoon walnut or canola oil

⅓ cup crumbled Gorgonzola cheese

¼ cup reduced-fat ricotta cheese

2 tablespoons chopped walnuts

1. In a medium saucepan, mix the pears, water, wine or juice, and pepper. Bring to a boil over high heat. Reduce the heat to low, cover, and simmer for 25 minutes. Remove from the heat and allow to cool for 5 minutes. Transfer to a blender or food processor. Add the vinegar and blend until coarsely chopped.

2. Preheat the oven to 450°F. Coat a large baking sheet with cooking spray. Unroll the dough onto the sheet. Using your hands, press it into a 12" circle, starting in the center. Brush with the oil. Spread the cooked pears evenly over the top, leaving a ½" border around the edge.

3. In a small bowl, mash together the Gorgonzola and ricotta with a fork. Sprinkle over the pears. Sprinkle with the walnuts. Bake on the lowest oven shelf for 12 to 15 minutes, or until the crust is crisp and the cheese is bubbly.

Makes 8 servings

Per serving: 135 calories, 5 g protein, 16 g carbohydrates, 5 g fat, 6 mg cholesterol, 1 g dietary fiber, 78 mg sodium

2 Carb Choices

QUICK
SWITCH • Replace the Gorgonzola with any other blue cheese and replace the walnuts with pecans.

Quickie Chili

This chili is so quick you can literally throw the ingredients into a pan while your friends are getting out of their cars to come into your house for dinner! Leftovers make ideal filling for tortillas along with lettuce, tomatoes, onions, and cheese.

1. In a large saucepan, mix the beans, tomatoes, peppers, sugar, and cumin. Bring to a boil over medium-high heat. Reduce the heat to medium-low and cook for 10 minutes. Serve topped with the cheese (if using).

Makes 4 servings

Per serving: 209 calories, 12 g protein, 37 g carbohydrates, 1 g fat, 0 mg cholesterol, 1 g dietary fiber, 921 mg sodium

2 Carb Choices

1 **can (30 ounces) chili beans, rinsed and drained**

1 **can (14½ ounces) chili-style tomatoes, undrained**

1 **can (4 ounces) diced green chile peppers**

1 **teaspoon sugar**

1 **teaspoon ground cumin**

1 **cup shredded reduced-fat Cheddar cheese (optional)**

Spicy Lentil Stew

[Photograph on page 125]

You can serve this versatile, tangy dish hot or at room temperature as a side dish
or cold as a salad. For an entrée, add a can of tuna or chicken.

1 **medium onion, chopped, or
  1½ cups frozen chopped
  onions**

2 **cloves garlic, minced**

1 **cup dry lentils**

1 **can (14½ ounces) fat-free,
  reduced-sodium chicken
  broth**

1 **can (14½ ounces) chopped
  Italian-style tomatoes,
  undrained**

1 **jar (4 ounces) spicy sliced
  pimientos**

¼ **cup water**

1 **teaspoon dried thyme,
  crushed**

¼ **teaspoon ground black
  pepper**

1 **cup shredded reduced-fat
  sharp Cheddar or Monterey
  Jack cheese (optional)**

1. Place the onion and garlic in a large saucepan, cover,
   and cook over low heat for 15 minutes, or until soft
   and translucent. (Add a little water, if necessary, to prevent scorching.)

2. Add the lentils and broth. Bring to a boil over high
   heat. Reduce the heat to low and simmer for 30 minutes, or until the lentils are tender and all the liquid
   has been absorbed.

3. Stir in the tomatoes, pimientos, water, thyme, and
   pepper. Simmer for 10 minutes. Serve sprinkled with
   the cheese (if using).

Makes 4 servings

Per serving: 288 calories, 24 g protein, 36 g carbohydrates, 5 g
fat, 0 mg cholesterol, 16 g dietary fiber, 343 mg sodium

2 Carb Choices

QUICK
SWITCH • Replace the thyme with rosemary.

Jeanne's **TOP 10** Fridge Essentials

The following items are always in my refrigerator. With these foods, I can add flavor and texture to practically anything I want to cook. Naturally, I choose low-fat versions whenever possible. Don't be surprised to find onions on the list—cold onions won't make you cry.

1. Milk
2. Yogurt
3. Cheese
4. Eggs and liquid egg substitute
5. Sour cream
6. Soy milk
7. Tofu
8. Onions
9. Lemons, limes, apples, lettuce, and coleslaw mix
10. All open condiments, including mayonnaise, ketchup, soy sauce, and mustard

Polenta with Creamy Sun-Dried Tomato Sauce

This is a quick, easy, and inexpensive vegetarian entrée that's sure to be a hit with the whole family. You can also serve the sauce over pasta or rice. To make your own dried tomatoes, halve plum tomatoes and sprinkle them lightly with kosher salt. Place them in a 250°F oven for 10 to 12 hours, or until dried.

1½ **cups water**

1 **cup oil-free sun-dried tomatoes**

1 **package (16 ounces) ready-to-serve unseasoned polenta**

1 **cup fat-free or 1% milk**

1 **cup fat-free or 1% cottage cheese**

1 **tablespoon extra-virgin olive oil**

1 **clove garlic, halved**

½ **teaspoon ground black pepper**

¼ **teaspoon red-pepper flakes**

¼ **teaspoon salt**

¾ **cup shredded Parmesan cheese**

1. Bring the water to a boil in a small saucepan. Add the tomatoes, remove from the heat, and allow to stand for 5 minutes.

2. Coat a large nonstick skillet with cooking spray and warm over medium heat. Cut the polenta into 8 rounds and arrange them in a single layer in the skillet. Cook for 5 minutes per side, or until lightly browned. Cover and keep warm.

3. Drain the tomatoes and place in a blender or food processor. Add the milk, cottage cheese, oil, garlic, black pepper, pepper flakes, salt, and ½ cup of the Parmesan cheese. Blend until smooth. Pour over the polenta, cover, and heat briefly to warm the sauce. Serve sprinkled with the remaining ¼ cup Parmesan cheese.

Makes 4 servings

Per serving: 411 calories, 17 g protein, 56 g carbohydrates, 19 g fat, 15 mg cholesterol, 0 g dietary fiber, 972 mg sodium

3½ **Carb Choices**

QUICK SWITCH • Replace the pepper flakes with ½ teaspoon crushed dried basil.

Basil-Garlic Polenta
with Marinara Sauce

This is perfect for those nights when you have only 10 minutes
to make dinner. It has just three ingredients.

1. Cut the polenta into 8 slices. Arrange in a single layer in a large nonstick skillet. Pour the sauce evenly over the polenta. Bring to a simmer over medium heat. Reduce the heat to low, cover, and simmer for 5 minutes.

2. Sprinkle with the cheese, cover, and cook for 2 minutes, or until the cheese is melted.

Makes 4 servings

Per serving: 166 calories, 8 g protein, 25 g carbohydrates, 3 g fat, 8 mg cholesterol, 2 g dietary fiber, 667 mg sodium

1½ Carb Choices

- 1 package (16 ounces) ready-to-serve basil-garlic polenta
- 1 jar (16 ounces) fat-free pasta sauce
- ½ cup shredded Parmesan cheese

QUICK
SWITCH • Use Mexican-style polenta, salsa, and Monterey Jack cheese.

Fish and Seafood

There's an incredibly wide variety of canned and frozen seafood products available these days. There is, of course, everybody's favorite—tuna. In addition to the water-packed canned tuna that we've been enjoying for many years, there are no-drain foil packets with an equally long shelf life and fresh taste. Feel free to use them in my recipes. Beyond that, there are very good salmon, clam, shrimp, and other seafood products that won't require a trip to the fishmonger's for fresh-from-the-ocean flavor. One thing's for sure: You won't have to fish for compliments when you dish out these recipes.

in this chapter . . .

Tuna Tailgate Gumbo

In less than 25 minutes, this gumbo can be on its way to a tailgate party or picnic. To complete the "pantry" menu for your next outing, take along a pan of cornbread.

1 medium onion, chopped, or 1½ cups frozen chopped onions

2 cloves garlic, sliced

3 cups shredded cabbage or coleslaw mix

1 cup water

1 bottle (8 ounces) clam juice

1 can (8 ounces) tomato sauce

1 jar (7 ounces) roasted red peppers, drained and chopped

½ cup uncooked white rice

¾ teaspoon celery salt

½ teaspoon ground black pepper

½ teaspoon dried thyme, crushed

¼ teaspoon red-pepper flakes

2 bay leaves

1 can (14½ ounces) chopped tomatoes, undrained

1 can (12 ounces) solid white tuna packed in water, drained and flaked

1 package (10 ounces) frozen sliced okra, thawed

Hot-pepper sauce (optional)

1. Place the onion and garlic in a large saucepan, cover, and cook over medium-low heat for 5 minutes, or until soft and translucent. (Add a little water, if necessary, to prevent scorching.)

2. Stir in the cabbage or coleslaw mix, water, clam juice, tomato sauce, red peppers, rice, celery salt, black pepper, thyme, pepper flakes, and bay leaves. Cover and cook over medium-low heat for 15 minutes, or until most of the liquid has been absorbed and the rice is tender. Stir in the tomatoes, tuna, and okra. Cover and cook for 2 minutes, or until heated through. Remove and discard the bay leaves. Serve with hot-pepper sauce (if using).

Makes 8 servings

Per serving: 148 calories, 14 g protein, 20 g carbohydrates, 2 g fat, 18 mg cholesterol, 2 g dietary fiber, 590 mg sodium

1 Carb Choice

QUICK
SWITCH • Replace the tuna with three 6½-ounce cans of crab.

THE SPICE RACK

THE MAGIC OF BAY LEAVES
Bay leaf is also called laurel leaf or bay laurel and grows on the evergreen bay laurel tree in the Mediterranean. Early Greeks and Romans attributed magical properties to these leaves. Both used laurel leaves as a symbol of honor and victory, as in "winning your laurels." A crown of laurel leaves was often placed on the head of the victor in early Olympic games. Today, bay leaves are most frequently used to season stews, soups, and other aromatic dishes and should be removed before serving the dish.

Gingerbread Pancakes garnished with red and green apple slices (page 20) and Apple Butter (page 237)

115

Cinnamon Quick Bread (page 24) and Spiced Cider (page 297)

Sourdough Milk Toast with Honeyed Peaches (page 23)

Clockwise: Curried Pumpkin Soup (page 39), Minestrone (page 46), and Clam Chowder (page 51)

Cheddar Cheese Soup (page 48) garnished with Garlic Croutons (page 85)

Dilled Tuna and Pasta Shell Salad (page 75)

Taco Salad (page 79)

Caraway-Ham Coleslaw (page 80)

Fettuccine with Shiitake Mushrooms (page 93)

Fusilli with Green Beans (page 97)

Spicy Lentil Stew (page 108) and Fast Focaccia (page 33)

Ultimate Quiche (page 132)

126

Crab Cakes (page 137) and Three-Bean Salad (page 68)

Pantry Paella (page 139)

Teriyaki Salmon and Vegetables on Brown Rice (page 142)

129

Chicken in Peachy Port Sauce on Spiced Couscous (page 159)

Tuna Tetrazzini

This easy and inexpensive dish appeals to people of all ages. Canned chicken and turkey substitute well for the tuna if you're in the mood for something different.

1. Preheat the oven to 400°F. Coat a 13" × 9" baking dish with cooking spray.

2. Cook the spaghetti in a large pot of boiling water according to the package directions until just tender. Drain and return to the pot.

3. In a large bowl, mix the mushroom soup, chicken soup, sherry or sherry extract, and pepper. Stir in the tuna, pimientos, and mushrooms. Pour over the spaghetti and mix well.

4. Spoon the mixture into the prepared baking dish and sprinkle the cheese evenly over the top. Bake for 20 minutes, or until bubbly.

Makes 6 servings

Per serving: 307 calories, 23 g protein, 40 g carbohydrates, 5 g fat, 25 mg cholesterol, 1 g dietary fiber, 755 mg sodium

2½ Carb Choices

8 ounces dry spaghetti

1 can (10¾ ounces) low-sodium, low-fat condensed cream of mushroom soup

1 can (10¾ ounces) low-sodium, low-fat condensed cream of chicken soup

3 tablespoons sherry or 3 teaspoons sherry extract

¼ teaspoon ground black pepper

1 can (12 ounces) solid white tuna packed in water, drained and flaked

1 jar (4 ounces) sliced pimientos, drained

1 can (4 ounces) sliced mushrooms, drained

⅓ cup shredded Parmesan cheese

Ultimate Quiche

[Photograph on page 126]

Many people tell me that although crustless quiches are popular on spa menus and get rave reviews at ladies' luncheons, they don't make the grade for family fare. So I am pleased to tell you that this quiche—crust and all—is so easy your children can make it and so low in calories and fat that I can still put it on spa menus.

CRUST

- **4 cups water**
- **½ cup uncooked wild rice**
- **1 cup shredded reduced-fat sharp Cheddar cheese**
- **½ cup fat-free or reduced-fat mayonnaise**

FILLING

- **1 can (6 ounces) solid white tuna packed in water, undrained**
- **1 can (8 ounces) sliced water chestnuts, drained**
- **1 package (10 ounces) frozen chopped broccoli, thawed**
- **½ cup fat-free or 1% milk**
- **1 egg**
- **1 egg white**
- **1 teaspoon dried tarragon, crushed**
- **¼ teaspoon salt**
- **¼ teaspoon ground black pepper**

1. *To make the crust:* In a medium saucepan, bring the water and rice to a boil over high heat. Reduce the heat to low, cover, and simmer for 30 minutes. Remove the pan from the heat but do not remove the lid. Allow to stand, covered, for 30 minutes.

2. Preheat the oven to 350°F. Coat a 9" or 10" quiche dish or pie plate with cooking spray. Drain the rice thoroughly and place in a large bowl. Stir in the cheese and mayonnaise. Press the mixture into the prepared baking dish. Bake for 10 minutes. Allow to cool slightly.

3. *To make the filling:* Drain the tuna, reserving the liquid. Flake the tuna and spread it evenly over the bottom of the crust. Spread the water chestnuts over the tuna and then spread the broccoli over the top.

4. In a small bowl, mix the milk, egg, egg white, tarragon, salt, pepper, and the reserved liquid from the tuna. Pour into the crust.

5. Bake for 55 minutes, or until lightly browned and firm. Allow to stand at room temperature for 10 minutes before serving.

Makes 6 servings

Per serving: 229 calories, 19 g protein, 22 g carbohydrates, 8 g fat, 65 mg cholesterol, 3 g dietary fiber, 512 mg sodium

1 Carb Choice

QUICK **SWITCH** • Replace the broccoli with frozen spinach.

Cheesy Smoked Tuna and Rice

To turn this simple treat into a one-dish meal, mix in your favorite vegetable.
I like baby peas, but almost any vegetable will work fine.

1. Combine the milk and dill in a medium saucepan and bring just to a boil over medium-low heat. Stir in the cheese and keep stirring until the cheese melts. Stir in the rice, tuna, parsley (if using), and liquid smoke.

2. Cover and remove from the heat. Allow to stand for 10 minutes, or until all the liquid is absorbed. Stir before serving.

Makes 4 servings

Per serving: 490 calories, 41 g protein, 66 g carbohydrates, 6 g fat, 44 mg cholesterol, 1 g dietary fiber, 584 mg sodium

4 Carb Choices

QUICK
SWITCH • Replace the dill with oregano.

1 **can (12 ounces) fat-free evaporated milk**

½ **teaspoon dried dill weed, crushed**

1 **cup shredded reduced-fat sharp Cheddar cheese**

1½ **cups uncooked quick-cooking white rice**

1 **can (12 ounces) tuna packed in water, undrained**

2 **tablespoons chopped fresh parsley (optional)**

¼ **teaspoon liquid smoke**

LIQUID SMOKE: A LITTLE DOES A LOT!

When using liquid smoke, be very careful not to use more than is called for in the recipe. A small amount gives a dish a truly authentic smoky taste. Too much of it tastes artificial. ∎

Tuna Tamale Pie

For a vegetarian tamale pie, omit the tuna.

1 **medium onion, chopped, or 1½ cups frozen chopped onions**

1 **clove garlic, minced**

1 **can (14½ ounces) chopped tomatoes, undrained**

1 **can (15 ounces) red kidney beans, rinsed and drained**

1 **box (10 ounces) frozen corn kernels, thawed**

2 **teaspoons chili powder**

¼ **teaspoon salt**

¼ **teaspoon ground black pepper**

2 **cans (12 ounces each) solid white tuna packed in water, drained and flaked**

1 **box (8½ ounces) cornbread mix**

½ **cup fat-free or 1% milk**

1 **egg**

1. Preheat the oven to 350°F. Coat a 13" × 9" baking dish with cooking spray.

2. Place the onion and garlic in a large saucepan, cover, and cook over medium-low heat for 10 minutes, or until soft and translucent. (Add a little water, if necessary, to prevent scorching.) Stir in the tomatoes, beans, corn, chili powder, salt, and pepper. Cover and simmer for 20 minutes. Stir in the tuna and spoon into the prepared baking dish.

3. In a medium bowl, stir together the cornbread mix, milk, and egg. Spoon evenly over the tuna mixture. Bake for 20 to 25 minutes, or until golden brown.

Makes 8 servings

Per serving: 331 calories, 30 g protein, 41 g carbohydrates, 6 g fat, 52 mg cholesterol, 7 g dietary fiber, 971 mg sodium

2½ Carb Choices

Tuna Veracruzana

This subtle south-of-the-border dish is typical of the state of Veracruz, Mexico.
It is usually made with fresh red snapper, but it is delicious with tuna.
Try serving it over quick-cooking brown rice.

1. Place the onion in a large saucepan, cover, and cook over medium-low heat for 10 minutes, or until soft and translucent. (Add a little water, if necessary, to prevent scorching.) Stir in the tomatoes, chile peppers, pimientos, parsley (if using), and capers. Simmer for 10 minutes. Stir in the tuna and heat through.

Makes 4 servings

Per serving: 163 calories, 24 g protein, 12 g carbohydrates, 1 g fat, 26 mg cholesterol, 3 g dietary fiber, 658 mg sodium

½ **Carb Choice**

1 **medium onion, chopped, or 1½ cups frozen chopped onions**

2 **cans (14½ ounces each) chopped tomatoes, undrained**

1 **can (4 ounces) diced green chile peppers, undrained**

1 **jar (2 ounces) sliced pimientos**

1 **tablespoon chopped fresh parsley (optional)**

2 **teaspoons capers**

1 **can (12 ounces) solid white tuna packed in water, drained and flaked**

Tuna Trifle

This extremely unusual and very tasty dish is actually just a chopped-up
sandwich. However, it is much less messy to eat than a sandwich,
and it's sure to be a conversation piece with your family and friends.
In fact, they will probably ask you for the recipe!

½ **loaf whole grain bread, unsliced**

½ **cup reduced-fat mayonnaise**

½ **cup fat-free or reduced-fat sour cream**

2 **tablespoons chopped pitted kalamata olives**

2 **tablespoons lemon juice**

1 **teaspoon grated lemon peel, yellow part only**

1 **tablespoon capers (optional)**

1 **can (12 ounces) solid white tuna packed in water, drained and flaked**

1 **jar (7 ounces) roasted red peppers, drained**

1. Cut the bread into 1" cubes.

2. In a medium bowl, combine the mayonnaise, sour cream, olives, lemon juice, lemon peel, and capers (if using).

3. Layer one-third of the bread cubes in the bottom of a glass trifle dish or bowl. Spread one-third of the mayonnaise mixture evenly over the top. Sprinkle with one-third of the tuna and then one-third of the peppers. Repeat the layers two more times to use all the ingredients.

Makes 6 servings

Per serving: 270 calories, 21 g protein, 31 g carbohydrates, 8 g fat, 24 mg cholesterol, 4 g dietary fiber, 585 mg sodium

2 Carb Choices

QUICK
SWITCH • Use ½ teaspoon pure lemon extract in place of the grated lemon peel.

Crab Cakes

[Photograph on page 127]

You can turn out very good crab cakes from canned crab. That means you can make these patties at the drop of a hat, without an extra trip to the fish store. Most crab cake recipes call for an egg, but these cakes hold together without one.

1. In a medium bowl, mix the mayonnaise, garlic, Worcestershire sauce, black pepper, celery seeds, mustard, pepper flakes, ginger, and paprika. Stir in the breadcrumbs and crab. Cover and refrigerate for at least 1 hour.

2. Form into 8 patties. Warm a large nonstick skillet over medium-low heat for 3 minutes. Add the patties and cook for 5 minutes per side, or until brown on both sides.

Makes 4 servings

Per serving: 134 calories, 19 g protein, 10 g carbohydrates, 2 g fat, 76 mg cholesterol, 0 g dietary fiber, 538 mg sodium

½ **Carb Choice**

QUICK
SWITCH • Replace the celery seeds with ½ teaspoon dried thyme.

⅓ **cup fat-free or reduced-fat mayonnaise**

1 **clove garlic, minced**

2 **teaspoons Worcestershire sauce**

¼ **teaspoon ground black pepper**

⅛ **teaspoon ground celery seeds**

⅛ **teaspoon dry mustard**

⅛ **teaspoon red-pepper flakes**

Pinch of ground ginger

Pinch of paprika

1 **cup soft breadcrumbs**

2 **cans (6½ ounces each) crab, rinsed and drained**

BETTER BREADCRUMBS

It's so easy to make your own breadcrumbs there's barely an excuse for buying packaged ones.

- *For fresh crumbs*—which I prefer using in most recipes—simply tear 2 slices of bread into pieces and grind in a blender or food processor. (Repeat until you have the amount of crumbs you need.)

- *For dry breadcrumbs,* leave the bread out on a counter for several hours, turning the slices occasionally until they're slightly stale. Then grind in a blender or food processor.

- *For toasted breadcrumbs,* toast the bread before blending or grind up homemade croutons. ∎

Pasta Shells with Dilled Crab Filling

This is a delightfully different taste combination. For a less-expensive dish, substitute water-packed white albacore tuna for the crab.

8 **dry jumbo pasta shells (2 ounces)**

1 **tablespoon butter**

1 **medium onion, finely chopped, or 1½ cups frozen chopped onions**

1 **clove garlic, minced**

2 **cups 1% cottage cheese**

1 **can (6½ ounces) crab, rinsed and drained**

1 **teaspoon dried dill weed, crushed**

1 **teaspoon grated lemon peel**

¼ **teaspoon salt**

¼ **teaspoon ground black pepper**

1 **jar (16 ounces) fat-free pasta sauce**

1. Preheat the oven to 350°F. Coat an 11" × 7" baking dish with cooking spray.

2. Cook the pasta in a large pot of boiling water according to the package directions until just tender. Drain.

3. Meanwhile, melt the butter in a large nonstick skillet over low heat. Add the onion and garlic. Cover and cook for 15 minutes, or until soft and translucent. Remove from the heat and stir in the cottage cheese, crab, dill, lemon peel, salt, and pepper. Spoon the mixture into the cooked shells.

4. Spread the pasta sauce evenly in the prepared baking dish. Arrange the shells on top of the sauce. Cover with foil and bake for 20 minutes.

Makes 4 servings

Per serving: 245 calories, 26 g protein, 24 g carbohydrates, 4 g fat, 51 mg cholesterol, 3 g dietary fiber, 1,033 mg sodium

2½ **Carb Choices**

QUICK
SWITCH • Replace the dill with crushed dried basil or oregano. • Or serve the crab filling over cooked pasta rather than filling shells.

Pantry Paella

[Photograph on page 128]

Here's the easiest recipe imaginable for this popular Spanish dish. For a more classic presentation, spoon the mixture into a large, flat serving dish and use the sliced pimientos to garnish the top instead of stirring them in at the end.

1. Warm the oil in a large nonstick skillet over low heat. Add the onion and garlic. Cover and cook for 5 minutes, or until soft and translucent. Stir in the rice and ham. Stir in the tomatoes, tomato sauce, red peppers, clam juice, wine, salt, and saffron.

2. Drain the juice from the clams into the skillet. Bring to a boil over medium heat. Reduce the heat to low, cover, and simmer for 20 minutes, or until the rice is tender.

3. Stir in the clams, chicken, peas, and pimientos. Cover, remove from the heat, and let stand for 5 minutes.

Makes 8 servings

Per serving: 324 calories, 15 g protein, 49 g carbohydrates, 5 g fat, 24 mg cholesterol, 3 g dietary fiber, 931 mg sodium

3 Carb Choices

1 tablespoon extra-virgin olive oil

1 medium onion, chopped, or 1½ cups frozen chopped onions

2 cloves garlic, minced

2 cups uncooked white rice

1 can (5 ounces) extra-lean chunk ham, drained and flaked

1 can (14½ ounces) ready-cut tomatoes, undrained

1 can (8 ounces) tomato sauce

1 jar (7 ounces) roasted red peppers, drained and cut into ½" strips

2 bottles (8 ounces each) clam juice

2 cups dry white wine

½ teaspoon salt

½ teaspoon saffron, crushed

2 cans (6½ ounces each) chopped clams, undrained

1 can (9¾ ounces) chunk white chicken packed in water, undrained

1½ cups frozen peas, thawed

1 jar (4 ounces) sliced pimientos, undrained

Bouillabaisse

This aromatic seafood stew is a staple of the fishermen on
the southern coast of France around Marseilles. They serve it over
crusty French bread, but I prefer to serve the bread on the side.

1 **medium onion, chopped, or
1½ cups frozen chopped
onions**

2 **cloves garlic, minced**

1 **can (14½ ounces) chopped
tomatoes, undrained**

2 **bottles (8 ounces each) clam
juice**

1 **cup dry white wine**

1 **bay leaf**

¼ **teaspoon ground fennel
seeds**

¼ **teaspoon dried thyme,
crushed**

¼ **teaspoon saffron, crushed**

⅛ **teaspoon ground black
pepper**

2 **cans (6½ ounces each) crab,
rinsed and drained**

1 **can (6½ ounces) chopped
clams, undrained**

1 **can (6 ounces) solid white
tuna packed in water, drained
and flaked**

1. Place the onion and garlic in a large saucepan, cover,
and cook over medium-low heat for 10 minutes, or
until soft and translucent. (Add a little water, if necessary, to prevent scorching.)

2. Add the tomatoes, clam juice, wine, bay leaf, fennel
seeds, thyme, saffron, and pepper. Bring to a boil over
medium heat. Reduce the heat to low, cover, and
simmer for 10 minutes. Stir in the crab, clams, and
tuna. Heat through. Remove and discard the bay leaf.

Makes 6 servings

Per serving: 136 calories, 21 g protein, 5 g carbohydrates, 1 g
fat, 64 mg cholesterol, 1 g dietary fiber, 504 mg sodium

0 Carb Choices

QUICK
SWITCH • Replace the crab with more tuna.

Cioppino

The Italian fishermen who came to San Francisco during the great Gold Rush combined the local seafood and their native marinara sauce to create this fabulous, spicy stew. Don't overcook the seafood after you add it to the sauce or you'll toughen it.

1. In a large saucepan, mix the pasta sauce, clam juice, wine, parsley (if using), and lemon juice. Bring to a boil over medium-high heat. Reduce the heat to low and simmer for 10 minutes. Stir in the crab, clams, and tuna. Heat through.

Makes 6 servings

Per serving: 144 calories, 19 g protein, 10 g carbohydrates, 1 g fat, 46 mg cholesterol, 2 g dietary fiber, 423 mg sodium

½ **Carb Choice**

1 **jar (26 ounces) fat-free tomato and basil pasta sauce**

1 **bottle (8 ounces) clam juice**

½ **cup dry white wine**

3 **tablespoons chopped fresh parsley (optional)**

1 **tablespoon lemon juice**

1 **can (6½ ounces) crab, rinsed and drained**

1 **can (6½ ounces) chopped clams, drained**

1 **can (6 ounces) solid white tuna packed in water, drained and flaked**

THE SPICE RACK

PARSLEY: THE ALL-PURPOSE HERB

Parsley is widely used as both a flavoring and a garnish and has a rewarding springtime freshness. It's probably the most versatile and adaptable herb there is. Although there are over 30 varieties to choose from, the most common ones are curly and Italian (flat leaf), which is slightly sweeter than curly. Both are so readily available there's hardly any reason to resort to dried parsley, which has a sadly inferior flavor. For best results, discard any less-than-perfect sprigs. Wash and thoroughly dry the remainder, and store it in a plastic bag in the refrigerator for up to a week.

Teriyaki Salmon and Vegetables on Brown Rice

[Photograph on page 129]

The flavor combination of teriyaki sauce and salmon is surprisingly good.
If you have any leftovers, combine the salmon and vegetables with
the rice and refrigerate for a memorable cold salad.

1¾ **cups water**

1 **cup uncooked quick-cooking brown rice**

⅓ **cup low-sodium teriyaki sauce**

1 **tablespoon lemon juice**

1 **bag (16 ounces) frozen stir-fry vegetables**

1 **can (14¾ ounces) red salmon, drained and broken into bite-size pieces**

1. Bring the water to a boil in a medium saucepan. Stir in the rice and return to a boil. Reduce the heat to low, cover, and cook for 5 minutes. Remove from the heat and stir. Cover and let stand for 5 minutes. Fluff with a fork.

2. Meanwhile, mix the teriyaki sauce and lemon juice in a wok or large nonstick skillet and bring to a boil over medium-high heat. Add the vegetables and cook, stirring constantly, for 2 minutes, or until thawed. Add the salmon and heat through. Serve over the rice.

Makes 4 servings

Per serving: 369 calories, 26 g protein, 48 g carbohydrates, 8 g fat, 57 mg cholesterol, 3 g dietary fiber, 931 mg sodium

3 Carb Choices

Salmon Mousse

In most recipes calling for canned salmon, you are told to discard the bones. I leave them in because they are enormously high in calcium and too soft to adversely affect the texture of most dishes. However, I often do remove and discard the skin to lower the fat content. I like to serve this mousse with sweet brown mustard or Dill Sauce (page 226) and whole grain rolls. You may also use this mousse as a sandwich spread or dip.

1. Coat a 3-quart mold with cooking spray.

2. Place the cool water in a small bowl and sprinkle with the gelatin. Let stand for 3 minutes to soften. Add the boiling water and stir until completely dissolved.

3. In a large bowl, mix the mayonnaise, sour cream, lemon juice, paprika, and salt. Stir in the dissolved gelatin.

4. Discard the skin from the salmon and flake the fish. Stir into the mayonnaise mixture. Spoon into the prepared mold and refrigerate for several hours or overnight before unmolding.

Makes 6 servings

Per serving: 179 calories, 27 g protein, 7 g carbohydrates, 4 g fat, 38 mg cholesterol, 0 g dietary fiber, 653 mg sodium

½ **Carb Choice**

QUICK
SWITCH • Replace the paprika with dried dill weed.

2 **tablespoons cool water**

1 **envelope unflavored gelatin**

¼ **cup boiling water**

½ **cup fat-free or reduced-fat mayonnaise**

½ **cup fat-free or reduced-fat sour cream**

3 **tablespoons lemon juice**

½ **teaspoon paprika**

⅛ **teaspoon salt**

1 **can (14¾ ounces) red salmon, drained**

Cajun Shrimp Pasta

For a vegetarian dish, substitute a can of drained beans for the shrimp.

1 tablespoon extra-virgin
   olive oil

3 cloves garlic, minced

¼ cup chopped scallions
   (optional)

2 teaspoons Cajun seasoning

1 can (12 ounces) fat-free
   evaporated milk

¼ teaspoon Worcestershire
   sauce

¼ teaspoon hot-pepper sauce

¼ teaspoon salt

½ cup shredded Parmesan
   cheese

1 package (12 ounces) frozen
   cooked peeled shrimp,
   thawed

8 ounces dry linguine

1. Combine the oil and garlic in a large nonstick skillet and stir over medium-high heat for 1 minute. Add the scallions (if using) and Cajun seasoning; stir for 1 minute. Add the milk and simmer for 5 minutes. Stir in the Worcestershire sauce, hot-pepper sauce, salt, and ¼ cup of the cheese; simmer for 3 minutes. Stir in the shrimp.

2. Meanwhile, cook the linguine in a large pot of boiling water according to the package directions until just tender. Drain and return to the pot. Add the sauce and toss to coat well. Serve sprinkled with the remaining ¼ cup cheese.

Makes 4 servings

Per serving: 406 calories, 32 g protein, 49 g carbohydrates, 8 g fat, 175 mg cholesterol, 2 g dietary fiber, 666 mg sodium

3 Carb Choices

QUICK
SWITCH • Replace the Cajun seasoning with another seasoning blend, such as Italian or Southwestern.

Angel Hair Nests with Clam Sauce

If you want to further reduce the fat in this easy 15-minute meal, just eliminate the
oil and add the garlic to the clam juice and tomatoes before heating them.

1. Cook the pasta in a large pot of boiling water according to the package directions until just tender. Drain, return to the pot, and keep warm.

2. Drain the clams, reserving the liquid.

3. Combine the oil and garlic in a large nonstick skillet. Stir over medium heat for 1 minute. Add the tomatoes and clam liquid. Bring to a boil. Remove from the heat and stir in the clams.

4. Divide the pasta among serving plates. Using a fork, twist each mound of pasta to form a nest. Top each nest with the clam sauce and sprinkle with the cheese.

Makes 4 servings

Per serving: 475 calories, 36 g protein, 52 g carbohydrates, 13 g fat, 70 mg cholesterol, 2 g dietary fiber, 461 mg sodium

3 Carb Choices

8 ounces dry angel hair pasta

2 cans (6½ ounces each) minced clams, undrained

2 tablespoons extra-virgin olive oil

2 cloves garlic, minced

1 can (14½ ounces) chopped Italian-style tomatoes, undrained

½ cup shredded Parmesan cheese

QUICK
SWITCH • Replace the Italian-style tomatoes with Mexican-style.

Linguine with Clam Sauce

This 15-minute marvel has long been one of my favorite pantry meals.
If you want to make it still lower in fat, just eliminate the oil and add the garlic
to the undrained clams before heating them.

6 ounces dry linguine

1 clove garlic, minced

1 tablespoon extra-virgin olive oil

1 can (6½ ounces) minced clams, undrained

¼ cup shredded Parmesan cheese

1. Cook the linguine in a large pot of boiling water according to the package directions until just tender. Drain, return to the pot, and keep warm.

2. In a large nonstick skillet over medium heat, cook the garlic in the oil for 1 minute, or until the garlic starts to sizzle. Stir in the clams and clam liquid and heat through. Serve over the linguine and sprinkle with the cheese.

Makes 6 servings

Per serving: 186 calories, 13 g protein, 23 g carbohydrates, 4 g fat, 23 mg cholesterol, 1 g dietary fiber, 99 mg sodium

4½ Carb Choices

QUICK
SWITCH • Add ½ teaspoon Italian herb blend.

PASTA PRIMER

There's an extraordinary variety of dried pasta sizes and shapes available. Each shape is best suited for a particular sauce or style of cooking. Here are some of the most common matchups.

PASTA NAME	COOKING TIME (MIN.)	SERVING SUGGESTIONS
Angel hair (capellini)	5	This is best combined with a light sauce that won't overwhelm the delicate noodles.
Bow ties (farfalle)	7–10	The butterfly shape collects dressings and seasonings.
Cannelloni	8	The noodles' thick, sturdy sides are ideal for casseroles.
Fettuccine	8–9	These firm ribbon shapes are often used with delicate cream sauces.
Lasagna	10	This thick, wide pasta holds up well during baking.
Linguine	5–7	The flat, slippery shape is often used with tomato or seafood sauces.
Macaroni	9–10	The sturdy curved elbows hold their shape and trap meat and vegetable pieces when used with robust sauces or in soups and stews. It's often used in salads, because the shape collects dressings and seasonings.
Shells	10	The shells are often used with meat or vegetable sauces, because the folds trap the pieces. They are also used with hearty soups like minestrone, since the shells can compete equally with beans and potatoes.
Spaghetti	7–9	The delicate shape goes well with light and spicy sauces.
Ziti	10	The grooved shape clings to meat and vegetable pieces, making it ideal for chunky sauces. It's also used in casseroles and salads.

Pasta with Tomatoes and Clams

You can use any type of pasta you want in this versatile dish.
When fresh basil is available, I like to stir in a big handful of the chopped herb.
Also, you may want to sprinkle a little Parmesan cheese over the top.

8 ounces dry pasta

2 cans (6½ ounces each) chopped clams, undrained

1 tablespoon extra-virgin olive oil

3 cloves garlic, minced

2 cans (14½ ounces each) chopped Italian-style tomatoes, undrained

2 tablespoons anchovy paste

¼ cup chopped fresh parsley (optional)

¼ teaspoon ground black pepper

2 teaspoons lemon juice

1. Cook the pasta in a large pot of boiling water according to the package directions until just tender. Drain, return to the pot, and keep warm.

2. Meanwhile, drain the clams, reserving the juice.

3. Warm the oil in a large saucepan over medium heat. Add the garlic and stir for 1 minute. Stir in the tomatoes, anchovy paste, parsley (if using), pepper, and clam juice. Bring to a boil. Reduce the heat to low and simmer for 15 minutes.

4. Add the clams and lemon juice; heat for 1 to 2 minutes. (Do not boil the sauce at this point or the clams will toughen.) Serve over the pasta.

Makes 4 servings

Per serving: 441 calories, 35 g protein, 57 g carbohydrates, 8 g fat, 62 mg cholesterol, 3 g dietary fiber, 431 mg sodium

3½ Carb Choices

QUICK
SWITCH • Replace the Italian-style tomatoes with Mexican-style.

Lobster and Broccoli Stir-Fry

You can chop your own fresh ginger for this recipe, but if you're short on time, jarred chopped ginger, which is available in many supermarkets, will work as well.

1. Place the sesame seeds in a small nonstick skillet over medium heat. Cook, stirring constantly, for 2 minutes, or until golden brown. (Watch carefully, because they burn easily.)

2. Combine the broth and cornstarch in a small bowl. Whisk to dissolve the cornstarch. Add the ginger and soy sauce.

3. Heat the oil in a wok or large skillet over medium heat. Add the garlic and cook just until it sizzles. Add the broccoli and cook, stirring constantly, for 2 minutes. Whisk the broth mixture and add to the pan. Cover and cook for 3 minutes, or until the broccoli is tender-crisp. Add the lobster or tuna. Cover and cook for 1 minute, or until heated through. Remove from the heat. Sprinkle with the sesame seeds.

Makes 4 servings

Per serving: 172 calories, 18 g protein, 14 g carbohydrates, 6 g fat, 14 mg cholesterol, 7 g dietary fiber, 376 mg sodium

½ **Carb Choice**

1 **tablespoon sesame seeds**

1 **cup fat-free, reduced-sodium chicken broth**

2 **teaspoons cornstarch**

2 **tablespoons finely chopped fresh ginger**

1 **tablespoon reduced-sodium soy sauce**

1 **tablespoon vegetable oil**

2 **cloves garlic, minced**

1 **package (16 ounces) frozen broccoli**

½ **pound cooked lobster, thinly sliced, or 1 can (12 ounces) solid white tuna packed in water, drained and flaked**

Lobster à la Newburg

This French-sounding dish was actually created by a chef
at Delmonico's in New York many years ago for a regular customer named Wenburg.
When the gentleman and the restaurant had a falling out, the chef renamed
the dish Newburg, which it is to this day. The original recipe is far more complicated
than this one, but this is equally opulent. Serve over rice or toast.

1 can (10¾ ounces) low-sodium, low-fat condensed cream of mushroom soup

½ cup sherry or 1 tablespoon sherry extract

½ teaspoon paprika

⅛ teaspoon ground nutmeg

12 ounces frozen lobster, thawed and diced

1 egg

1. In a medium saucepan, mix the soup, sherry or sherry extract, paprika, and nutmeg. Stir in the lobster and bring to a boil over medium-low heat.

2. Place the egg in a small bowl and whisk lightly. Slowly whisk in about ¼ cup of the soup mixture. Whisk this mixture back into the saucepan. Whisk over low heat for 1 minute to thicken.

Makes 4 servings

Per serving: 185 calories, 20 g protein, 9 g carbohydrates, 4 g fat, 114 mg cholesterol, 0 g dietary fiber, 643 mg sodium

½ **Carb Choice**

QUICK
SWITCH • Substitute solid white tuna in water for the lobster.

Scallops with Sage and Corn

If you've never had this combination of flavors, you're in for a treat.
Leftovers are great cold over salad greens.

1. Place the scallops on a plate and sprinkle with the lemon juice, salt, and pepper.

2. Combine the oil, sage, and garlic in a large nonstick skillet and stir over medium heat for 1 minute. Add the scallops and cook, stirring frequently, for 3 minutes, or until opaque. Remove from the skillet and set aside.

3. Add the corn and pimientos to the skillet. Cook, stirring frequently, for 3 minutes, or until heated through. Stir in the scallops and remove from the heat.

Makes 4 servings

Per serving: 187 calories, 21 g protein, 19 g carbohydrates, 4 g fat, 37 mg cholesterol, 2 g dietary fiber, 320 mg sodium

1 Carb Choice

QUICK
SWITCH • Replace the scallops with shrimp.

- **1 package (16 ounces) frozen scallops, thawed**
- **1 tablespoon lemon juice**
- **¼ teaspoon salt**
- **¼ teaspoon ground black pepper**
- **2 teaspoons extra-virgin olive oil**
- **1 tablespoon dried sage, crushed**
- **1 clove garlic, minced**
- **1 package (10 ounces) frozen corn kernels, thawed**
- **1 jar (2 ounces) sliced pimientos, drained**

THE SPICE RACK **SAGE ADVICE**
This Mediterranean herb with narrow greenish-gray leaves has a bit of a bitter, musty, mint taste and aroma. It's most often used in recipes with beans, cheese, and pork, but it also pairs well with chicken and other types of poultry. Look for crumbled or powdered leaves.

Chicken

Of all the canned poultry products, my favorite is chunk white chicken packed in water. It's very tender, low in fat, and quite versatile. Other poultry options include canned turkey and mixed dark and light chicken meat. I find the latter to be very good in sauces and soups, and it's less expensive than the all-white meat if you want to economize. The following recipes also work very well with leftover chicken or turkey. Around the holidays, freeze cooked meat in 1-cup portions. That's the amount of chicken in a $9^3/_4$-ounce can, so the conversion is simple.

in this chapter . . .

Tortilla Soup

One of my favorite Mexican dishes is this delicious Tortilla Soup.
It is hearty enough to serve as an entrée for parties. You can also serve
this soup buffet-style and allow your guests to add the chicken, cheese,
and tortilla strips to their soup bowls themselves.

6 corn tortillas (6" diameter)

6 cloves garlic

2 tablespoons chopped cilantro

2 quarts (8 cups) fat-free chicken broth

1 large onion, chopped, or 2 cups frozen chopped onions

1 can (28 ounces) diced tomatoes, drained

2 teaspoons ground cumin

2 teaspoons chili powder

2 bay leaves, crumbled

½ teaspoon salt (omit if using salted broth)

⅛ teaspoon cayenne pepper

3 boneless, skinless chicken breasts halves, cooked and julienne cut

¾ cup shredded reduced-fat Monterey Jack cheese

Cilantro sprigs for garnish

1. Preheat the oven to 350°F. Cut 3 of the tortillas into thin strips, about ¼" wide, and place them on a non-stick baking sheet. Bake for 15 minutes, or until crisp and a rich, golden brown. (Watch carefully because they burn easily.) Set aside.

2. Chop the remaining tortillas coarsely and place them in a large, heavy saucepan over medium-high heat. Add the garlic, cilantro, and 2 cups of broth and bring to a boil. Reduce the heat to low and simmer for 5 minutes, or until the tortillas are soft.

3. Combine the onion and 1 cup of the remaining broth in a blender and puree. Pour the pureed onion into the pan with the tortillas. Put the tomatoes in the blender and puree, then add to the saucepan. Mix well and continue to simmer. Add the cumin, chili powder, bay leaves, salt, and cayenne. Add the remaining 5 cups broth and bring to a boil over medium-high heat. Reduce the heat to low and simmer, stirring frequently, for 30 minutes.

4. Strain the soup and pour into warm bowls. Top with the cooked chicken strips and the cheese. Garnish with toasted tortilla strips and cilantro sprigs.

Makes 6 servings

Per serving: 193 calories, 17 g protein, 21 g carbohydrates, 4 g fat, 32 mg cholesterol, 3 g dietary fiber, 564 mg sodium

1 Carb Choice

Chicken Stew Provençal

This flavorful stew is wonderful with crusty French bread and garlic-flavored mayonnaise. (Just add a little minced garlic and 1 or 2 teaspoons of extra-virgin olive oil to fat-free mayonnaise. Or make the cholesterol-free Light Aïoli on page 000.)

1. In a large saucepan, mix the onion, tomatoes, garlic, bay leaves, thyme, pepper, and pepper flakes. Bring to a boil over medium-high heat. Stir in 2 tablespoons of the Pernod or $\frac{1}{2}$ teaspoon of the anise extract. Reduce the heat to medium and simmer for 30 minutes.

2. Stir in the broth, mixed vegetables, potatoes, and the remaining 2 tablespoons Pernod or $\frac{1}{2}$ teaspoon anise extract. Cook for 10 minutes. Drain the liquid from the chicken into the saucepan. Break the chicken into bite-size pieces and stir in. Heat through. Remove and discard the bay leaves.

Makes 8 servings

Per serving: 138 calories, 14 g protein, 15 g carbohydrates, 2 g fat, 30 mg cholesterol, 4 g dietary fiber, 652 mg sodium

1 Carb Choice

QUICK
SWITCH • Replace the thyme with dried herbes de Provence.

1 **medium onion, chopped, or 1½ cups frozen chopped onions**

1 **can (28 ounces) chopped tomatoes, undrained**

3 **cloves garlic, minced**

2 **bay leaves**

2 **teaspoons dried thyme, crushed**

½ **teaspoon ground black pepper**

¼ **teaspoon red-pepper flakes**

4 **tablespoons Pernod or 1 teaspoon anise extract**

1 **can (14½ ounces) fat-free, reduced-sodium chicken broth**

1 **package (16 ounces) frozen mixed vegetables**

1 **can (15 ounces) new potatoes, drained**

2 **cans (9¾ ounces each) chunk white chicken packed in water, undrained**

Country Chicken and Corn Stew

This stew is also very good made with turkey or ham.

1 tablespoon extra-virgin olive oil

1 medium onion, finely chopped, or 1½ cups frozen chopped onions

2 packages (10 ounces each) frozen corn kernels, thawed

1 can (14½ ounces) fat-free, reduced-sodium chicken broth

1½ teaspoons sugar

½ teaspoon salt

¼ teaspoon ground black pepper

¼ cup fat-free or 1% milk

1½ teaspoons cornstarch

2 cans (9¾ ounces each) chunk white chicken packed in water, drained and broken into bite-size pieces

1. Warm the oil in a large saucepan over medium heat. Add the onion, cover, and cook for 5 minutes, or until soft and translucent. Add the corn, broth, sugar, salt, and pepper. Simmer for 3 minutes.

2. Combine the milk and cornstarch in a cup and stir until the cornstarch is dissolved. Add to the corn mixture. Stir in the chicken. Mix well and simmer for 3 minutes, or until slightly thickened.

Makes 4 servings

Per serving: 305 calories, 27 g protein, 35 g carbohydrates, 7 g fat, 60 mg cholesterol, 4 g dietary fiber, 934 mg sodium

2 Carb Choices

QUICK **SWITCH** • Stir in a 14½-ounce can of undrained ready-cut tomatoes.

White Chili

One of my own favorite recipes, in which clove is an essential ingredient,
is this tasty White Chili. I often add cooked cubes of chicken breast,
turkey breast, rabbit, veal, or drained water-packed white albacore just
before serving. It adds extra protein and still keeps the chili white!

1. In a large heavy saucepan, bring the beans, broth, half of the onions, the garlic, and salt to a boil. Reduce the heat to low, cover, and simmer for 2 hours, or until the beans are very tender, adding more broth if needed.

2. Add the chicken, the remaining onions, the chiles, cumin, oregano, coriander, cloves, and cayenne. Mix well, cover, and cook for 30 minutes.

3. Spoon chili into individual bowls and top with cheese (if using).

Makes 6 servings

Per serving: 370 calories, 30 g protein, 54 g carbohydrates, 5 g fat, 20 mg cholesterol, 17 g dietary fiber, 960 mg sodium

4 Carb Choices

1 **pound dry great Northern beans, picked over, soaked overnight in water to cover, and drained**

4 **cups fat-free, reduced-sodium chicken broth**

2 **medium onions, coarsely chopped, or 3 cups frozen chopped onions**

3 **cloves garlic, minced**

½ **teaspoon salt**

1 **can (9¾ ounces) chunk white chicken packed in water**

1 **can (4 ounces) diced green chile peppers**

2 **teaspoons ground cumin**

1½ **teaspoons dried oregano, crushed**

1 **teaspoon ground coriander**

¼ **teaspoon ground cloves**

¼ **teaspoon cayenne pepper**

¾ **cup shredded reduced-fat Monterey Jack cheese (optional)**

Chicken in Papaya Cups

This delightfully refreshing combination of papaya and chicken
is perfect for a luncheon when the weather is still warm. You can even serve it
in its own "bowl," which makes it an extra-easy entrée to serve.

2 ripe papayas, halved
lengthwise and seeded

2 cans (9¾ ounces each) chunk
white chicken packed in
water, drained and flaked

2 tablespoons finely chopped
chives or scallion tops

¾ teaspoon curry powder

2 tablespoons toasted
sunflower seeds

Parsley or mint sprigs for
garnish (optional)

1. Using a melon baller, remove the papaya pulp, being
careful not to tear the peel. Set the papaya "bowls"
aside.

2. In a large bowl, combine the papaya balls, chicken,
chives or scallions, curry powder, and sunflower seeds.
Evenly divide the mixture among the papaya bowls.
Garnish with a sprig of parsley or mint (if using).

Makes 4 servings

Per serving: 207 calories, 24 g protein, 16 g carbohydrates, 5 g
fat, 60 mg cholesterol, 3 g dietary fiber, 655 mg sodium

1 Carb Choice

QUICK
SWITCH • Replace the chicken with white albacore tuna.

Chicken in Peachy Port Sauce on Spiced Couscous

[Photograph on page 130]

Here's an unusually good combination of flavors and textures. If you don't have couscous, serve the chicken and sauce over rice or any type of pasta.

1. *To make the couscous:* In a small saucepan, mix the water, pepper, allspice, and bay leaf. Bring to a boil over medium-high heat. Stir in the couscous. Remove from the heat, cover tightly, and let stand for 5 minutes, or until all the liquid is absorbed. Fluff with a fork. Remove and discard the bay leaf.

2. *To make the chicken and sauce:* Drain the liquid from both the peaches and the chicken into a blender or food processor. Add half of the peaches and the port, oregano, salt, pepper, and nutmeg. Blend until smooth. Pour into a medium saucepan. Bring to a boil over medium-high heat. Reduce the heat to medium-low and simmer, stirring frequently, for 10 minutes.

3. Break the chicken into bite-size pieces. Serve the couscous topped with the chicken and the remaining peaches. Drizzle with the sauce.

Makes 2 servings

Per serving: 334 calories, 17 g protein, 54 g carbohydrates, 2 g fat, 28 mg cholesterol, 5 g dietary fiber, 587 mg sodium

3½ Carb Choices

QUICK **SWITCH** • Replace the peaches with apricots or pears.

COUSCOUS

- **1 cup water**
- **⅛ teaspoon ground black pepper**
- **⅛ teaspoon ground allspice**
- **1 bay leaf**
- **½ cup dry quick-cooking couscous**

CHICKEN AND SAUCE

- **1 can (16 ounces) sliced peaches packed in water, undrained**
- **1 can (4½ ounces) chunk white chicken packed in water, undrained**
- **¼ cup white port wine**
- **½ teaspoon dried oregano, crushed**
- **¼ teaspoon salt**
- **¼ teaspoon ground black pepper**
- **⅛ teaspoon ground nutmeg**

Tarragon Chicken and Pasta Bake

With just a few minutes of preparation time, you can get
an old-fashioned comfort food ready for the oven.

8 ounces dry ziti

1 can (10¾ ounces) low-sodium, low-fat condensed cream of chicken soup

1 cup fat-free or 1% milk

2 teaspoons dried tarragon, crushed

½ teaspoon ground black pepper

2 cans (9¾ ounces each) chunk white chicken packed in water, drained and broken into bite-size pieces

¼ cup shredded Parmesan cheese

1. Preheat the oven to 350°F. Coat a 13" × 9" baking dish with cooking spray.

2. Cook the ziti in a large pot of boiling water according to the package directions until just tender. Drain and return to the pot.

3. In a medium bowl, mix the soup, milk, tarragon, and pepper. Pour over the ziti. Add the chicken and mix well. Transfer to the prepared baking dish. Sprinkle with the cheese. Bake for 30 minutes, or until heated through.

Makes 4 servings

Per serving: 422 calories, 34 g protein, 54 g carbohydrates, 7 g fat, 72 mg cholesterol, 1 g dietary fiber, 1,067 mg sodium

3½ Carb Choices

QUICK SWITCH • Replace the tarragon with 1 teaspoon curry powder. • Or replace the chicken with a 16-ounce package of thawed frozen broccoli florets. • Or use cream of celery or cream of mushroom soup in place of the cream of chicken soup.

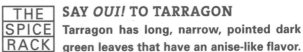
THE SPICE RACK

SAY *OUI!* TO TARRAGON

Tarragon has long, narrow, pointed dark green leaves that have an anise-like flavor. It's frequently used in classic French cooking to season a variety of foods, including vegetables, chicken, and fish. It is also used in many sauces, most notably Béarnaise sauce, which is frequently served with steak. Because of its assertive, aromatic flavor, tarragon can easily overpower a dish. Although most people prefer fresh tarragon, dried and powdered forms are available. When substituting dried tarragon for fresh, use only one-third as much of it.

Chicken Linguine with Red Pepper Sauce

[Photograph on page 261]

This is a true cupboard combination! It's divine
with freshly grated Parmesan or Romano cheese.

1. Cook the linguine in a large pot of boiling water according to the package directions until just tender. Drain, return to the pot, and keep warm.

2. In a medium saucepan, mix the pasta sauce and rosemary. Bring to a boil over medium-low heat. Reduce the heat to low and simmer for 5 minutes. Drain the liquid from the chicken into the sauce. Break the chicken into bite-size pieces and stir in. Serve over the linguine. Sprinkle with the cheese (if using).

Makes 4 servings

Per serving: 444 calories, 25 g protein, 77 g carbohydrates, 3 g fat, 31 mg cholesterol, 5 g dietary fiber, 632 mg sodium

4 Carb Choices

QUICK **SWITCH** • Replace the red-pepper pasta sauce with basil and tomato pasta sauce.

12 **ounces dry linguine**

1 **jar (26 ounces) spicy fat-free red-pepper pasta sauce**

¾ **teaspoon dried rosemary, crushed**

1 **can (9¾ ounces) chunk white chicken packed in water, undrained**

¾ **cup shredded Parmesan cheese (optional)**

Sweet-and-Sour Chicken on Jasmine Rice

[Photograph on page 260]

If you prefer, you can combine the rice and the chicken mixture. This works particularly well for a buffet party because you need put only one dish on the table.

2 cups water

1 cup uncooked jasmine rice or white rice

1 can (8 ounces) pineapple chunks packed in juice, undrained

1½ tablespoons cornstarch

2 tablespoons cider vinegar

1½ teaspoons reduced-sodium soy sauce

1½ teaspoons sugar

¼ teaspoon salt

1 package (16 ounces) frozen sugar snap pea stir-fry mix

1 can (8 ounces) sliced water chestnuts, drained

1 small onion, thinly sliced, or 1 cup frozen chopped onions

1 can (9¾ ounces) chunk white chicken packed in water, undrained

1. In a medium saucepan, mix the water and rice. Bring to a boil over medium-high heat. Reduce the heat to low, cover, and simmer for 15 minutes, or until all the liquid is absorbed. Fluff with a fork.

2. Pour the juice from the pineapple into a large saucepan. Stir in the cornstarch until completely dissolved. Stir in the vinegar, soy sauce, sugar, and salt. Cook over medium heat, stirring constantly, for 5 minutes, or until the mixture comes to a boil and thickens. Stir in the pineapple, snap pea mix, water chestnuts, and onion. Cook for 5 minutes, or until the vegetables are crisp-tender. Stir in the liquid from the chicken. Break the chicken into bite-size pieces and stir in. Serve over the rice.

Makes 4 servings

Per serving: 329 calories, 16 g protein, 61 g carbohydrates, 2 g fat, 31 mg cholesterol, 4 g dietary fiber, 656 mg sodium

5 Carb Choices

QUICK
SWITCH • Replace the snap pea mix with broccoli florets or a brightly colored combination of stir-fry vegetables.

Hawaiian-Style Chicken Curry

This practically instant meal can be served hot, at room temperature, or cold.
When serving it hot, I like to spoon it over rice or rice noodles.
When serving it at room temperature, I add soy milk to make an Asian soup.
For a salad, I serve it cold over shredded Napa cabbage.

1. Preheat the oven to 325°F.

2. In a large bowl, combine the pineapple (with juice), curry powder, vanilla, and coconut extract. Add the water chestnuts and chicken and mix well. Place in a casserole or shallow baking dish.

3. Bake for 30 minutes, or until hot and bubbly.

   Makes 6 servings

   Per serving: 113 calories, 15 g protein, 8 g carbohydrates, 2 g fat, 40 mg cholesterol, 1 g dietary fiber, 434 mg sodium

   ½ **Carb Choice**

QUICK
   SWITCH • Replace the coconut extract with almond extract.

1 **can (20 ounces) crushed pineappple packed in juice, undrained**

2 **teaspoons curry powder**

½ **teaspoon vanilla extract**

½ **teaspoon coconut extract**

1 **can (8 ounces) sliced water chestnuts, drained**

2 **cans (9¾ ounces each) chunk white chicken packed in water, drained**

Chicken Florentine

This recipe also works well with fish. You can make it
ahead of time and reheat it just before serving.

1 can (10¾ ounces) low-
sodium, low-fat condensed
cream of chicken soup

½ cup shredded reduced-fat
mozzarella cheese

⅛ teaspoon ground nutmeg

⅛ teaspoon ground black
pepper

1 package (10 ounces) frozen
chopped spinach, thawed

2 cans (9¾ ounces each) chunk
white chicken packed in
water, drained and broken
into bite-size pieces

2 tablespoons shredded
Parmesan cheese

1. Preheat the oven to 350°F. Coat a 13" × 9" baking dish
   with cooking spray.

2. In a medium saucepan, mix the soup, mozzarella
   cheese, nutmeg, and pepper. Stir over medium-low
   heat until the mozzarella is melted.

3. Spread the spinach in the bottom of the prepared
   baking dish. Top with the chicken and cover with the
   cheese sauce. Sprinkle with the Parmesan cheese. Bake
   for 10 minutes. Change the heat to the broil setting.
   Broil until the top is lightly browned.

Makes 4 servings

Per serving: 235 calories, 30 g protein, 11 g carbohydrates, 8 g
fat, 76 mg cholesterol, 2 g dietary fiber, 1,112 mg sodium

½ **Carb Choice**

QUICK
SWITCH • Replace the cream of chicken soup with cream
of mushroom. Add 1 teaspoon crushed dried oregano.

THE
SPICE
RACK

NUTMEG AND MACE: A SPICY PAIR
These two spices come from the same
plant, the nutmeg tree. For this reason, and
because their flavors so nicely complement each other,
I often group them together. The brown nutmeg seed
has a spicy, slightly sweet flavor. It is sold both whole
and ground. For a better flavor, buy the whole seeds
and grind or grate just what you need. Mace is the
bright orange covering of the nutmeg seed. When
dried and ground, it smells and tastes like a pungent
version of nutmeg. Use either for flavoring poultry
marinades, rice, vegetable sauces, puddings, cakes,
muffins, sweet breads, and fruit desserts.

Chicken Italian-Style

I particularly like this dish for dinner parties because I can cook
the polenta and the sauce ahead of time and just reheat them before serving.
It can be made even faster by using sliced, precooked chicken.

1. In a large saucepan over medium-high heat, combine the polenta and broth and bring to a boil. Reduce the heat to low and simmer for 5 minutes, stirring frequently. Cover and set aside.

2. Heat 2 teaspoons of the oil in a large skillet over medium-high heat. Add the garlic and onion and cook, stirring frequently, for 5 minutes, or until soft. Add the mushrooms and cook for 5 minutes, or until the mushrooms are soft. Add the wine, salt, pepper, tarragon, and oregano and simmer for 5 minutes. Add the tomatoes (with juice), 2 tablespoons of the parsley (if using), and the lemon peel and mix well. Remove from the heat and cover to keep warm.

3. Sprinkle the chicken with the lemon juice. Heat the remaining 2 teaspoons oil in another large skillet over high heat. Add the chicken and cook for 5 minutes on each side, or until a thermometer inserted in the thickest portion registers 160°F and the juices run clear when the chicken is cut with a knife. (Do not overcook the chicken or it will become tough.)

4. Evenly divide the polenta among 4 plates. Top with the chicken, spooning the sauce evenly over the chicken. Top with the cheese and garnish with the remaining parsley.

Makes 4 servings

Per serving: 291 calories, 28 g protein, 20 g carbohydrates, 9 g fat, 57 mg cholesterol, 3 g dietary fiber, 857 mg sodium

1 Carb Choice

- 1 **cup polenta**
- 4 **cups fat-free, reduced-sodium chicken broth**
- 4 **teaspoons extra-virgin olive oil**
- 2 **cloves garlic, minced**
- 1 **medium onion, chopped, or 1½ cups frozen chopped onions**
- 1 **can (8 ounces) sliced mushrooms**
- ½ **cup dry red wine**
- ¼ **teaspoon salt**
- ½ **teaspoon ground black pepper**
- ½ **teaspoon dry tarragon, crushed**
- ½ **teaspoon dry oregano, crushed**
- 1 **can (14½ ounces) chopped Italian-style tomatoes, undrained**
- 3 **tablespoons chopped fresh parsley (optional)**
- 2 **tablespoons very finely chopped fresh lemon peel, yellow part only**
- 4 **boneless, skinless chicken breast halves, pounded thin**
- 2 **tablespoons lemon juice**
- ½ **cup grated Parmesan cheese**

Chicken and Broccoli Amandine

[Photograph on page 259]

This is also good served with pasta.

1 cup uncooked brown rice

2 tablespoons chopped raw almonds

1 medium onion, chopped, or 1½ cups frozen chopped onions

1 package (16 ounces) frozen chopped broccoli, thawed

1 can (10¾ ounces) low-sodium, low-fat condensed cream of mushroom soup

1 can (4 ounces) sliced mushrooms, drained

½ teaspoon ground black pepper

1 cup shredded reduced-fat sharp Cheddar cheese

1 can (9¾ ounces) chunk white chicken packed in water, undrained

1. Cook the rice according to the package directions.

2. Put the almonds in a small skillet and cook over medium heat, stirring frequently, for 3 minutes, or until well toasted. Set aside.

3. Place the onion in a large saucepan, cover, and cook over medium-low heat for 10 minutes, or until soft and translucent. (Add a little water, if necessary, to prevent scorching.) Add the broccoli and cook, stirring frequently, for 5 minutes, or until the broccoli is hot. Stir in the soup, mushrooms, and pepper. Stir in the cheese and continue to cook, stirring frequently, for 3 minutes, or until the cheese is melted.

4. Stir in the rice and the liquid from the chicken. Break the chicken into bite-size pieces and stir in. Serve sprinkled with the almonds.

Makes 6 servings

Per serving: 279 calories, 19 g protein, 35 g carbohydrates, 8 g fat, 31 mg cholesterol, 3 g dietary fiber, 632 mg sodium

2 Carb Choices

QUICK
SWITCH • Replace the almonds and broccoli with pecans and peas.

Greek Chicken with Orzo

[Photograph on page 262]

Here's a useful tip: It is easier to cut dried tomatoes into strips using scissors rather than a knife. This dish is great served hot as a one-dish meal for buffet entertaining, and it is also good served cold or at room temperature as a pasta salad.

1. Warm the oil and garlic in a large nonstick skillet over medium heat for 1 minute, or until the garlic sizzles. Stir in the tomatoes, wine, red peppers, honey, cinnamon, oregano, salt, and black pepper. Reduce the heat to medium-low and simmer, stirring frequently, for 15 minutes.

2. Cook the orzo in a large pot of boiling water according to the package directions until just tender. Drain and stir into the skillet. Stir in the liquid from the chicken. Break the chicken into bite-size pieces and stir in along with the scallions.

Makes 4 servings

Per serving: 421 calories, 19 g protein, 60 g carbohydrates, 8 g fat, 31 mg cholesterol, 2 g dietary fiber, 496 mg sodium

4 Carb Choices

QUICK
SWITCH • Replace the cinnamon with ¼ teaspoon ginger.

1 tablespoon extra-virgin olive oil

3 cloves garlic, minced

1 cup oil-free sun-dried tomatoes, cut into thin strips

1 cup dry white wine

1 jar (7 ounces) roasted red peppers, cut into thin strips

2 teaspoons honey

1 teaspoon ground cinnamon

½ teaspoon dried oregano, crushed

¼ teaspoon salt

¼ teaspoon ground black pepper

8 ounces dry orzo

1 can (9¾ ounces) chunk white chicken packed in water, undrained

5 scallions, cut into ½" pieces

PASTA: HOW MUCH DO YOU NEED?

Pasta, a boon to pantry cooks, is one of the easiest and quickest ingredients to help you to get dinner on the table quickly. Here are a few tricks for serving up perfectly cooked pasta—and just the right amount—every time.

- Pasta expands considerably during cooking, so a single serving of dried pasta looks deceptively skimpy. (That's why many cooks, nervous about running short, end up with enough to feed the whole neighborhood.)

A rule of thumb is to allow 2 ounces of dry pasta per serving. Here's how to gauge the amount needed of different shapes.

PASTA	DRY MEASURE (4 SERVINGS)
Long, skinny pastas, such as spaghetti	1½"-diameter bunch
Broad noodles	4 cups
Fine or medium noodles	4½ cups
Macaroni	2 cups
Rigatoni	4 cups
Fusilli, rotini, or ziti	3 cups
Ditalini or orzo	1⅓ cups

- Use a big pot and plenty of water to boil your pasta so that it can move freely and not stick together. Most chefs recommend 4 quarts of water for each pound of pasta.

- Frequently taste-test the pasta before it is scheduled to be done. Start timing as soon as the water returns to a boil. Lift a piece of the pasta out of the boiling water using tongs or a long-handled fork. Let cool slightly, then bite into it. It should be tender but slightly resistant.

- Drain pasta immediately once it's done. Pasta continues to cook from residual heat and can easily overcook.

- Never rinse pasta unless it will be baked or used in a salad. The starch on the surface of the pasta will help the sauce cling to the pasta.

- Pasta will stay warm longer when served in shallow bowls rather than on flat plates. For best results, warm your serving dishes.

- Always prepare the sauce before cooking the pasta so that the pasta never has to sit (and turn sticky and gluey) while the sauce finishes cooking. If the pasta finishes cooking before the sauce is ready, toss the warm pasta with a small amount of olive oil and keep it warm while the sauce finishes cooking.

- To unstick stuck pasta, submerge it in hot water and separate it gently with a fork. ■

Chicken Enchilada Casserole

You can assemble this casserole ahead of time, refrigerate it, and bake it
just before serving. Allow a few extra minutes of baking time.

1. Preheat the oven to 350°F. Coat a 13" × 9" baking dish with cooking spray.

2. In a large bowl, mix the soup, milk, sour cream, onion, and peppers.

3. Spread half of the tortillas evenly in the bottom of the prepared baking dish. Top with half of the chicken and half of the soup mixture. Repeat. Sprinkle with the cheese. Bake for 30 minutes, or until hot and bubbly.

Makes 6 servings

Per serving: 285 calories, 23 g protein, 35 g carbohydrates, 6 g fat, 50 mg cholesterol, 3 g dietary fiber, 821 mg sodium

2 Carb Choices

QUICK
SWITCH • Replace the cream of chicken soup with cream of mushroom soup. • Or add ½ teaspoon ground cumin.

1 can (10¾ ounces) low-sodium, low-fat condensed cream of chicken soup

½ cup fat-free or 1% milk

½ cup fat-free or reduced-fat sour cream

1 medium onion, finely chopped, or 1½ cups frozen chopped onions

1 can (4 ounces) diced green chile peppers

12 corn tortillas (6" diameter), cut into shreds

2 cans (9¾ ounces each) chunk white chicken packed in water, drained and broken into bite-size pieces

½ cup shredded reduced-fat sharp Cheddar cheese

Chicken Tonnato Pasta

Tonnato sauce contains tuna. It is usually served over veal, but it is just as good over chicken. If you'd like, you can replace the pasta with rice. For a wonderful appetizer, use the sauce as a dip with toast, chips, or crackers.

12 ounces dry pasta shells

½ cup fat-free or reduced-fat mayonnaise

1 can (6 ounces) solid white tuna packed in water, drained

1 tablespoon anchovy paste

1 tablespoon lemon juice

Pinch of cayenne pepper

1 tablespoon extra-virgin olive oil

2 cans (9¾ ounces each) chunk white chicken packed in water, drained and broken into bite-size pieces

1. Cook the pasta in a large pot of boiling water according to the package directions until just tender. Drain.

2. In a blender or food processor, combine the mayonnaise, tuna, anchovy paste, lemon juice, and cayenne. Blend until smooth. With the motor running, slowly add the oil.

3. Serve the shells topped with the chicken and sauce or mix the shells, chicken, and sauce.

Makes 6 servings

Per serving: 546 calories, 44 g protein, 68 g carbohydrates, 8 g fat, 73 mg cholesterol, 2 g dietary fiber, 1,039 mg sodium

4½ Carb Choices

Chicken and Spinach Frittata

This frittata is good served hot or cold, for brunch, lunch, or a light supper entrée.
When serving it for breakfast, I like to serve it warm accompanied by toasted bread
and three colors of melon. For brunch, supper, or picnics, I like it cold or at room
temperature, with crusty Italian bread and a variety of whole, fresh fruits.

1. Preheat the broiler.

2. Heat the oil in an 8" skillet or omelet pan. Add the onion and cook for 2 minutes, or until translucent and soft.

3. In a medium bowl, combine the egg substitute, 2 tablespoons of the cheese, the oregano, pepper, spinach, and chicken and mix well. Pour the mixture into the skillet with the onion and cook over very low heat until the edges are lightly browned. Sprinkle the remaining 2 tablespoons cheese over the top and place under a broiler until the cheese is lightly browned. Cut into wedges.

Makes 4 servings

Per serving: 141 calories, 18 g protein, 1 g carbohydrates, 6 g fat, 35 mg cholesterol, 0 g dietary fiber, 512 mg sodium

0 Carb Choices

1 tablespoon extra-virgin olive oil

1 tablespoon minced onion

¾ cup fat-free liquid egg substitute

¼ cup grated Parmesan cheese

½ teaspoon dried oregano, crushed

⅛ teaspoon ground black pepper

1 package (10 ounces) frozen chopped spinach, very well drained

1 can (9¾ ounces) chunk white chicken packed in water, drained and flaked

QUICK
SWITCH • Substitute another vegetable or a combination of vegetables for the spinach. (If you are using mushrooms, add them to the olive oil along with the onions.) • Substitute 1 cup leftover chopped chicken or turkey for the canned chicken.

Creamed Chicken on Toast

This is a healthier version of chicken à la king, which I revised for a reader
so she could serve it to her bridge club. She wrote back and told me
it was a big hit with her group.

¼ **cup unbleached all-purpose flour**

1 **tablespoon canola oil**

1 **can (12 ounces) fat-free evaporated milk**

¾ **teaspoon dried tarragon, crushed**

¼ **teaspoon salt**

¼ **teaspoon ground black pepper**

2 **cans (9¾ ounces each) chunk white chicken packed in water, drained and broken into bite-size pieces**

1 **jar (4 ounces) sliced pimientos, drained**

1 **tablespoon sherry or 1 teaspoon sherry extract**

4 **slices whole wheat bread, toasted**

1. In a large nonstick skillet, whisk together the flour and oil. Slowly whisk in the milk, tarragon, salt, and pepper until smooth. Whisk over medium heat until the mixture comes to a simmer. Reduce the heat to low and cook, stirring frequently, for 3 minutes, or until slightly thickened.

2. Stir in the chicken, pimientos, and sherry or sherry extract. Heat through. Spoon over the toast.

Makes 4 servings

Per serving: 321 calories, 30 g protein, 31 g carbohydrates, 8 g fat, 61 mg cholesterol, 3 g dietary fiber, 1,049 mg sodium

2 Carb Choices

QUICK
SWITCH • Stir in a 4-ounce can of drained sliced mushrooms. • Or replace the tarragon with crushed dried thyme.

Chicken Sausage

These chicken sausage patties are perfect for a brunch on chilly fall and winter mornings. They are easy to make, and the cooked sausage patties can be frozen in individual zip-top plastic bags so they can easily be reheated in a microwave. They're also great in sandwiches or crumbled over pasta, pizzas, salads, and soups.

1. in a large bowl, combine the chicken and egg white. Add the apple, onion, salt, and pepper and mix well.

2. Divide the mixture into 20 balls, 2 tablespoons each. Place the balls on a flat surface, cover with plastic wrap, and flatten into ¼"-thick patties.

3. Heat a large nonstick skillet over high heat. Place half of the patties in the skillet with ½ cup of the apple juice. Cook for 5 minutes on each side, or until the apple juice evaporates and the patties are firm and no longer pink. Repeat with the remaining patties and apple juice.

Makes 10 servings

Per serving: 78 calories, 11 g protein, 7 g carbohydrates, 1 g fat, 26 mg cholesterol, 1 g dietary fiber, 143 mg sodium

½ Carb Choice

1 pound ground chicken breast without skin

1 egg white

1 apple, peeled and finely chopped

1 small onion, finely chopped, or 1 cup frozen chopped onions

½ teaspoon salt

½ teaspoon ground black pepper

1 cup apple juice

Jambalaya

This Creole dish varies widely from one southern cook to another,
but all versions contain rice, onions, tomatoes, peppers, and ham. In fact,
the name comes from the French word for ham, *jambon*. However, since there
is more chicken than ham in this recipe, I consider it a poultry dish.

1 **medium onion, chopped, or 1½ cups frozen chopped onions**

1 **clove garlic, minced**

1 **can (14½ ounces) fat-free, reduced-sodium chicken broth**

1 **can (8 ounces) tomato sauce**

1 **jar (7 ounces) roasted red peppers, drained and chopped**

2 **bay leaves**

½ **teaspoon ground black pepper**

½ **teaspoon paprika**

½ **teaspoon dried oregano, crushed**

½ **teaspoon dried thyme, crushed**

½ **teaspoon dried basil, crushed**

¼ **teaspoon cayenne pepper**

1 **can (5 ounces) extra-lean chunk ham, undrained**

1 **cup uncooked white rice**

1 **can (9¾ ounces) chunk white chicken packed in water, undrained**

Hot-pepper sauce

1. Place the onion and garlic in a large saucepan, cover, and cook over medium-low heat for 10 minutes, or until soft and translucent. (Add a little water, if necessary, to prevent scorching.)

2. Stir in the broth, tomato sauce, red peppers, bay leaves, black pepper, paprika, oregano, thyme, basil, cayenne, and the liquid from the ham. Flake the ham and stir in. Bring to a boil.

3. Stir in the rice. Reduce the heat to low, cover, and cook for 20 minutes, or until the rice is tender. Stir in the liquid from the chicken. Break the chicken into bite-size pieces and stir in. Remove and discard the bay leaves. Serve with hot-pepper sauce.

Makes 4 servings

Per serving: 360 calories, 22 g protein, 46 g carbohydrates, 8 g fat, 48 mg cholesterol, 2 g dietary fiber, 1,175 mg sodium

3 Carb Choices

Curried Chicken Pita Pockets

You can also use this same recipe for a curried chicken salad. Just add more lettuce and spoon it onto a chilled plate. When serving this as a salad, I usually sprinkle roasted peanuts over the top and accompany it with toasted pita bread.

1. Place the raisins in a small bowl and cover with boiling water. Let stand for 5 minutes and drain.

2. In a large bowl, mix the mayonnaise, curry powder, and ginger. Stir in the raisins, apple, and onion. Stir in the chicken. Serve stuffed in the pita pockets.

Makes 6 servings

Per serving: 175 calories, 11 g protein, 29 g carbohydrates, 2 g fat, 21 mg cholesterol, 4 g dietary fiber, 553 mg sodium

1 Carb Choice

QUICK
SWITCH • Replace the curry powder with Thai spice blend.

¼ **cup raisins**

¼ **cup fat-free or reduced-fat mayonnaise**

1 **teaspoon curry powder**

¼ **teaspoon ground ginger**

1 **small Red or Golden Delicious apple, cored and finely chopped**

¼ **cup finely chopped onion**

1 **can (9¾ ounces) chunk white chicken packed in water, drained and broken into bite-size pieces**

3 **whole wheat pitas, cut in half**

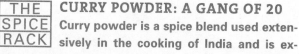 **CURRY POWDER: A GANG OF 20**
Curry powder is a spice blend used extensively in the cooking of India and is extremely popular throughout the rest of the world. The up-to-20 spices most commonly used to make curry powder are ground fresh daily in India, where curry powders vary dramatically according to the region, traditions, and tastes of the cook. In the United States, standard and hotter versions called Madras curry powder are available. Always store curry powder tightly sealed and out of sunlight. It will begin to lose its pungency after about 2 months.

Meat

It's amazing what you can do with a can of beef in gravy. Now, I'll be the first to admit I don't particularly like the flavor of this product—at least not straight from the can. But I've found that if I drain, rinse, and shred the beef, it absorbs the taste of other ingredients in the recipe and turns out great. The Beef Stroganoff, for instance, totally floored me. (If canned roast beef in gravy isn't available in your area, you can substitute packaged roast beef in gravy, found in the refrigerated section. For the same amount as a 12-ounce can, you'll need 1½ cups of the packaged variety.) Another product I find indispensable is the 5-ounce can of ham. It's just the perfect no-leftovers size and so much more convenient than large canned hams.

in this chapter . . .

Beef and Vegetable Stew

[Photograph on cover]

Enjoy the flavor of long-cooking beef stew in a fraction of the time
and with none of the fuss.

 1 **medium onion, chopped, or
   1½ cups frozen chopped
   onions**

 1 **can (8 ounces) sliced
   mushrooms, drained**

 1 **clove garlic, minced**

12 **frozen new potatoes or
   2 cans (15 ounces each)
   new potatoes, drained**

 1 **can (12 ounces) roast beef in
   gravy, rinsed, drained, and
   shredded**

 1 **cup frozen baby carrots or
   1 can (16 ounces) whole
   carrots, drained**

 2 **cups dry red wine**

 ½ **teaspoon dried thyme,
   crushed**

 ½ **teaspoon dried dill weed,
   crushed**

 ½ **teaspoon dried summer
   savory, crushed**

 ½ **teaspoon ground black
   pepper**

 1 **bay leaf**

1¾ **cups water**

 2 **cups frozen peas or 2 cans
   (8½ ounces each) peas,
   drained**

 3 **tablespoons unbleached
   all-purpose flour**

1. In a large pot, mix the onion, mushrooms, and garlic.
   Cover and cook over medium-low heat for 5 minutes.
   Stir in the potatoes, beef, carrots, wine, thyme, dill, savory, pepper, bay leaf, and 1½ cups of the water. Cover
   and simmer for 30 minutes. Stir in the peas and cook
   for 10 minutes.

2. In a cup, stir together the flour and the remaining ¼
   cup water until smooth. Stir into the pot and cook, stirring constantly, for 2 minutes, or until slightly thickened. Remove and discard the bay leaf.

Makes 6 servings

Per serving: 223 calories, 16 g protein, 34 g carbohydrates,
2 g fat, 26 mg cholesterol, 7 g dietary fiber, 404 mg sodium

2 Carb Choices

Beef Barbecue Cups

[Photograph on page 263]

These tasty little treats are also good served at room temperature
and make an excellent addition to picnics or school lunches.

1. Preheat the oven to 400°F. Coat 10 of the 12 muffin cups in a standard-size muffin tin with cooking spray.

2. Place the onion in a medium saucepan, cover, and cook over low heat for 10 minutes, or until soft and translucent. (Add a little water, if necessary, to prevent scorching.) Stir in the beef, barbecue sauce, and brown sugar.

3. Place a biscuit in each sprayed muffin cup. Make an indentation in the center of each biscuit and fill with the beef mixture. Bake for 10 minutes, or until the biscuits are golden brown. Remove from the oven and sprinkle with the cheese.

Makes 5 servings

Per serving: 234 calories, 15 g protein, 25 g carbohydrates, 9 g fat, 31 mg cholesterol, 1 g dietary fiber, 924 mg sodium

1½ Carb Choices

1 small onion, chopped, or 1 cup frozen chopped onions

1 can (12 ounces) roast beef in gravy, rinsed, drained, and shredded

¼ cup barbecue sauce

1 tablespoon packed dark brown sugar

1 can (7½ ounces) refrigerated biscuits (10 biscuits)

½ cup shredded reduced-fat sharp Cheddar cheese

Meat Loaf in an Onion

This innovative, satisfying, and healthy meal was created by Dian Thomas, who has appeared frequently on major television shows with her imaginative and practical solutions to the problems faced when camping out of doors. For example, she tells us how to make this tasty and healthy meat loaf in an onion over a fire.

1 **pound extra-lean ground beef**

2 **egg whites**

¼ **cup tomato sauce**

½ **teaspoon dry mustard**

½ **teaspoon salt**

⅛ **teaspoon ground black pepper**

6 **medium onions, peeled and halved horizontally**

1. Cut 6 rectangles (12" × 14" each) of heavy foil. Preheat the grill.

2. In a medium bowl, combine the beef, egg whites, tomato sauce, mustard, salt, and pepper. Mix well.

3. Remove the centers of the onions, leaving a ¼" shell. Finely chop the center from one of the onions and stir into the meat mixture. Tightly wrap the 5 remaining onion centers and refrigerate or freeze for future use.

4. Spoon the meat mixture into 6 of the onion halves, rounding it on top. Place the remaining onion halves on top of the filled halves and press together tightly. Place the filled onions on top of each piece of foil. Bring the ends of foil up over the onions and fold down tightly. Flatten the ends and roll tightly around each onion. Cook the onion packages for 15 minutes on each side, or until the onions are softened and the beef is no longer pink. (Or you can bake the onions in a 350°F oven for 45 minutes.)

Makes 6 servings

Per serving: 183 calories, 17 g protein, 10 g carbohydrates, 8 g fat, 39 mg cholesterol, 2 g dietary fiber, 314 mg sodium

½ **Carb Choice**

Beef-Stuffed Bell Peppers

These stuffed peppers are easy to prepare, and they make
an impressive presentation for parties or dinner gatherings. For a more
colorful presentation, try using red bell peppers.

1. Preheat the oven to 375°F. Coat a 1½-quart casserole with cooking spray. Prepare the rice according to the package directions.

2. Cut the tops off the peppers and carefully remove and discard the seeds. Steam the peppers over boiling water for 4 minutes, or until fork-tender.

3. Heat a nonstick skillet coated with cooking spray over medium heat until hot enough for drops of water to "dance" on the surface. Add the beef and cook, stirring frequently, for 4 minutes, or until no longer pink. Add the onion and cook, stirring frequently, for 4 minutes, or until the onion is soft and translucent.

4. Remove from the heat. Add 1 cup of the tomato soup, the Worcestershire sauce, salt, and black pepper and mix well. Spoon about ¾ cup of the mixture into each pepper. Place the stuffed peppers in the prepared casserole and bake for 30 minutes, or until the peppers begin to brown.

5. Heat the remaining soup in a small saucepan. Spoon over the top of each pepper.

Makes 4 servings

Per serving: 353 calories, 25 g protein, 32 g carbohydrates, 13 g fat, 59 mg cholesterol, 2 g dietary fiber, 540 mg sodium

2 Carb Choices

½ **cup uncooked white rice**

4 **medium green bell peppers**

1 **pound extra-lean ground beef**

1 **medium onion, finely chopped, or 1½ cups frozen chopped onions**

1 **can (10¾ ounces) reduced-sodium tomato soup**

1½ **teaspoons Worcestershire sauce**

¼ **teaspoon salt**

¼ **teaspoon ground black pepper**

Beef Stroganoff

You can make this dish ahead of time, but don't add the sour cream
until you have reheated it to serve.

1 tablespoon arrowroot

1 cup fat-free or 1% milk

8 ounces dry no-yolk or egg noodles

1 tablespoon butter

1 onion, thinly sliced

1 can (12 ounces) roast beef with gravy, rinsed, drained, and shredded

1 tablespoon tomato paste

1½ teaspoons paprika

½ teaspoon dried basil, crushed

¼ teaspoon ground nutmeg

⅛ teaspoon red-pepper flakes

½ cup reduced-fat sour cream

1. Place the arrowroot in a small bowl and gradually stir in the milk until smooth.

2. Cook the noodles in a large pot of boiling water according to the package directions until just tender. Drain and keep warm.

3. Melt the butter in a large nonstick skillet over medium heat. Add the onion and cook, stirring frequently, for 5 minutes, or until soft and translucent. Stir in the beef, tomato paste, paprika, basil, nutmeg, and pepper flakes. Stir in the milk mixture, reduce the heat to low, and simmer for 3 minutes, or until thickened.

4. Stir in the sour cream and heat through. Do not boil. Serve over the noodles.

Makes 4 servings

Per serving: 390 calories, 24 g protein, 54 g carbohydrates, 7 g fat, 94 mg cholesterol, 2 g dietary fiber, 492 mg sodium

3 Carb Choices

QUICK
SWITCH • Replace the basil with tarragon or dill. • Or replace the beef with canned chicken or turkey.

THE SPICE RACK

PIQUANT PAPRIKA

Paprika is a dark red powder made from certain dried peppers. The flavor can vary from mildly sweet to downright hot. Most people sprinkle paprika on all manner of savory dishes. In Hungary, however, paprika is a dominant flavor in foods such as chicken paprikash and goulash. It's also great in chowders, chili, and fish or potato dishes.

Southwestern Beef and Bean Lasagna

[Photograph on page 264]

Who'd have thought Mexican and Italian influences could blend so smoothly?
You can prepare the tomato sauce ahead of time and even assemble
the lasagna a few hours ahead and refrigerate it until needed.

1. Place the onion and garlic in a large nonstick skillet, cover, and cook over medium-low heat for 10 minutes, or until soft and translucent. (Add a little water, if necessary, to prevent scorching.) Stir in the tomatoes, chile peppers, chili powder, oregano, and cumin. Bring to a boil. Reduce the heat to low and simmer for 20 minutes.

2. Preheat the oven to 350°F. Coat a 13" × 9" baking dish with cooking spray.

3. In a small bowl, mix the beef and beans. In another bowl, mix the cottage cheese, egg white, cilantro (if using), black pepper, and ½ cup of the Cheddar cheese.

4. Spoon ¾ cup of the tomato sauce in the bottom of the prepared baking dish. Top with a layer of noodles and half of the beef mixture. Add another layer of noodles, the cottage cheese mixture, and the remaining beef mixture. Top with the remaining noodles and the remaining tomato sauce. Sprinkle the remaining 1 cup of Cheddar cheese over the top.

5. Pour the water around the edges and cover tightly with foil. Bake for 1¼ hours, or until the noodles are tender. Allow to cool for 10 minutes before cutting.

Makes 8 servings

Per serving: 290 calories, 25 g protein, 38 g carbohydrates, 5 g fat, 32 mg cholesterol, 4 g dietary fiber, 850 mg sodium

2½ Carb Choices

1 **medium onion, chopped, or 1½ cups frozen chopped onions**

1 **clove garlic, minced**

1 **can (28 ounces) chopped tomatoes**

1 **can (4 ounces) diced green chile peppers**

2 **teaspoons chili powder**

1 **teaspoon dried oregano, crushed**

½ **teaspoon ground cumin**

1 **can (12 ounces) roast beef in gravy, rinsed, drained, and shredded**

1 **can (15 ounces) pinto beans, rinsed and drained**

8 **ounces fat-free or 1% cottage cheese**

1 **egg white**

¼ **cup chopped fresh cilantro leaves (optional)**

½ **teaspoon ground black pepper**

1½ **cups shredded reduced-fat sharp Cheddar cheese**

8 **ounces dry no-boil lasagna noodles**

1 **cup water**

Beef and Noodle Casserole

You can use frozen beef and bacon in this recipe for a complete pantry
ingredient list. You can also prepare the casserole dish in the morning
or even a day ahead of the time you bake it. If using a Pyrex-style casserole,
be sure to take it out of the refrigerator at least 1 hour before baking
so that the cold glass dish won't crack in the hot oven.

4 ounces dry medium egg
noodles

3 slices turkey bacon, cut into
1" pieces

1 pound extra-ground beef

1 onion, finely chopped, or
1 cup frozen chopped onions

2 teaspoons chili powder

¼ teaspoon salt

¼ teaspoon ground black
pepper

1 can (10¾ ounces) reduced-
sodium tomato soup

¼ cup water

½ small green bell pepper, finely
chopped

½ cup shredded reduced-fat
sharp Cheddar cheese

1 package (10 ounces) frozen
corn kernels

1. Preheat the oven to 350°F. Coat a 1½-quart casserole
with cooking spray.

2. Prepare the noodles according to the package directions until just tender. Drain.

3. Cook the bacon in a large nonstick skillet over
medium-high heat for 3 minutes, or until crisp. Remove to a plate. Add the beef, onion, chili powder, salt,
and black pepper to the skillet and mix well. Add the
soup and water and mix well.

4. Layer the noodles, half of the beef mixture, bacon, bell
pepper, cheese, and corn in the prepared casserole.
Layer the rest of the beef mixture on the top. Bake for
30 minutes, or until hot and bubbly.

Makes 6 servings

Per serving: 335 calories, 11 g protein, 34 g carbohydrates, 11 g
fat, 59 mg cholesterol, 3 g dietary fiber, 478 mg sodium

2 Carb Choices

Beef Spaghetti Pie Olé

This is a slightly modified version of the recipe that won the first prize for
Sherry Druary in the Alabama state Beef Cook Off. I met Sherry at the National Beef
Cook Off in Little Rock in 1995. She's committed to keeping daily dinners as a time
for the family to be together, despite her busy schedule. For this reason,
she frequently makes use of healthy convenience foods.

1. Preheat the oven to 350°F.

2. *To make the shell:* Prepare the spaghetti according to the package directions until just tender. Drain.

3. In a large bowl, whisk together the cheese, egg, salt, and garlic powder. Add the spaghetti and toss to coat. Place in a 9" pie plate. Press evenly in the bottom and up the sides to form a shell.

4. *To make the filling:* Heat a large nonstick skillet over medium heat until drops of water sprinkled into the skillet "dance" on the surface. Crumble the beef into the pan and cook, stirring often, for about 5 minutes, or until lightly browned. Drain and return the beef to the skillet. Sprinkle with the garlic powder, cumin, and salt.

5. Stir in the tomatoes and bring to a boil. Cook, stirring occasionally, for 5 minutes, or until most of the liquid has evaporated.

6. Reserve 2 tablespoons of the beef mixture for a garnish. Stir the sour cream into the remaining beef mixture and spoon it into the prepared shell. Sprinkle the cheese over the top, leaving a 2" border around the edge. Spoon the reserved beef mixture onto the center of the cheese. Bake for 15 minutes, or until heated through.

Makes 6 servings

Per serving: 570 calories, 46 g protein, 47 g carbohydrates, 20 g fat, 132 mg cholesterol, 2 g dietary fiber, 772 mg sodium

3 Carb Choices

SHELL

- **7 ounces dry spaghetti**
- **⅓ cup shredded reduced-fat Monterey Jack or Cheddar cheese**
- **1 egg**
- **¼ teaspoon salt**
- **¼ teaspoon garlic powder**

FILLING

- **1 pound extra-lean ground beef**
- **1 teaspoon garlic powder**
- **½ teaspoon ground cumin**
- **¼ teaspoon salt**
- **1 can (10 ounces) diced tomatoes with green chiles**
- **¾ cup fat-free or reduced-fat sour cream**
- **1 cup shredded reduced-fat Monterey Jack or Cheddar cheese**

Macronade

[Photograph on page 265]

This hearty meat and pasta dish is popular in the region of Sète in
the south of France. It is usually served over rigatoni for a party.

1 medium onion, chopped, or
  1½ cups frozen chopped
  onions

3 cloves garlic, minced

1 can (28 ounces) chopped
  tomatoes, undrained

1 can (6 ounces) tomato paste

1 tablespoon sugar

1 can (12 ounces) roast beef in
  gravy, rinsed, drained, and
  shredded

1 can (5 ounces) extra-lean
  chunk ham, drained and
  flaked

¾ cup dry red wine

¼ teaspoon ground black
  pepper

16 ounces dry rigatoni

1. Place the onion and garlic in a large saucepan, cover,
   and cook over medium-low heat for 10 minutes, or
   until soft and translucent. (Add a little water, if necessary, to prevent scorching.)

2. Stir in the tomatoes, tomato paste, and sugar. Bring to
   a boil over medium heat. Reduce the heat to low, cover,
   and simmer, stirring occasionally, for 1 hour. Stir in the
   beef, ham, wine, and pepper. Cover and cook for 30
   minutes.

3. Cook the rigatoni in a large pot of boiling water according to the package directions until just tender.
   Drain. Serve topped with the sauce.

Makes 6 servings

Per serving: 463 calories, 26 g protein, 73 g carbohydrates, 7 g
fat, 38 mg cholesterol, 5 g dietary fiber, 862 mg sodium

4½ Carb Choices

Beef and Tomato Curry

Try this hearty curry over rice or Asian noodles. And accompany it with chutney
and other curry condiments, such as peanuts and diced pineapple.

1. Place the onion and garlic in a large saucepan, cover, and cook over medium-low heat for 10 minutes, or until soft and translucent. (Add a little water, if necessary, to prevent scorching.)

2. Stir in the tomatoes, beef, water, raisins, honey, curry powder, cinnamon, allspice, ginger, and pepper. Simmer for 10 minutes.

Makes 4 servings

Per serving: 176 calories, 17 g protein, 25 g carbohydrates, 2 g fat, 39 mg cholesterol, 3 g dietary fiber, 774 mg sodium

1½ Carb Choices

QUICK
SWITCH • Replace the cinnamon, allspice, and ginger with ¾ teaspoon pumpkin pie spice.

1 **medium onion, chopped, or
1½ cups frozen chopped
onions**

1 **clove garlic, minced**

1 **can (14½ ounces) chopped
tomatoes, undrained**

1 **can (12 ounces) roast beef in
gravy, rinsed, drained, and
shredded**

½ **cup water**

¼ **cup raisins**

1 **tablespoon honey**

2 **teaspoons curry powder**

¼ **teaspoon ground cinnamon**

¼ **teaspoon ground allspice**

¼ **teaspoon ground ginger**

¼ **teaspoon ground black pepper**

Speedy Sukiyaki

If you are not in a hurry, allow the meat to marinate for 1 hour. Start cooking the rice about 10 minutes ahead so it will be ready to serve when the topping is finished. For variety, replace the rice with soba noodles tossed with a teaspoon or two of toasted sesame oil. Leftover sukiyaki is wonderful as a chilled salad.

1 cup uncooked white rice

½ cup mirin (rice wine)

¼ cup water

3 tablespoons reduced-sodium soy sauce

1 can (12 ounces) roast beef in gravy, rinsed, drained, and shredded

1 medium onion, thinly sliced

1 package (16 ounces) frozen spinach leaves

1 package (10½ ounces) low-fat silken extra-firm tofu, drained and cubed

1. Cook the rice according to the package directions.

2. In a medium bowl, mix the mirin, water, and soy sauce. Stir in the beef and let stand for 10 minutes.

3. In a large nonstick skillet, combine the onion and spinach. Cook over medium heat, stirring constantly, until the spinach is thawed. Add the beef mixture and cook for 1 minute. Carefully stir in the tofu and heat through. Serve over the rice.

Makes 4 servings

Per serving: 656 calories, 33 g protein, 120 g carbohydrates, 4 g fat, 39 mg cholesterol, 5 g dietary fiber, 956 mg sodium

8½ **Carb Choices**

QUICK
SWITCH • Replace the soy sauce with teriyaki sauce.

Red Flannel Hash

This hearty New England dish traditionally makes good use of leftover corned beef and vegetables. Although every recipe I have ever seen for this hash uses only beets and potatoes with the corned beef, I occasionally add other leftover vegetables such as cooked cabbage, carrots, and parsnips. For a really fast last-minute meal, combine just the canned ingredients and brown them in a skillet.

1. Warm the oil in a large nonstick skillet over medium heat. Add the onion and bacon bits and cook for 5 minutes, or until soft and browned. Transfer to a large bowl.

2. Stir in the beets, potatoes, corned beef, sour cream, parsley (if using), and pepper. Mix well. Spoon the mixture back into the skillet and press down firmly with a wide spatula. Cook over medium-low heat, stirring frequently, for 20 minutes, or until evenly browned.

Makes 6 servings

Per serving: 249 calories, 19 g protein, 18 g carbohydrates, 12 g fat, 49 mg cholesterol, 2 g dietary fiber, 877 mg sodium

1 Carb Choice

QUICK
SWITCH • Add ½ teaspoon dried dill weed.

1 tablespoon canola oil

1 medium onion, chopped, or 1½ cups frozen chopped onions

1 tablespoon imitation bacon bits

1 can (16 ounces) julienned beets, drained

1 package (16 ounces) frozen new potatoes, thawed and chopped

1 can (12 ounces) lean corned beef, crumbled

3 tablespoons reduced-fat sour cream

2 tablespoons chopped fresh parsley (optional)

¼ teaspoon ground black pepper

Shepherd's Pie

Shepherd's pie is a delicious and satisfying British dish.
It is a meat and vegetable combination baked under a "crust" of mashed potatoes.

4–5 **medium potatoes, peeled and cubed**

1 **tablespoon butter, melted**

½ **cup 1% milk**

¼ **cup finely chopped fresh parsley**

½ **teaspoon ground black pepper**

1½ **pounds extra-lean ground beef**

1 **clove garlic, minced**

4 **carrots, peeled and chopped**

6 **ounces mushrooms, chopped**

1 **medium onion, chopped, or 1½ cups frozen chopped onions**

1 **teaspoon dried thyme, crushed**

1 **tablespoon unbleached all-purpose flour**

1 **cup fat-free, reduced-sodium chicken broth**

1 **package (10 ounces) frozen corn kernels, thawed**

1. Preheat the oven to 375°F. Coat a 2-quart baking dish with cooking spray.

2. Place the potatoes in a large saucepan. Cover with water. Bring to a boil over high heat. Reduce the heat to low, cover, and cook for 20 minutes, or until tender. Drain and place in a bowl. Add the butter, milk, parsley, and ¼ teaspoon of the pepper. Mash the mixture. Set aside.

3. Heat a large nonstick skillet over medium-high heat until hot enough for drops of water to "dance" on the surface. Add the beef and garlic and cook, stirring frequently, for 10 minutes, or until browned. Remove the meat to a bowl and set aside. (Do not wash the skillet.)

4. In the same skillet, combine the carrots, mushrooms, and onion and cook, stirring frequently, for 5 minutes, or until fork-tender. Stir in the thyme and the remaining ¼ teaspoon pepper.

5. In a small bowl, combine the flour and broth and stir until smooth. Add the flour mixture to the skillet and mix well. Bring to a boil over high heat, reduce the heat to low, and simmer, uncovered, stirring occasionally, for 10 minutes, or until slightly thickened. Add the corn, beef mixture, and any juices that have collected in the bowl and mix well. Spread the mixture in the prepared baking dish.

6. Using a spoon, decorate the top with small mounds of mashed potato. Bake for 30 minutes, or until bubbly. Remove from the oven and allow to stand for 5 minutes before serving.

Makes 6 servings

Per serving: 466 calories, 28 g protein, 40 g carbohydrates, 22 g fat, 40 mg cholesterol, 5 g dietary fiber, 144 mg sodium

2½ **Carb Choices**

Popeye's Spinach Hash

When Popeye credited spinach for his superior strength
and endurance, he encouraged millions of kids to eat their greens.
In his honor, I have created Popeye's Spinach Hash as my way of saying
"thank you." This recipe also pays tribute to Popeye's scrawny girlfriend,
Olive Oyl, because extra-virgin olive oil is an important ingredient.

1. In a medium bowl, combine the egg whites, salt, and pepper and beat until well mixed.

2. Heat the oil in a heavy skillet over medium-high heat. Add the onion and cook, stirring frequently, for 5 minutes, or until soft and translucent. Add the beef and cook, stirring frequently, for 3 minutes, or until no longer pink. Add the spinach and cook, stirring constantly, for 1 minute, or until wilted.

3. Add the egg white mixture to the beef mixture in the skillet and stir until all moisture is absorbed.

Makes 4 servings

Per serving: 274 calories, 29 g protein, 7 g carbohydrates, 15 g fat, 59 mg cholesterol, 4 g dietary fiber, 490 mg sodium

½ **Carb Choice**

3 **egg whites**

½ **teaspoon salt**

¼ **teaspoon ground black pepper**

2 **teaspoons extra-virgin olive oil**

1 **medium onion, chopped, or 1½ cups frozen chopped onions**

1 **pound extra-lean ground beef**

3 **packages (6 ounces each) prewashed baby spinach leaves**

Ham in Orange Sauce on Wild Rice

If you can find quick-cooking wild rice, so much the better. If you can't
and don't want to wait 45 minutes for regular wild rice, use quick-cooking
brown rice instead. It takes only 10 minutes—and is less expensive!

1 box (5 ounces) uncooked
   wild rice

1 cup water

1 tablespoon arrowroot

⅓ cup frozen orange juice
   concentrate, thawed

1½ tablespoons packed light
   brown sugar

½ teaspoon ground cinnamon

¼ teaspoon red-pepper flakes

⅛ teaspoon ground cloves

2 cans (5 ounces each) extra-
   lean chunk ham, drained and
   flaked

1. Cook the wild rice according to the package directions.

2. Meanwhile, combine the water and arrowroot in a
   medium saucepan and stir until the arrowroot is dissolved. Stir in the juice concentrate, brown sugar, cinnamon, pepper flakes, and cloves. Cook over
   medium-low heat, stirring frequently, for 5 minutes, or
   until thickened. Stir in the ham and heat through.
   Serve over the wild rice.

Makes 4 servings

Per serving: 326 calories, 17 g protein, 26 g carbohydrates, 4 g
fat, 33 mg cholesterol, 2 g dietary fiber, 972 mg sodium

1½ **Carb Choices**

QUICK
SWITCH • Replace the cinnamon with ¼ teaspoon ginger.

Ham and Pineapple with Spiced Couscous

This is a wonderful holiday recipe, perfect for buffet parties.
Serve it hot or chill it for a marvelous couscous salad.

1. Drain the juice from the pineapple into a medium saucepan. Stir in the water, cinnamon, salt, allspice, and cloves. Bring to a boil over medium-high heat.

2. Add the couscous and mix well. Cover and remove from the heat. Let stand for 5 minutes, or until the liquid has been absorbed. Fluff with a fork. Stir in the pineapple and ham.

Makes 5 servings

Per serving: 344 calories, 19 g protein, 60 g carbohydrates, 4 g fat, 27 mg cholesterol, 3 g dietary fiber, 816 mg sodium

4½ Carb Choices

1 **can (20 ounces) crushed pineapple packed in juice, undrained**

1 **cup water**

½ **teaspoon ground cinnamon**

¼ **teaspoon salt**

¼ **teaspoon ground allspice**

⅛ **teaspoon ground cloves**

1 **box (10 ounces) dry quick-cooking couscous**

2 **cans (5 ounces each) extra-lean chunk ham, drained and flaked**

Alsatian Ham and Sauerkraut with New Potatoes

In the Alsace region of northeastern France, a popular dish is sauerkraut cooked with wine and juniper berries, served with potatoes and either sausage or ham. For a lower-sodium variation, serve only ¼ cup of ham and sauerkraut over large baked potatoes.

1 **can (16 ounces) sauerkraut, rinsed and drained**

1 **cup dry white wine**

2 **teaspoons juniper berries**

1 **package (16 ounces) frozen new potatoes, thawed**

1 **can (5 ounces) extra-lean chunk ham, drained and flaked**

1. In a large saucepan, combine the sauerkraut, wine, and juniper berries. Bring to a boil over medium-high heat. Reduce the heat to low, cover, and simmer for 15 minutes. Stir in the potatoes and ham. Cover and cook for 5 minutes.

Makes 4 servings

Per serving: 168 calories, 10 g protein, 26 g carbohydrates, 2 g fat, 17 mg cholesterol, 5 g dietary fiber, 1,264 mg sodium

1½ Carb Choices

Jeanne's **TOP 10** *Freezer Favorites*

I never skimp on keeping the freezer stocked. It saves me from unnecessary trips to the store. Some foods I use right from the freezer or give a quick zap in the microwave. Others—like raw chicken, fish, or meat—I thaw overnight in the refrigerator. (Believe me, that makes a really big difference in the quality of fish and other seafood.) As for freezing bread: It doesn't get stale and toasts beautifully.

1. **Ice cream and frozen yogurt**

2. **Whipped topping**

3. **Phyllo dough**

4. **Fruits and vegetables**

5. **Fruit juice concentrates**

6. **Fish and seafood**

7. **Poultry**

8. **Meat**

9. **Bread**

10. **Ice cubes**

Ham and Cheese Calzone

A calzone is a stuffed pizza that resembles a large turnover. I make a large
one here, but you can also prepare small ones. The calzone is equally good
hot or at room temperature. Using a ready-to-bake packaged pizza crust
makes this recipe as easy to prepare as it is easy to eat!

⅓ **cup reduced-fat ricotta
cheese**

½ **teaspoon dried oregano,
crushed**

½ **teaspoon ground black
pepper**

¾ **cup shredded reduced-fat
mozzarella cheese**

¼ **cup shredded Parmesan
cheese**

1 **can (5 ounces) extra-lean
chunk ham, drained and
flaked**

1 **tube (10 ounces) ready-to-
bake pizza dough**

1. Preheat the oven to 425°F. Coat a large baking sheet
   with cooking spray.

2. In a medium bowl, mix the ricotta, oregano, and
   pepper. Stir in the mozzarella cheese, Parmesan
   cheese, and ham.

3. Unroll the dough onto the prepared baking sheet.
   Using your hands, press it into a 10" circle, starting in
   the center. Spoon the cheese mixture onto half of the
   circle, leaving a 1" border. Fold the other half of the
   crust over the filling, making a half-moon shape. Press
   the edges together tightly, pinching the dough to seal
   it shut.

4. Bake for 8 minutes. Turn the calzone over and bake for
   7 minutes, or until well browned. Cool slightly before
   cutting into wedges.

Makes 4 servings

Per serving: 312 calories, 21 g protein, 32 g carbohydrates, 10 g
fat, 38 mg cholesterol, 0 g dietary fiber, 739 mg sodium

2 Carb Choices

QUICK
SWITCH • Omit the ham and use ¼ cup dry-pack sun-dried
tomato bits for a vegetarian dish.

Frankfurters with Baked Beans

Kids will love this recipe! If you keep frankfurters stored
in the freezer, place them in a pot of boiling water for a few minutes
to thaw them before proceeding with the recipe.

1. Preheat the oven to 375°F. Coat a 3-quart baking dish with cooking spray.

2. Squeeze 1 tablespoon juice from one of the lemon halves. Cut the remaining half into thin slices and set aside.

3. Melt the butter in a large nonstick skillet over medium heat. Add the onion and cook, stirring frequently, for 7 minutes, or until translucent. Add the lemon juice, beans, molasses, mustard, nutmeg, and baking soda. Stir to mix well. Spoon the mixture into the prepared baking dish.

4. Score the frankfurters on one side in a crisscross fashion and arrange them on top of the bean mixture. Coat lightly with cooking spray. Place the lemon slices on top. Bake for 1 hour, or until the frankfurters are browned.

Makes 6 servings

Per serving: 264 calories, 9 g protein, 26 g carbohydrates, 15 g fat, 33 mg cholesterol, 4 g dietary fiber, 882 mg sodium

1½ Carb Choices

1 **lemon, halved**

1 **tablespoon butter**

1 **onion, finely chopped, or
   1 cup frozen chopped onions**

2 **cans (16 ounces each) baked
   beans**

3 **tablespoons molasses**

½ **teaspoon dry mustard**

¼ **teaspoon ground nutmeg**

   Pinch of baking soda

6 **all-beef frankfurters**

Side Dishes

If little things mean a lot, side dishes are worth their weight in gold (or is that saffron?). They take a plain Jane entrée and turn it into something interesting. Whether you're feeding your family or catering to guests who materialize out of nowhere, you can be sure everybody will leave the table satisfied if you add a side dish to your meal. Rice and other grains are one part of the equation. Quick-cooking varieties from the cupboard and ready-made items like polenta in the fridge get that component of the meal dispatched in a jiffy. As for vegetables and condiments, they're just as easy with a little help from pantry foods.

in this chapter . . .

Dirty Rice

To lighten this Cajun specialty, I left out the traditional high-cholesterol organ meats and browned the flour for the roux in a very small amount of oil rather than chicken fat. For extra fiber, I used brown rice instead of white. This dish makes a wonderful base for leftovers, and it can be made ahead and reheated just before serving.

2 cups uncooked quick-cooking brown rice

1 tablespoon canola oil

2 tablespoons unbleached all-purpose flour

1 medium onion, finely chopped, or 1½ cups frozen chopped onions

1 can (4 ounces) diced green chile peppers

2 cloves garlic, minced

1 bay leaf

½ cup water

½ teaspoon dried oregano, crushed

½ teaspoon dried thyme, crushed

½ teaspoon salt

¼ teaspoon cayenne pepper

¼ teaspoon ground black pepper

1. Cook the rice according to the package directions.

2. Warm the oil in a large nonstick skillet over medium-high heat. Stir in the flour until completely moistened. Reduce the heat to medium and continue stirring for 3 minutes, or until the flour is dark brown.

3. Add the onion, chile peppers, garlic, and bay leaf. Cook, stirring frequently, for 5 minutes. Stir in the water, oregano, thyme, salt, cayenne, and black pepper. Bring to a boil. Remove and discard the bay leaf. Stir in the rice and heat through.

Makes 4 servings

Per serving: 410 calories, 8 g protein, 78 g carbohydrates, 6 g fat, 0 mg cholesterol, 1 g dietary fiber, 291 mg sodium

5 Carb Choices

ONE POT OF RICE, THREE GREAT DISHES

Rice is a busy cook's friend. It's a breeze to make, it keeps for up to a week in the refrigerator, and it can be used for main courses, side dishes, and even desserts.

Two cups of rice and 4 cups of water make about 5 cups of cooked rice. So cook up a big batch all at once and try some of the following recipes. Or experiment on your own, adding interesting leftovers or some of your favorite flavors to dress up the taste of this standard fare.

Cuban black beans and rice. Mix 1 can (16 ounces) rinsed and drained black beans, 1/2 cup frozen chopped onion, 1 tablespoon minced garlic, 1 teaspoon olive oil, 1/2 teaspoon ground cumin, and a pinch of salt and pepper. Cook for 5 minutes. Add 3 cups cooked rice. Serve with salsa.

Quick pilaf. Cook 1 cup frozen mixed vegetables, 1 tablespoon chopped almonds, and 1 teaspoon minced garlic for 5 minutes. Add 3 cups cooked rice, 1/4 cup chicken broth, 2 tablespoons chopped parsley, and a pinch of salt and pepper. Cook for 5 minutes, or until the liquid has evaporated and the rice is golden brown.

Rice and broccoli salad. Mix 2 cups cooked rice, 1 cup thawed broccoli florets, 1 jar (2 ounces) chopped roasted red peppers, 2 tablespoons olive oil, 1 teaspoon toasted chopped walnuts, 1/4 teaspoon salt, and balsamic vinegar or lemon juice to taste. ▪

Honeyed Rice

For a higher-fiber dish, use 2 cups quick-cooking brown rice in place of
the white and prepare according to the package directions.

1 cup uncooked white rice

2 cups water

2 tablespoons honey

**1 tablespoon reduced-sodium
soy sauce**

2 teaspoons dried mint

**1 teaspoon sherry or apple
juice**

1. Combine the rice and water in a medium saucepan
and bring to a boil over high heat. Reduce the heat to
low, cover, and cook for 15 minutes, or until the liquid
is absorbed. Remove from the heat and fluff with a
fork.

2. Stir in the honey, soy sauce, mint, and sherry or apple
juice.

Makes 6 servings

Per serving: 141 calories, 2 g protein, 33 g carbohydrates,
0 g fat, 0 mg cholesterol, 1g dietary fiber, 81 mg sodium

2 Carb Choices

QUICK
SWITCH • Stir in raisins and diced apples. • Or replace the
soy sauce with frozen orange juice concentrate and add ¼
teaspoon ground nutmeg or cinnamon.

THE SPICE RACK **MANY KINDS OF MINT**
This ancient herb is known for its forest-
green to dark green leaves and its refreshing, palate-cleansing taste. It comes in many
varieties, including peppermint, spearmint, lemon,
pineapple, apple, and orange. The first two are the
most common dried mints you'll encounter. Use mint
in fruit salads, lamb and game condiments, tabbouleh,
yogurt sauces, desserts, jelly, and teas.

Spicy Thai Rice

This piquant Asian rice dish is good served hot, cold, or at room temperature.
It can be used as a side dish or as a vegetarian entrée.

1. In a large saucepan, combine the water, sugar, and salt. Bring to a boil over high heat. Stir in the rice. Reduce the heat to low, cover, and simmer for 15 minutes, or until the rice is tender and the water has been absorbed. Remove from the heat and fluff with a fork.

2. In a blender, combine the peanut butter, vinegar, soy sauce, lime juice, oil, garlic, and pepper flakes. Blend until smooth. Pour over the rice and mix well. Stir in the scallions (if using) and cilantro (if using).

Makes 6 servings

Per serving: 202 calories, 6 g protein, 30 g carbohydrates, 7 g fat, 0 mg cholesterol, 1 g dietary fiber, 260 mg sodium

2 Carb Choices

QUICK
SWITCH • Stir a 9¾-ounce can of chunk white chicken (drained and broken into bite-size pieces) into the cooked rice. • Or add a 10½-ounce package of low-fat silken extra-firm tofu (drained and cubed) to the cooked rice.

2 **cups water**

2 **teaspoons sugar**

½ **teaspoon salt**

1 **cup uncooked jasmine or white rice**

⅓ **cup unhomogenized creamy peanut butter**

2 **tablespoons rice vinegar**

1 **tablespoon reduced-sodium soy sauce**

2 **teaspoons lime juice**

1 **teaspoon toasted sesame oil**

1 **clove garlic, halved**

¼ **teaspoon red-pepper flakes**

4 **scallions, chopped (optional)**

½ **cup chopped fresh cilantro (optional)**

Rice Pilaf

You can turn this pilaf into an entrée by adding cooked fish, poultry, meat, or beans.

1 **tablespoon canola oil**

1 **cup uncooked white rice**

1 **medium onion, thinly sliced**

1 **can (14½ ounces) fat-free, reduced-sodium chicken broth**

2 **tablespoons reduced-sodium soy sauce**

1 **teaspoon dried thyme, crushed**

1. Warm the oil in a large saucepan over medium heat. Add the rice and onion. Cook, stirring frequently, for 5 minutes, or until lightly browned.

2. Add the broth, soy sauce, and thyme. Bring to a boil. Reduce the heat to low, cover, and cook for 20 minutes, or until the liquid has been absorbed. Fluff with a fork.

Makes 8 servings

Per serving: 109 calories, 2 g protein, 20 g carbohydrates, 2 g fat, 0 mg cholesterol, 1 g dietary fiber, 125 mg sodium

1 Carb Choice

QUICK **SWITCH** • Replace the soy sauce with frozen orange juice concentrate. Add 2 tablespoons dried currants.

THE SPICE RACK **JUST IN THYME**
Thyme, a member of the mint family, has a pungent, earthy flavor that gets stronger over time. The most commonly used variety is garden thyme, which has the aroma of mint laced with lemon. Use thyme to season all manner of meat, poultry, vegetable, and fish dishes, as well as soups.

Parmesan Polenta

Precooked polenta is wonderful to have on hand for no-fuss side dishes, instant hors d'oeuvres, and the basis for myriad entrées. (You can top it with most any kind of sauce.) It is available seasoned and unseasoned; look for it in the produce section. Serve leftovers for breakfast in place of toast.

1. Preheat the broiler. Coat a large baking sheet with cooking spray.

2. Slice the polenta into 8 rounds and arrange them on the sheet. Mist lightly with cooking spray. Sprinkle with the cheese. Broil for 3 to 4 minutes, or until the cheese starts to brown lightly.

Makes 4 servings

Per serving: 97 calories, 4 g protein, 16 g carbohydrates, 1 g fat, 3 mg cholesterol, 0 g dietary fiber, 371 mg sodium

1 Carb Choice

1 package (16 ounces) ready-to-serve unseasoned polenta

3 tablespoons shredded Parmesan cheese

Herbed Quinoa

Quinoa (pronounced *keen*-wah) is a tiny bead-shaped, ivory-colored grain with a
bland flavor and a slightly chewy texture. It can be used like rice and cooks in half
the time. It contains more protein than most other grains and is a balanced source of
many vital nutrients. Quinoa is becoming increasingly popular in this country and
is available in most supermarkets and all health food stores.

1 can (14½ ounces) fat-free,
reduced-sodium chicken
broth

3 tablespoons water

¼ teaspoon ground black
pepper

1 cup uncooked quinoa, rinsed

1 tablespoon extra-virgin
olive oil

¾ teaspoon dried thyme,
crushed

½ teaspoon dried oregano,
crushed

1. In a medium saucepan, mix the broth, water, and
pepper. Bring to a boil over medium-high heat. Stir in
the quinoa. Reduce the heat to low, cover, and cook for
12 minutes, or until all the liquid has been absorbed.

2. Remove from the heat and stir in the oil, thyme, and
oregano. Cover and let stand for 5 minutes. Fluff with a
fork.

Makes 3 cups

Per ½-cup serving: 129 calories, 4 g protein, 20 g carbohydrates, 4 g fat, 0 mg cholesterol, 2 g dietary fiber, 9 mg sodium

1 Carb Choice

QUICK
SWITCH • Replace the thyme with savory and the
oregano with basil.

Asparagus au Gratin

This easy-to-make combination of asparagus and cheese makes a great side dish as well as an entrée. If you don't have frozen asparagus, you may use a 15-ounce can; save ½ cup of the liquid to mix with the soup.

1. Preheat the oven to 350°F. Coat an 11" × 7" baking dish with cooking spray.

2. Arrange the asparagus in the prepared baking dish and top with half of the potato chips. Cover with half of the soup and then the remaining potato chips. Mix the water into the remaining soup and pour evenly over the potato chips.

3. Sprinkle with the cheese, breadcrumbs, and paprika. Bake for 30 minutes, or until bubbly.

Makes 6 servings

Per serving: 243 calories, 12 g protein, 25 g carbohydrates, 11 g fat, 10 mg cholesterol, 3 g dietary fiber, 380 mg sodium

1½ Carb Choices

2 **boxes (10 ounces each) frozen asparagus spears, thawed**

1 **bag (4 ounces) unsalted fat-free or reduced-fat potato chips, crushed**

1 **can (10¾ ounces) low-sodium, low-fat condensed cream of mushroom soup**

½ cup water

1 **cup shredded reduced-fat sharp Cheddar cheese**

½ cup dry breadcrumbs

¼ teaspoon paprika

QUICK
SWITCH • Replace the paprika with chili powder or ⅛ teaspoon cayenne pepper.

STOCK UP ON GRAINS

Grains are ideal pantry items because they store well and can form the base for an endless variety of meals. Used both as side dishes and main courses, grains can be teamed with meats, poultry, fish, and vegetables to make satisfying, family-pleasing meals.

There are literally thousands of grains, ranging from "exotics" like quinoa to the very familiar white rice. All have one thing in common: They're remarkably easy to cook. Essentially, grains require nothing more than water and a stint on the stove until they're done.

Store grains in tightly covered jars either at room temperature or in the refrigerator or freezer. Grains with a high oil content, such as wheat germ, should always be refrigerated.

Here are cooking instructions for some of the most common grains—and a few unusual ones that you really should get to know. To give grains a deliciously aromatic flavor, toast them in a dry, heavy nonstick skillet for a few minutes. Stir frequently until the grains are golden. Then cook as directed, slightly reducing the cooking time. You can also cook grains in a flavorful stock or in canned broth instead of water. ∎

GRAIN	COOKING TIPS	USE
Amaranth	Simmer 1 part amaranth in 3 parts water for 20 to 25 minutes	Cereal
Barley, pearl	Simmer 1 part barley in 4 parts water for 30 to 40 minutes	Side dishes, pilafs
Buckwheat groats	Simmer 1 part groats in 2 parts water for 15 minutes	Kasha, pilafs
Bulgur	Pour 1½ cups boiling water over 1 cup bulgur and let stand for 30 minutes	Side dishes, cold salads
Cornmeal	Simmer 1 part cornmeal in 4 parts water for 30 minutes	Cereal, polenta
Couscous	Pour 1½ cups boiling water over 1⅓ cups couscous and let stand for 5 minutes	Side dishes

GRAIN	COOKING TIPS	USE
Hominy	Soak overnight, then simmer 1 part hominy in 3 parts water for 2½ to 3 hours	Cereal, side dishes
Millet	Simmer 1 part millet in 2 parts water for 25 to 30 minutes	Soups, stews, side dishes
Oats, old-fashioned rolled	Simmer 1 part oats in 2 parts water for 10 minutes and let stand for 2 minutes	Cereal, baking
Oats, steel-cut	Simmer 1 part oats in 4 parts water for 30 to 40 minutes	Cereal
Quinoa	Rinse before using. Simmer 1 part quinoa in 2 parts water for 15 to 20 minutes	Side dishes
Rice, brown	Simmer 1 part rice in 2 parts water for 30 to 40 minutes	Side dishes, casseroles, pilafs, soups
Rice, white	Simmer 1 part rice in 2 parts water for 15 to 20 minutes	Side dishes, casseroles, pilafs, soups
Wheat berries	Soak overnight, then simmer 1 part wheat berries in 3 parts water for 2 hours	Stuffings, casseroles, side dishes, cereals
Wheat, cracked	Simmer 1 part cracked wheat in 2 parts water for 25 minutes	Cereal, side dishes, salads, casseroles
Wild rice	Simmer 1 part rice in 3 parts water for 45 to 60 minutes	Stuffings, casseroles, side dishes

Pickled Asparagus with Herbed Lemon Dressing

Serve these asparagus as a first course. They're also good chopped up in salads or added to pasta. The dressing is amazingly rich tasting. Use it immediately or chill it first. To pickle your own asparagus, blanch spears and marinate them in ¼ cup vinegar. Refrigerate and allow to stand for 2 to 4 hours.

¼ **cup fat-free or reduced-fat mayonnaise**

½ **teaspoon dried thyme, crushed**

½ **teaspoon grated lemon peel**

⅛ **teaspoon cayenne pepper**

1 **jar (16 ounces) pickled asparagus spears, chilled and undrained**

1. In a small bowl, mix the mayonnaise, thyme, lemon peel, and cayenne. Spoon out 1 tablespoon of the liquid from the asparagus and add to the bowl; mix well. Discard the remaining liquid.

2. Divide the asparagus among serving plates and drizzle with the dressing.

Makes 4 servings

Per serving: 32 calories, 3 g protein, 5 g carbohydrates, 1 g fat, 0 mg cholesterol, 2 g dietary fiber, 562 mg sodium

0 Carb Choices

Hawaiian Green Beans

Pineapple gives these beans their island flair. It's an unusually good way to dress up a plain vegetable.

1. Drain the juice from the pineapple into a medium saucepan. Add the vinegar, sugar, cornstarch, and pepper and stir until the cornstarch is dissolved.

2. Bring the mixture to a boil over medium-low heat and simmer, stirring constantly, for 3 minutes, or until thickened. Stir in the beans and pineapple; heat through.

Makes 4 servings

Per serving: 79 calories, 2 g protein, 20 g carbohydrates, 0 g fat, 0 mg cholesterol, 2 g dietary fiber, 3 mg sodium

1 Carb Choice

1 **can (8 ounces) crushed pineapple packed in juice, undrained**

3 **tablespoons rice vinegar**

1 **tablespoon sugar**

1 **tablespoon cornstarch**

⅛ **teaspoon ground black pepper**

1 **package (10 ounces) frozen french-cut green beans, thawed**

QUICK
SWITCH • Replace the rice vinegar with white vinegar.

Herbed Green Beans

An easy way to thaw the beans is in the microwave.
Leftover herbed beans make a fine addition to salads.

1 teaspoon canola oil

¼ cup chopped fresh parsley (optional)

½ teaspoon dried basil, crushed

¼ teaspoon dried thyme, crushed

⅛ teaspoon salt

1 package (16 ounces) cut green beans, thawed

1. Warm the oil in a large nonstick skillet over medium heat. Add the parsley (if using), basil, thyme, and salt. Stir for 1 minute, or until the mixture starts to sizzle. Stir in the beans and heat through.

Makes 4 servings

Per serving: 47 calories, 2 g protein, 9 g carbohydrates, 1 g fat, 0 mg cholesterol, 3 g dietary fiber, 70 mg sodium

½ **Carb Choice**

QUICK
SWITCH • Replace the basil with dried tarragon and the thyme with grated lemon peel. • Or replace the green beans with frozen brussels sprouts, cauliflower, or broccoli.

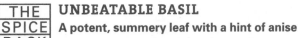

UNBEATABLE BASIL

A potent, summery leaf with a hint of anise and mint, basil is a mainstay in Mediterranean cooking and most associated with traditional pesto. Dried leaves are acceptable in a pinch, but they just don't measure to up fresh. Fortunately, it's easy to find fresh basil in stores most of the year. Wrap the leaves in a damp paper towel and place in a zip-top bag for up to 4 days. Or finely chop the leaves, mix with a little bit of oil, spoon it into ice cube trays, and freeze. Drop the cubes into a freezer bag and use as needed.

Honeyed Beets

This sweet-and-sour side dish is good hot or cold.

1. Drain the liquid from the beets into a medium saucepan. Stir in the honey, vinegar, and oil. Add the onions and bring to a boil over medium heat. Remove from the heat and allow to cool for 5 minutes, or just until the onions are crisp-tender.

2. Stir in the beets. If serving hot, heat through. If serving cold, refrigerate for at least 1 hour. Drain the beets and onions before serving.

Makes 4 servings

Per serving: 138 calories, 2 g protein, 29 g carbohydrates, 4 g fat, 0 mg cholesterol, 2 g dietary fiber, 300 mg sodium

1½ Carb Choices

QUICK
SWITCH • Add ½ teaspoon dried dill weed.

1 **can (16 ounces) sliced beets, undrained**

¼ **cup honey**

1 **tablespoon cider vinegar**

1 **tablespoon extra-virgin olive oil**

1 **medium red onion, thinly sliced and separated into rings**

Corn Casserole

If you have any leftovers, crumble them and toast them in the oven
to use as a topping on soups and salads. To turn this dish into an entrée,
sprinkle cheese over the top before baking.

1 can (16½ ounces) cream-style corn

1 can (16 ounces) corn kernels

1 box (8½ ounces) corn muffin mix

1 cup reduced-fat sour cream

1 egg

1. Preheat the oven to 350°F. Coat a 13" × 9" baking dish with cooking spray.

2. In a large bowl, mix the cream-style corn, corn kernels, muffin mix, sour cream, and egg until well-blended. Spoon into the prepared baking dish. Bake for 30 minutes.

Makes 6 servings

Per serving: 294 calories, 7 g protein, 54 g carbohydrates, 7 g fat, 38 mg cholesterol, 4 g dietary fiber, 873 mg sodium

3½ Carb Choices

QUICK
SWITCH • Add 1 teaspoon ground cumin or 1 teaspoon ground cinnamon.

Mushroom and Pea Medley

You can turn this simple side dish into a main course by tossing it with cooked pasta or rice. You can also add canned chicken or tuna.

1. Warm the oil in a large nonstick skillet over medium heat. Add the garlic and stir for 1 minute. Add the mushrooms and cook, stirring frequently, for 3 minutes. Stir in the onion powder, salt, and pepper. Stir in the peas and heat through.

Makes 6 servings

Per serving: 98 calories, 5 g protein, 15 g carbohydrates, 3 g fat, 0 mg cholesterol, 5 g dietary fiber, 495 mg sodium

1 Carb Choice

QUICK
SWITCH • Add ½ teaspoon crushed dried mint.

1 tablespoon extra-virgin olive oil

2 cloves garlic, minced

2 cans (8 ounces each) sliced mushrooms, drained

¼ teaspoon onion powder

¼ teaspoon salt

¼ teaspoon ground black pepper

1 package (16 ounces) frozen peas, thawed

SUPER SPUD STUFFERS

If you keep a bag of baking potatoes handy, you can have an easy feast whenever you want. Here are some of my favorite ideas—meatless and otherwise—but you can experiment with toppings to create your very own spud specialties.

First, here's the best method for baking potatoes for stuffing.

The basic spud. Scrub large baking potatoes (12 ounces each) with cold water and pat dry. Pierce several times with a fork to keep the skins from bursting. (Do not rub the potatoes with oil or butter or wrap them in foil because you will soften the skins in the process. You want tough-textured shells so they can be stuffed without tearing.) Bake on a baking sheet at 400°F for 1 hour, or until easily pierced with a skewer. Set aside until cool enough to handle. They're now ready for stuffing!

The following recipes each make 2 servings. For all but the Irish taco spuds, lox 'n' spuds, pizza spuds, and cut a thin slice from the top of 2 baked potatoes. Scoop out the potato pulp, leaving a 1/4"-thick shell. Mash the pulp, cover, and set aside. Set the shells on a baking sheet and keep warm.

Anchovy spuds. Cook 1 chopped onion and 1 tablespoon butter in a skillet over low heat for 5 minutes. Add 1 can (2 ounces) flat an-chovy fillets (rinsed, dried, and chopped) and cook, stirring, for 5 minutes. Stir in the mashed potatoes, 1/2 cup milk, and a pinch of pepper. Cook until the liquid is absorbed. Spoon into the potato shells and sprinkle with fine bread crumbs. Bake at 350°F for 20 minutes.

Chicken surprise spuds. Melt 1 tablespoon butter in a saucepan. Add 1 cup thawed frozen french-cut green beans, 1/2 cup milk, and 2 tablespoons soy sauce; heat slowly, stirring constantly. Stir in 1/2 cup sour cream, 1 can (9 3/4 ounces) chunk white chicken packed in water (drained and flaked), 1/2 cup drained canned water chestnuts, and the mashed potatoes. Heat through and spoon into the potato shells. Sprinkle with paprika.

Clam spuds. Mix together 1/2 package dehydrated leek soup mix and 1/2 cup boiling water. Stir in the mashed potatoes, 1 can (6 1/2 ounces) chopped clams (drained), and a pinch of pepper. Spoon into the potato shells. Sprinkle with chopped parsley.

Irish taco spuds. Split the tops of 2 baked potatoes. Scoop the pulp from the potatoes and place the pulp from one of the potatoes in a plastic bag; freeze to use at another time. Mash the remaining potato pulp in a bowl. Flatten the two potato shells to form "taco shells" and keep warm. Stir 3/4 cup cooked lean ground beef into the pulp. Stir in $\frac{1}{2}$ cup taco sauce and $\frac{1}{2}$ cup shredded reduced-fat sharp Cheddar cheese. Spoon into the potato shells. Top each with shredded lettuce and diced tomato.

Lox 'n' spuds. Cut 2 baked potatoes lengthwise into halves. Cut slits about $\frac{1}{2}$" apart in the edges of the potato skins and flatten the halves to form the "crust." Using a fork, work $1\frac{1}{2}$ teaspoons butter, 2 tablespoons sour cream, and a pinch **each** of salt and pepper into each potato half. Top each with 1 red onion slice and some smoked salmon (lox) from a 3-ounce can. Spread 1 tablespoon light cream cheese over each. Top with any remaining salmon and 1 teaspoon sour cream.

Onion au gratin spuds. Cook 2 chopped onions and 1 teaspoon oil in a covered skillet over low heat until soft. Add water if needed to prevent scorching. Uncover and cook, stirring occasionally, for 20 minutes, or until browned. Stir in the mashed potatoes and heat through. Spoon into the potato shells and sprinkle with shredded Swiss cheese. Bake at 375°F for 20 minutes, or until lightly browned.

Pizza spuds. Cut 2 baked potatoes lengthwise into halves. Cut slits about $\frac{1}{2}$" apart in the edges of the potato skins and flatten the halves to form the "crust." Place on a baking sheet. Using a fork, work $\frac{1}{2}$ teaspoon shredded Parmesan cheese, $\frac{1}{4}$ teaspoon oregano, and pinches of salt and pepper into the pulp of each half. Top each with $\frac{1}{4}$ cup pizza sauce and $\frac{1}{4}$ cup shredded mozzarella cheese. Bake at 400°F for 10 minutes, or until the cheese is melted.

Sloppy Joe spuds. In a skillet, combine 1 tablespoon oil, 1 cup cooked ground beef, $\frac{1}{4}$ cup chopped scallions, 3 tablespoons Sloppy Joe seasoning mix, 1 can (8 ounces) tomato sauce, and a dash of hot-pepper sauce. Cook for 10 minutes, stirring often. Mix in the mashed potatoes and heat through. Spoon into the potato shells.

Spa spuds. Cook 1 chopped onion in a skillet over low heat until soft. Add water if needed to prevent scorching. Stir in the mashed potatoes, $\frac{1}{2}$ cup cottage cheese, $\frac{1}{4}$ cup buttermilk, and 3 tablespoons shredded Parmesan cheese. Heat through and spoon into the potato shells. Bake at 350°F for 12 minutes, or until hot.

Vegetarian spuds. Combine $\frac{1}{2}$ cup **each** white sauce and grated Monterey Jack cheese with $\frac{1}{4}$ cup **each** cooked frozen peas and carrots. Season with salt and combine with the mashed potatoes. Spoon into the potato shells. Bake at 375°F for 20 minutes, or until lightly browned. ∎

Herbed Scalloped Potatoes

[Photograph on page 266]

If you thought scalloped potatoes were too much bother, this recipe will change
your mind. It's ready for the oven in less than 10 minutes.

1 **package (16 ounces) frozen
hash-brown-cut potatoes,
thawed**

2 **tablespoons unbleached
all-purpose flour**

¾ **teaspoon dried oregano,
crushed**

¾ **teaspoon dried basil, crushed**

½ **teaspoon salt**

½ **teaspoon ground black
pepper**

¾ **cup shredded Parmesan
cheese**

1 **onion, thinly sliced**

1 **can (12 ounces) fat-free
evaporated milk**

1. Preheat the oven to 350°F. Coat a 13" × 9" baking dish
with cooking spray.

2. Spread one-third of the potatoes in the prepared
baking dish. In a cup, mix the flour, oregano, basil, salt,
and pepper; sprinkle half over the potatoes. Sprinkle ¼
cup of the cheese over the top and cover with half of
the onion. Repeat the layers. Top with the remaining
potatoes and cheese.

3. Pour the milk over the top. Bake for 1 hour, or until
bubbling and lightly browned.

Makes 8 servings

Per serving: 211 calories, 9 g protein, 40 g carbohydrates, 2 g
fat, 7 mg cholesterol, 4 g dietary fiber, 322 mg sodium

2½ Carb Choices

QUICK
SWITCH • Replace the basil with 1 teaspoon freeze-dried
chives.

Tuscan Potatoes

[Photograph on page 267]

My favorite recipe for new potatoes is one that I learned at Lorenzo de Medici's picturesque villa and cooking school in Tuscany. These tender garlic-and-rosemary potatoes are a perfect accompaniment for grill menus. If you have any potatoes left over, serve them cold for an unusual potato salad.

1. Preheat the oven to 400°F. Coat a 13" × 9" baking dish with cooking spray.

2. Place the potatoes, oil, and garlic in the prepared baking dish. Toss to mix well. Sprinkle with the rosemary. Bake, stirring occasionally, for 45 minutes, or until evenly browned.

Makes 3 servings

Per serving: 112 calories, 3 g protein, 16 g carbohydrates, 5 g fat, 0 mg cholesterol, 3 g dietary fiber, 456 mg sodium

1 Carb Choice

QUICK
SWITCH • Replace the rosemary with Southwestern spice blend.

1 can (15 ounces) new potatoes, drained and halved

1 tablespoon extra-virgin olive oil

6 cloves garlic, peeled

2 teaspoons dried rosemary, crushed

 FRESH-SCENTED ROSEMARY
Rosemary grows wild in Mediterranean regions, but it's also grown commercially in the United States and Europe. A relative of mint, this fragrant herb has an evergreen scent and a flavor that suggests both pine and lemon. Dried rosemary is available in whole-leaf and powdered form. Crush the whole leaves with a mortar and pestle, because they don't disintegrate during cooking. Rosemary is a natural with lamb and also perks up pork, poultry, vegetables, focaccia, and marinades.

Mashed Potatoes with Horseradish

Try adding diced cooked fish, poultry, or meat to these tasty potatoes for
a satisfying main dish. If you have any leftover mashed potatoes,
form them into patties and brown them in a nonstick skillet.

2 pounds boiling potatoes, peeled and cubed

2 tablespoons butter

½ teaspoon salt

½ teaspoon ground black pepper

½ cup reduced-fat sour cream

3 tablespoons prepared horseradish

1. Place the potatoes in a large saucepan. Cover with cold water and bring to a boil over high heat. Cook for 8 to 10 minutes, or until tender. Drain thoroughly and place in a large bowl.

2. Add the butter, salt, and pepper. Mash with a potato masher. Mix in the sour cream and horseradish.

Makes 6 servings

Per serving: 163 calories, 4 g protein, 29 g carbohydrates, 4 g fat, 12 mg cholesterol, 3 g dietary fiber, 239 mg sodium

1½ Carb Choices

QUICK
SWITCH • Replace the sour cream with buttermilk and add ½ teaspoon crushed dill weed. • Or replace the horseradish with crumbled feta cheese.

Sweet Dill Pickles

If you find dill pickles too sour and sweet pickles too sweet, here is the perfect compromise. These treats are so good they can become habit forming. They also make a uniquely different hostess gift.

1. Cut the pickles into ½" slices. Place in a bowl and mix in the sugar, mustard seeds, and garlic. Spoon into the jar, cover, and refrigerate. Allow to stand for several days, turning the jar daily.

Makes 3 cups

Per ¼-cup serving: 69 calories, 0 g protein, 18 g carbohydrates, 0 g fat, 0 mg cholesterol, 0 g dietary fiber, 209 mg sodium

1 Carb Choice

1 jar (32 ounces) kosher dill pickles, drained

1 cup sugar

1 teaspoon mustard seeds

1 clove garlic, quartered

THE SPICE RACK | THE MOODS OF MUSTARD

When young, the green leaves of the mustard plant can be cooked and eaten like turnip greens. When the plant blooms, its luminous flowers produce flavor-rich mustard seeds, which are used whole or ground (dry mustard). Or they're made into prepared mustard, the base for countless sauces and an essential condiment for backyard barbecues and picnics. Try mixing your favorite prepared brown mustard with a little honey as a sweet-and-spicy baste for chicken.

Sweet Potato Dip

[Photograph on page 268]

While I was working on this unusual dip, I had lots of fun asking people what they thought the ingredients were. Very few guessed correctly.

1½ **pounds sweet potatoes**

1½ **teaspoons dried marjoram, crushed**

½ **teaspoon ground nutmeg**

¼ **teaspoon salt**

⅛ **teaspoon ground black pepper**

⅛ **teaspoon red-pepper flakes (optional)**

1 **tablespoon extra-virgin olive oil**

1. Preheat the oven to 400°F.

2. Scrub and dry the sweet potatoes and poke holes in them with a fork. Place them on a baking sheet and bake for 1 hour, or until soft. Set aside until cool enough to handle. Remove and discard the skins.

3. Transfer the flesh to a food processor. Add the marjoram, nutmeg, salt, pepper, and pepper flakes (if using). Blend until smooth. With the motor running, slowly pour the oil in through the feed tube and mix well.

Makes 1¾ cups

Per 2-tablespoon serving: 60 calories, 1 g protein, 12 carbohydrates, 1 g fat, 0 mg cholesterol, 2 g dietary fiber, 45 mg sodium

½ **Carb Choice**

QUICK
SWITCH • Replace the sweet potatoes with a 16-ounce can of solid-pack pumpkin. Add 2 tablespoons sugar and an additional ¼ teaspoon salt.

THE SPICE RACK

SIMPLY MARJORAM There are many species of this ancient herb, which dates back to early Greek times, but the most frequently used is sweet marjoram (generally labeled just marjoram). The small oval leaves have a slightly sweet taste and a flavor very similar to oregano but much more mild. When using marjoram, always add it near the end of the cooking time as its delicate flavor is easily destroyed. Marjoram is used primarily to season meats such as lamb and veal.

Artichoke Dip

[Photograph on page 268]

This has literally become my favorite dip. You can serve it warm, at room temperature, or cold. It also makes a fine vegetable side dish or cold salad.

1. Preheat the oven to 350°F.

2. In a 1-quart baking dish, mix the artichokes, peppers, mayonnaise, and all but 2 tablespoons of the cheese. Spread evenly in the dish. Sprinkle with the remaining cheese. Bake for 50 minutes, or until the top is lightly browned.

Makes 1½ cups

Per 1-tablespoon serving: 26 calories, 2 g protein, 2 g carbohydrates, 1 g fat, 3 mg cholesterol, 0 g dietary fiber, 160 mg sodium

0 Carb Choices

1 can (8½ ounces) artichoke hearts, drained and chopped

1 can (4 ounces) diced green chile peppers

¾ cup fat-free or reduced-fat mayonnaise

¾ cup shredded Parmesan cheese

Southwestern Soybean Dip

I like to serve this dip with baked corn tortilla chips. Leftovers make
a great filling for burritos and omelets.

1 can (16 ounces) black soybeans, rinsed and drained

1 cup shredded reduced-fat sharp Cheddar cheese

½ cup fat-free or reduced-fat mayonnaise

1 can (4 ounces) diced green chile peppers

¼ teaspoon red-pepper flakes

1. Preheat the oven to 350°F. Coat a 9" × 5" loaf pan with cooking spray.

2. Place the soybeans in a large bowl. Mash using a pastry blender or a heavy fork. Stir in the cheese, mayonnaise, peppers, and pepper flakes. Spoon into the prepared pan and bake for 50 minutes, or until the top is golden brown.

Makes 2¼ cups

Per 2-tablespoon serving: 40 calories, 4 g protein, 4 g carbohydrates, 1 g fat, 3 mg cholesterol, 1 g dietary fiber, 92 mg sodium

0 Carb Choices

QUICK
SWITCH • Replace the Cheddar cheese with pepper Jack cheese.

DIP TIPS

Beans have a firm texture and smooth interior that makes them ideal for dips. And with canned beans in your pantry, dips are a snap to prepare. Here are three quick ones to get you started.

- For a chunky dip, add black beans to your favorite salsa.

- For a smooth Southwestern dip, puree black or red beans, drained canned chile peppers, cumin, and garlic powder.

- For a Middle Eastern dip, mash up chickpeas with tahini, minced garlic, lemon juice, and cumin. ∎

Barbecue Sauce

Too many barbecue sauces are sky-high in sodium.
This one is lower in sodium, tastes better, and takes only a short time
to whip up. It keeps well for several weeks in the refrigerator.

1. In a medium saucepan, mix the onion and water. Cook over medium heat for 10 minutes, or until soft and translucent. Add the ketchup, juice concentrate, lemon peel, lemon juice, Worcestershire sauce, vinegar, and mustard. Mix well and bring to a boil over medium-high heat. Reduce the heat to medium and cook, stirring occasionally, for 30 minutes, or until thick.

2. Remove from the heat and stir in the liquid smoke. Let cool for 5 minutes. Transfer to a blender or food processor and blend until smooth. Cool to room temperature. Spoon into a container with a tight-fitting lid and store in the refrigerator.

Makes 1½ cups

Per ¼-cup serving: 62 calories, 1 g protein, 16 g carbohydrates, 0 g fat, 0 mg cholesterol, 1 g dietary fiber, 285 mg sodium

½ Carb Choice

1 **medium onion, finely chopped, or 1½ cups frozen chopped onions**

2 **tablespoons water**

½ **cup ketchup**

6 **tablespoons frozen unsweetened apple juice concentrate, thawed**

½ **teaspoon grated lemon peel**

2 **tablespoons lemon juice**

1½ **tablespoons Worcestershire sauce**

1 **tablespoon cider vinegar**

¾ **teaspoon dry mustard**

¼ **teaspoon liquid smoke**

Dill Sauce

This sauce is wonderful on vegetables as well as seafood of all types. (I always serve it with Salmon Mousse; see page 143.) And it's also a very good salad dressing. When possible, make this sauce a day before you plan to serve it so the flavors can blend.

1 cup fat-free or reduced-fat sour cream

½ cup fat-free or reduced-fat mayonnaise

1½ teaspoons dried dill weed, crushed

1 teaspoon dried tarragon, crushed

½ teaspoon salt

1. In a small bowl, mix the sour cream, mayonnaise, dill, tarragon, and salt. Cover and refrigerate (overnight, if possible) until needed.

Makes 1½ cups

Per 1-tablespoon serving: 13 calories, 1 g protein, 2 g carbohydrates, 0 g fat, 0 mg cholesterol, 0 g dietary fiber, 102 mg sodium

0 Carb Choices

Horseradish Sauce

This sauce is best if made ahead of time to give the flavors a chance to "marry."
If you want to use it immediately, however, it is still a very tasty topping
for vegetables, seafood, poultry, and meat of all types.

1. In a small bowl, mix the mayonnaise, sour cream, horseradish, lemon juice, mustard, salt, and pepper. Cover and refrigerate (overnight, if possible) until needed.

Makes 1 cup

Per 1-tablespoon serving: 14 calories, 1 g protein, 3 g carbohydrates, 0 g fat, 0 mg cholesterol, 0 g dietary fiber, 112 mg sodium

0 Carb Choices

QUICK
SWITCH • Add 1 teaspoon dried dill, basil, thyme, or other herb.

½ **cup fat-free or reduced-fat mayonnaise**

½ **cup fat-free or reduced-fat sour cream**

¼ **cup prepared horseradish**

1 **teaspoon lemon juice**

½ **teaspoon Dijon mustard**

¼ **teaspoon salt**

⅛ **teaspoon ground black pepper**

Holiday Cranberry Ketchup

I like to make a large quantity of this tasty condiment, put it in small decorative jars, and take it to holiday parties as a hostess gift. It is great served with a traditional turkey dinner in place of cranberry sauce. And it's a wonderful no-fat spread for turkey sandwiches.

2 cups cranberries

½ cup chopped onion

¼ cup water

¼ cup frozen unsweetened apple juice concentrate, thawed

¼ cup white vinegar

½ teaspoon ground allspice

½ teaspoon ground cinnamon

½ teaspoon salt

⅛ teaspoon ground cloves

⅛ teaspoon ground black pepper

1. In a medium saucepan, mix the cranberries, onion, and water. Bring to a boil over medium-high heat. Reduce the heat to medium-low and cook, stirring frequently, for 5 to 10 minutes, or until the cranberries are soft.

2. Let cool for 5 minutes. Transfer to a blender or food processor and blend until smooth.

3. Pour the pureed mixture back into the saucepan and add the juice concentrate, vinegar, allspice, cinnamon, salt, cloves, and pepper. Cook over medium heat, stirring frequently to prevent scorching, for 10 minutes, or until thick. Cool to room temperature before serving.

Makes 1 cup

Per 2-tablespoon serving: 23 calories, 0 g protein, 6 g carbohydrates, 0 g fat, 0 mg cholesterol, 0 g dietary fiber, 135 mg sodium

½ Carb Choice

THE SPICE RACK

ALLSPICE: A FLAVOR TRIO
Allspice is the round reddish or dark brown berry of the tropical evergreen pimiento tree. It got its name because it tastes like a combination of cinnamon, nutmeg, and cloves. The largest quantity of allspice is grown in Jamaica, where it is sometimes called Jamaica pepper. The dried berries can be purchased whole or ground. This extremely versatile spice is perfect for both sweet and savory dishes, among them soups, marinades, sauces, chutney, spice cake, puddings, and fruit desserts.

Salsa

There are lots of really good, already prepared salsas available.
But when you don't have any on hand and need salsa immediately,
this easy recipe uses only standard pantry ingredients.

1. In a medium bowl, mix the tomatoes, chile peppers,
   onion, cilantro (if using), lemon or lime juice, garlic,
   oregano, cumin, and black pepper.

Makes 2 cups

Per ¼-cup serving: 20 calories, 1 g protein, 3 g carbohydrates,
0 g fat, 0 mg cholesterol, 1 g dietary fiber, 94 mg sodium

0 Carb Choices

- **1 can (14½) ounces chopped tomatoes, drained**
- **1 can (4 ounces) diced green chile peppers**
- **½ medium onion, chopped, or ¾ cup frozen chopped onions**
- **3 tablespoons chopped fresh cilantro (optional)**
- **1 tablespoon lemon or lime juice**
- **1 clove garlic, minced**
- **¾ teaspoon ground oregano, crushed**
- **¾ teaspoon ground cumin**
- **¼ teaspoon ground black pepper**

Sweets

It's no accident this chapter is the longest in the book. There isn't anybody who doesn't like dessert, and nobody will guess how easy these are to throw together using ingredients from your cupboard, refrigerator, or freezer. There's truly something for everybody here, whether your tastes run from fruit to chocolate, from pudding to pie, or from cookies to compote. Once you try them, you may find—as I did—that many will become part of your everyday repertoire, no matter how much time you have to make dessert. It just doesn't get any better than this!

in this chapter . . .

Secret Sauce

This sauce is my own "secret weapon." Whenever I don't have anything for dessert, I just open a can of fruit and spoon some of this sauce over the top. Guests always think it is an outrageously rich crème anglaise.

1 cup vanilla ice milk or reduced-fat ice cream, melted

1½ teaspoons orange liqueur

1. In a small bowl, mix the ice milk and liqueur.

Makes 1 cup

Per 2-tablespoon serving: 26 calories, 1 g protein, 4 g carbohydrates, 1 g fat, 2 mg cholesterol, 0 g dietary fiber, 14 mg sodium

0 Carb Choices

QUICK
SWITCH • Replace the orange liqueur with brandy or almond, coffee, or raspberry liqueur.

Orange Meringue Sauce

[Photograph on page 270]

Use this satin-smooth meringue as a sauce or dip for fruit or cake.
Or serve it like sherbet. For a really incredible dessert, try topping it with
drained mandarin orange segments and a little Secret Sauce (opposite page)
flavored with orange liqueur. The egg white powder is a great alternative
to raw egg whites in recipes that don't require cooking.

¾ cup frozen orange juice concentrate, slightly warmed

¼ cup 100% egg white powder

½ cup sugar

1. In a medium bowl, combine the juice concentrate and egg white powder. Using an electric mixer on low speed, beat until mixed well. Increase the speed to medium and beat until the mixture starts to thicken. Slowly add the sugar and continue beating until soft peaks form when you lift the beaters.

Makes 2 cups

Per ¼-cup serving: 62 calories, 1 g protein, 15 g carbohydrates, 0 g fat, 0 mg cholesterol, 0 g dietary fiber, 13 mg sodium

1 Carb Choice

QUICK
SWITCH • Replace the orange juice concentrate with lemonade or limeade concentrate. Reduce the sugar to ¼ cup or to taste.

OUT OF EGGS?

Or perhaps you're just nervous about using egg whites in uncooked desserts because of concerns about salmonella. Dried egg whites to the rescue. Look for products like Just Whites, which are 100 percent dried egg whites. They keep a long time without refrigeration and are wonderful for meringues, mousses, sauces (like this Orange Meringue Sauce), and baked products. They're available in health food stores and many supermarkets. ∎

Whipped Maple Topping

The surprise ingredient in this versatile dessert topping is tofu,
but no one will ever guess. Use it on plain cake, fruit, pancakes, waffles,
or anything else that needs a little pizzazz.

1 **package (10½ ounces) low-fat silken firm tofu, drained**

3 **tablespoons maple syrup**

1 **teaspoon vanilla extract**

⅛ **teaspoon ground cinnamon**

1. In a blender or food processor, combine the tofu, maple syrup, vanilla, and cinnamon. Blend until very smooth. Use at room temperature on hot foods or chilled for at least 30 minutes on cold ones.

Makes 1½ cups

Per 2-tablespoon serving: 22 calories, 2 g protein, 4 g carbohydrates, 0 g fat, 0 mg cholesterol, 0 g dietary fiber, 17 mg sodium

0 Carb Choices

QUICK SWITCH • Replace the maple syrup with sugar or honey.

Chocolate Sauce

[Photograph on page 270]

This sauce thickens when chilled and is wonderful served over ice milk, frozen yogurt, or sliced angel food cake—use your imagination!

1. In a small saucepan, whisk together the cocoa, sugar, corn syrup, and milk. Bring to a boil over medium-low heat, whisking continuously. Remove from the heat and stir in the vanilla. Cover and refrigerate for at least 1 hour.

Makes 1⅓ cups

Per 2-tablespoon serving: 99 calories, 1 g protein, 26 g carbohydrates, 1 g fat, 0 mg cholesterol, 1 g dietary fiber, 27 mg sodium

1½ Carb Choices

½ **cup unsweetened cocoa powder**

½ **cup sugar**

½ **cup corn syrup**

½ **cup fat-free or 1% milk**

½ **teaspoon vanilla extract**

QUICK
SWITCH • Replace the vanilla with coffee extract.

Raspberry Sauce

My favorite way to serve this colorful sauce is
over Blueberry Mousse (page 243).

1 package (12 ounces) frozen
  unsweetened raspberries,
  thawed

¼ cup sugar

1 tablespoon orange liqueur or
  frozen orange juice
  concentrate, thawed

1 teaspoon lemon juice

1. Combine the raspberries, sugar, liqueur or juice concentrate, and lemon juice in a blender or food
processor. Blend until smooth. If desired, use a spatula
to press the sauce through a fine strainer (to remove
the seeds) into a medium bowl. Cover and refrigerate
until ready to serve.

Makes about 1¾ cups

Per 2-tablespoon serving: 30 calories, 0 g protein, 7 g carbohydrates, 0 g fat, 0 mg cholesterol, 0 g dietary fiber, 0 mg sodium

X Carb Choices

**QUICK
SWITCH** • Replace the liqueur with 1 teaspoon almond
extract.

Apple Butter

[Photograph on page 115]

Although you can buy sugar-free apple butter, I prefer to make my own.
It is tastier and less expensive, and it keeps for weeks in the refrigerator. You usually
have to go to a health food store to find unsulfured dried apples, but it is well
worth the trip. They make a better-quality apple butter than lighter-colored,
treated fruit. For variety, replace the apples with dried pears.

1. In a large saucepan, mix the apples, juice, cinnamon, allspice, and cloves. Bring to a boil over medium heat. Cover, reduce the heat to low, and simmer for 20 minutes, stirring occasionally.

2. Remove from the heat and let cool for 5 minutes. Transfer to a blender or food processor and blend until smooth. Cool to room temperature. Spoon into a container with a tight-fitting lid and store in the refrigerator.

Makes 2 cups

Per 1-tablespoon serving: 42 calories, 0 g protein, 11 g carbohydrates, 0 g fat, 0 mg cholesterol, 1 g dietary fiber, 9 mg sodium

½ Carb Choice

- **2 cups unsulfured dried apple slices**
- **2 cups unsweetened apple juice**
- **1 teaspoon ground cinnamon**
- **½ teaspoon ground allspice**
- **⅛ teaspoon ground cloves**

THE SPICE RACK — **WARM AND WONDERFUL CLOVES** Cloves grow on extremely tall trees, and because all of the buds must be picked by hand, it is often said that someone risked his life for every clove. The sensory characteristics of cloves include a pungent, sweet, menthol aroma with a minty, warm, spicy taste. After tasting cloves, the mouth often has a numb sensation due the essential oil eugenol. When using ground cloves, always be careful when measuring—a small amount adds greatly to the flavor, but just a bit too much can ruin a dish.

Lemon-Ginger Ice Milk

This fabulous fat-free frozen dessert will remind you of the richest, creamiest, highest-fat ice cream you ever tasted. If you just can't wait for the ice milk to freeze, serve it as a custard sauce.

¾ **cup packed light brown sugar**

2 **cartons (16 ounces each) fat-free or reduced-fat sour cream**

1 **carton (8 ounces) fat-free or reduced-fat lemon yogurt**

2 **tablespoons minced candied ginger**

2 **tablespoons light corn syrup**

2 **teaspoons vanilla extract**

2 **teaspoons grated lemon peel**

⅛ **teaspoon salt**

1. Push the brown sugar through a large-mesh strainer to remove any lumps. Transfer to a blender or food processor. Add the sour cream, yogurt, ginger, corn syrup, vanilla, lemon peel, and salt. Blend well. Transfer to a large bowl and place in the freezer for 10 minutes.

2. Transfer the mixture to an ice-cream maker and freeze according to the manufacturer's directions. (Or pour into a metal bowl and freeze until almost solid. Break into pieces and blend in a food processor until smooth.)

Makes 8 servings

Per serving: 202 calories, 9 g protein, 38 g carbohydrates, 0 g fat, 3 mg cholesterol, 0 g dietary fiber, 270 mg sodium

2½ **Carb Choices**

Tropical Sorbet

When making this refreshing dessert, put the drained pineapple into a large self-sealing plastic bag and press it out flat before freezing. Do the same thing with the banana slices. Break the fruit pieces apart before putting them into the blender or food processor—it is much easier to puree the mixture that way.

1. Place one-quarter each of the pineapple and banana in a blender or food processor. Add the orange juice, sugar, and coconut extract. Blend until smooth.

2. Add the remaining pineapple and banana a little at a time, blending until smooth after each addition, until the mixture is smooth, light, and frothy. Pour into a large bowl. Cover and freeze for 1 hour before serving.

Makes 8 servings

Per serving: 45 calories, 1 g protein, 12 g carbohydrates, 0 g fat, 0 mg cholesterol, 1 g dietary fiber, 1 mg sodium

½ **Carb Choice**

1 **can (20 ounces) crushed pineapple packed in juice, drained and frozen**

1 **large banana, sliced and frozen**

¼ **cup orange juice**

1 **tablespoon sugar**

½ **teaspoon coconut extract**

Spa Strawberry Mousse

This is a delicious, fat-free dessert. You can serve it
as a cold soup if you eliminate the gelatin.

2 tablespoons cool water

2 envelopes unflavored gelatin

¼ cup boiling water

1 package (16 ounces) frozen
unsweetened strawberries,
thawed

½ cup sugar

2 cups fat-free or reduced-fat
plain yogurt

1. Place the cool water in a small bowl. Sprinkle with the
gelatin and let stand for 5 minutes, or until the gelatin
is softened. Add the boiling water and stir until the
gelatin is completely dissolved.

2. Place the strawberries, sugar, and gelatin mixture in a
blender or food processor and blend until smooth. Add
the yogurt and blend just until mixed. Divide among 4
dessert dishes. Cover and refrigerate for at least 3
hours, or until firm.

Makes 4 servings

Per serving: 253 calories, 9 g protein, 58 g carbohydrates, 0 g
fat, 2 mg cholesterol, 2 g dietary fiber, 84 mg sodium

3½ **Carb Choices**

QUICK
SWITCH • Replace the strawberries with raspberries,
peaches, or blueberries.

Piña Colada Mousse

You can spoon this mousse into a prepared reduced-fat
graham cracker pie crust for a sensational tropical pie.

1. In a large bowl, mix the pineapple, whipped topping,
sour cream, sugar, vanilla, and coconut extract. Cover
and refrigerate for at least 4 hours.

Makes 8 servings

Per serving: 105 calories, 2 g protein, 22 g carbohydrates, 0 g
fat, 0 mg cholesterol, 0 g dietary fiber, 68 mg sodium

1 Carb Choice

1 can (8 ounces) crushed
pineapple packed in juice,
undrained

1 container (8 ounces) frozen
fat-free or reduced-fat
whipped topping, thawed

1 cup fat-free or reduced-fat
sour cream

2 tablespoons sugar

1 teaspoon vanilla extract

1 teaspoon coconut extract

Milk Chocolate–Raspberry Mousse

This opulent-tasting dessert can be made in minutes
and is sure to put smiles on your guests' faces.

2 cups fat-free or 1% milk

1 package (4-serving-size) fat-free instant chocolate pudding mix

1 cup fat-free or reduced-fat sour cream

1 container (8 ounces) frozen fat-free or reduced-fat whipped topping, thawed

1 package (12 ounces) frozen unsweetened raspberries, thawed and drained

16 reduced-fat chocolate graham crackers, broken into pieces

1. Pour the milk into a large bowl. Add the pudding mix and whisk for 1 full minute, or until smooth and creamy. Whisk in the sour cream and whipped topping until smooth. Fold in the raspberries.

2. Pour into a 13" × 9" baking dish and spread evenly with a rubber spatula. Press the graham cracker pieces into the mousse, distributing them evenly. Cover and refrigerate for at least 3 hours.

Makes 16 servings

Per serving: 91 calories, 2 g protein, 23 g carbohydrates, 0 g fat, 1 mg cholesterol, 1 g dietary fiber, 161 mg sodium

1½ Carb Choices

MIX UP SOME MOO JUICE!

Always keep a box of fat-free milk powder in your pantry. (After opening the box, store it in the refrigerator.) It is just like having a cow in the kitchen—if you run out of milk, simply make some more! ■

Blueberry Mousse

Although this dessert requires a fair amount of refrigerator time,
your hands-on involvement is quite limited. You can make this mousse in individual
molds or custard cups if you prefer. For a superlative frozen dessert, freeze the mousse
(or the leftovers). Top it with Raspberry Sauce (page 236).

1. Several hours ahead, put the can of milk in the refrigerator to chill. Place a large metal or glass bowl and the beaters from an electric mixer in the freezer. (Chilling these items ensures that the milk will whip properly.)

2. Place the cool water in a small bowl. Sprinkle with the gelatin and let stand for 5 minutes, or until the gelatin is softened. Add the boiling water and stir until the gelatin is completely dissolved.

3. Place the blueberries in a blender or food processor. Add the liqueur or juice concentrate, lemon juice, and gelatin mixture. Blend until smooth. Transfer to a medium bowl and refrigerate until needed.

4. Remove the bowl and beaters from the freezer. Pour the chilled milk into the bowl and beat until soft peaks form when the beaters are lifted. Slowly add the sugar and continue beating until firm peaks form.

5. Pour the blueberry mixture over the whipped milk. Using a rubber spatula, carefully fold in the blueberry mixture until no streaks of white show. Pour into a large bowl, cover, and refrigerate for at least 4 hours. To serve, spoon into dessert bowls.

Makes 12 servings

Per serving: 77 calories, 3 g protein, 14 g carbohydrates, 0 g fat, 0 mg cholesterol, 1 g dietary fiber, 40 mg sodium

1 Carb Choice

1 **can (12 ounces) fat-free evaporated milk**

¼ **cup cool water**

2 **envelopes unflavored gelatin**

¼ **cup boiling water**

1 **package (16 ounces) frozen unsweetened blueberries, thawed**

3 **tablespoons orange liqueur or frozen orange juice concentrate, thawed**

2 **tablespoons lemon juice**

¼ **cup sugar**

QUICK
SWITCH • Replace the blueberries with frozen peaches.

Jelled Cappuccino

This speedy dessert is perfect following an Italian meal. It is also
a satisfying snack or an unusual breakfast treat. For a chilled latte,
place in a blender with fat-free milk and blend until frothy.

2 **tablespoons cool water**

1 **envelope unflavored gelatin**

¼ **cup boiling water**

3 **tablespoons instant
cappuccino powder**

2 **tablespoons sugar**

1 **can (12 ounces) fat-free
evaporated milk**

1. Place the cool water in a medium bowl. Sprinkle with the gelatin and let stand for 5 minutes, or until the gelatin is softened. Add the boiling water and stir until the gelatin is completely dissolved.

2. Stir in the cappuccino powder and sugar until completely dissolved. Add the milk and mix well. Cover and refrigerate for at least 3 hours.

Makes 4 servings

Per serving: 86 calories, 5 g protein, 16 g carbohydrates, 1 g fat, 1 mg cholesterol, 0 g dietary fiber, 73 mg sodium

1 Carb Choice

Pink Panna Cotta with Red Raspberries

Panna cotta is a rich, smooth-textured Italian pudding that is like a custard without the eggs. It's usually white, but the addition of berry syrup gives it a delightful pink color. I use red Italian coffee syrup such as raspberry or strawberry.

1. Place the water in a cup. Sprinkle with the gelatin and let stand for 5 minutes, or until the gelatin is softened.

2. In a medium saucepan, combine the milk and sugar. Cook over medium heat, stirring frequently, until the mixture just comes to the boiling point. Remove from the heat, add the softened gelatin, and stir until it is completely dissolved.

3. Stir in the vanilla, almond extract, and ¼ cup of the berry syrup. Pour into six 6-ounce custard cups. Cover and refrigerate for at least 4 hours.

4. Shortly before serving, thaw the raspberries just until icy cold but not mushy. Dip the custard cups briefly into hot water and then loosen the panna cotta with a knife, if necessary. Unmold each panna cotta onto a dessert plate. Surround with the raspberries and drizzle with the remaining ¼ cup berry syrup.

Makes 6 servings

Per serving: 202 calories, 8 g protein, 44 g carbohydrates, 0 g fat, 3 mg cholesterol, 3 g dietary fiber, 94 mg sodium

2½ Carb Choices

¼ **cup cool water**

2 **envelopes unflavored gelatin**

3¾ **cups fat-free or 1% milk**

2 **tablespoons sugar**

2 **teaspoons vanilla extract**

¾ **teaspoon almond extract**

½ **cup red berry syrup**

1 **package (12 ounces) frozen unsweetened raspberries**

QUICK **SWITCH** • Replace the almond extract with orange extract or 1 tablespoon frozen orange juice concentrate.

Rice Pudding

Because rice pudding is an American icon, I have purposely
made this a very basic recipe. It's a wonderful way to use up leftover plain
cooked rice. Add your favorite spices or ½ teaspoon almond, coconut,
maple, or rum extract, along with the vanilla extract.

3 egg whites

1 egg

1 can (12 ounces) fat-free evaporated milk

⅓ cup sugar

1 teaspoon vanilla extract

1 cup cooked white rice

½ cup raisins

1. Preheat the oven to 325°F. Coat a 1½-quart baking dish with cooking spray.

2. In a medium bowl, whisk together the egg whites, egg, milk, sugar, and vanilla. Stir in the rice and raisins. Pour into the prepared baking dish.

3. Bake for 30 minutes. Stir the pudding. Bake for 20 minutes longer, or until the liquid is absorbed.

Makes 6 servings

Per serving: 189 calories, 8 g protein, 37 g carbohydrates, 1 g fat, 37 mg cholesterol, 1 g dietary fiber, 105 mg sodium

2 Carb Choices

Prune Pudding

You might call it gilding the lily, but this rich-tasting dessert can be made even better
with a little brandy-flavored Secret Sauce (page 232) spooned over each serving.

1. In a small bowl, combine the prunes and ¾ cup boiling water. Cover and allow to stand for at least 1 hour. Pour into a blender or food processor.

2. Place the cool water in a cup. Sprinkle with the gelatin and let stand for 5 minutes, or until the gelatin is softened. Add ¼ cup boiling water and stir until the gelatin is completely dissolved. Pour into the blender or food processor.

3. Add the cold water, milk powder, vanilla, and cinnamon. Blend until smooth. Pour into a serving bowl or individual cups. Refrigerate for at least 3 hours, or until firm.

Makes 6 servings

Per serving: 163 calories, 18 g protein, 24 g carbohydrates, 0 g fat, 3 mg cholesterol, 2 g dietary fiber, 109 mg sodium

1½ Carb Choices

1 **cup pitted prunes**

1 **cup boiling water**

2 **tablespoons cool water**

1 **envelope unflavored gelatin**

1 **cup cold water**

¾ **cup fat-free milk powder**

1 **teaspoon vanilla extract**

½ **teaspoon ground cinnamon**

Pecan Pudding

Would you believe there's a lower-calorie version of Southern pecan pie?
Leftovers (if you should be so lucky) make a marvelous sauce for pancakes
and waffles; just blend the pudding until smooth.

½ cup chopped pecans

2 tablespoons cool water

1½ teaspoons unflavored gelatin

1 can (12 ounces) fat-free
evaporated milk

⅓ cup packed dark brown sugar

1 tablespoon butter

1 teaspoon vanilla extract

1. Put the pecans in a small skillet and cook over medium heat, stirring frequently, for 3 minutes, or until toasted. Divide among four 6-ounce custard cups.

2. Place the water in a cup. Sprinkle with the gelatin and let stand for 5 minutes, or until the gelatin is softened.

3. In a medium saucepan, combine the milk, brown sugar, and butter. Bring slowly just to the boiling point over medium-low heat. Remove from the heat and add the vanilla and softened gelatin. Stir until the gelatin is completely dissolved. Allow to cool slightly.

4. Pour into the custard cups. Cover and refrigerate for at least 4 hours.

Makes 4 servings

Per serving: 196 calories, 5 g protein, 18 g carbohydrates, 12 g fat, 9 mg cholesterol, 1 g dietary fiber, 78 mg sodium

1 Carb Choice

Fiesta Grapefruit

This is a delightfully refreshing dessert. It is particularly good following a Mexican or Southwestern meal. A nice way to garnish it is with whole coffee beans.

1. Pour 1 tablespoon of the juice from the grapefruit into a small bowl; discard the remaining juice or reserve for another use. Stir the liqueur or coffee into the bowl. Add the grapefruit sections and mix well. Cover and refrigerate for at least 1 hour.

Makes 4 servings

Per serving: 57 calories, 1 g protein, 13 g carbohydrates, 0 g fat, 0 mg cholesterol, 1 g dietary fiber, 2 mg sodium

½ **Carb Choice**

QUICK
SWITCH • Replace the coffee liqueur with orange liqueur or orange juice concentrate.

1 can (16 ounces) grapefruit sections packed in juice, undrained

1 tablespoon coffee liqueur or very strong coffee

Tropical Fruit Compote

At first glance, this might not look like a real pantry recipe because of the banana. However, I always keep bags of sliced bananas in my freezer to make Banana Shakes (page 291) and other recipes. They work beautifully here, too.

1 cup fat-free or reduced-fat plain yogurt

1 banana, peeled and sliced

1 can (20 ounces) pineapple chunks packed in juice, chilled and drained

Ground cinnamon (optional)

1. In a blender or food processor, combine the yogurt and banana. Blend until smooth. Serve over the pineapple and sprinkle with a little cinnamon (if using).

Makes 4 servings

Per serving: 139 calories, 4 g protein, 34 g carbohydrates, 0 g fat, 1 mg cholesterol, 2 g dietary fiber, 39 mg sodium

2 Carb Choices

QUICK SWITCH • Add ½ teaspoon coconut extract.

Instant Cherry Trifle

If you like trifle but don't have the time to make the traditional custard
it contains, this is an ideal recipe for you. It uses light cherry pie filling,
fat-free instant pudding mix, and angel food cake. Layer them in
a straight-sided glass bowl for an impressive dessert.

1. Pour the milk into a large mixing bowl. Add the pudding mix and whisk for 1 minute, or until smooth and creamy. Whisk in the sherry or sherry extract.

2. Line the bottom of a trifle dish or a glass bowl with one-third of the angel food cake; top with one-third of the pudding mixture, then one-third of the cherry filling. Repeat twice. Cover and refrigerate for at least 2 hours.

Makes 16 servings

Per serving: 107 calories, 2 g protein, 29 g carbohydrates, 0 g fat, 1 mg cholesterol, 0 g dietary fiber, 197 mg sodium

1½ Carb Choices

QUICK
SWITCH • Replace the cherry pie filling with blueberry or apple. • Or replace the vanilla pudding with chocolate.

2 **cups fat-free or 1% milk**

1 **package (4-serving-size) fat-free instant vanilla pudding mix**

2 **tablespoons sherry or 1 teaspoon sherry extract**

1 **prepared (10 ounces) angel food cake, cut into 1" cubes**

1 **container (21 ounces) light cherry pie filling**

Poached Dried Apricots

These apricots have so many uses. Serve them for breakfast topped
with vanilla yogurt or spooned over cereal. They're great in fruit salads,
on frozen yogurt, or over angel food cake. If desired, puree them
with a little of the poaching liquid to make a nice sauce.

1 cup dried apricot halves

1 teaspoon sugar

1 teaspoon vanilla extract

1 teaspoon ground cinnamon

1. Place the apricots in a medium saucepan and cover with water to a depth of 2". Bring to a boil, cover, and remove from the heat. Let stand for 1 hour.

2. Add the sugar, vanilla, and cinnamon. Bring to a boil over high heat. Reduce the heat to medium and simmer, uncovered, for 15 minutes. Remove from the heat and set aside to cool. To serve, remove the apricots from the poaching liquid with a slotted spoon.

Makes 4 servings

Per serving: 102 calories, 2 g protein, 26 g carbohydrates, 0 g fat, 0 mg cholesterol, 0 g dietary fiber, 4 mg sodium

1½ Carb Choices

QUICK
SWITCH • Replace the apricots with dried peaches, pears, or apples. • Or replace the vanilla with ½ teaspoon almond, lemon, or brandy extract. • Or replace the cinnamon with ½ teaspoon ground nutmeg or ginger.

Peaches with Almond Sauce

This speedy Italian dessert tastes so delicious it is bound to become
a family favorite. Besides, you can make it in 5 minutes!

1. In a small bowl, mix the ice cream, vanilla, and almond extract.

2. Shortly before serving, thaw the peaches until icy cold but not mushy. Spoon the almond sauce over the peaches.

Makes 4 servings

Per serving: 92 calories, 2 g protein, 18 g carbohydrates, 2 g fat, 10 mg cholesterol, 1 g dietary fiber, 22 mg sodium

1 Carb Choice

QUICK **SWITCH** • Replace the peaches with frozen strawberries, raspberries, or blueberries. • Or replace the almond extract with orange, lemon, or coconut extract.

1 cup reduced-fat frozen vanilla ice cream, melted

1 teaspoon vanilla extract

½ teaspoon almond extract

1 package (16 ounces) frozen unsweetened sliced peaches

Gingered Fruit Compote with Cinnamon Sauce

This simple dessert is perfect for winter menus, when really good fresh fruits are more difficult to find and very expensive. For a sensation breakfast treat, spoon the fruit and sauce over oatmeal.

1½ **cups water**

  1 **cup chopped unsulfured dried apples**

  ¾ **cup chopped dried apricots**

  1 **teaspoon ground ginger**

  ¼ **cup dried currants**

  1 **cup reduced-fat sour cream**

  ¼ **cup frozen unsweetened apple juice concentrate, thawed**

1½ **teaspoons vanilla extract**

  ½ **teaspoon ground cinnamon**

1. In a medium saucepan, combine the water, apples, apricots, and ginger. Bring to a boil over high heat. Reduce the heat to low, cover, and simmer for 25 minutes. Stir in the currants. Cool to room temperature, then refrigerate for at least 2 hours.

2. In a small bowl, mix the sour cream, juice concentrate, vanilla, and cinnamon. Serve spooned over the fruit.

Makes 8 servings

Per serving: 90 calories, 1 g protein, 21 g carbohydrates, 1 g fat, 2 mg cholesterol, 1 g dietary fiber, 19 mg sodium

1 Carb Choice

QUICK
SWITCH • Replace the ginger with ¼ teaspoon ground cardamom. • Or replace the cinnamon with 1 teaspoon grated lemon peel.

THE SPICE RACK

SAVORY, FLAVORY GINGER
Ginger is a tropical plant with a knobby root. The flavor of fresh ginger is pungent, peppery, and a little sweet. Ground ginger has quite a different flavor and is not recommended as a substitute for fresh. Dried ginger is still a fabulous spice, however, and enhances the flavor of many savory dishes as well as baked goods. Use ginger when preparing Asian dishes, curries, vegetables, poultry, and meat.

Peach Risotto

Risotto isn't just an entrée—it can also be a memorable dessert. As with all risotto, the tricks are to use arborio rice (which becomes creamy when cooked), to add the liquid in small batches, and to stir until most of the liquid is absorbed before adding more. There should always be a veil of liquid over the rice, and the finished risotto should have a creamy, cereal-like consistency. The entire process should take about 20 minutes.

1. Place the milk in a small saucepan and warm over medium-low heat; keep warm. Drain the peaches, reserving the liquid. Dice the peaches and set aside.

2. Melt the butter in a medium saucepan over medium heat. Add the rice and stir for 1 minute. Add the rum and stir until almost dry. Add the peach liquid and stir until almost dry.

3. Add half of the apple juice and stir until almost dry. Add the peaches, brown sugar, cinnamon, salt, and the remaining apple juice. Stir until most of the liquid is gone.

4. Add the milk ½ cup at a time and stir frequently until most of the milk has been absorbed before adding more. Do not allow the last addition of milk to be completely absorbed. Remove from the heat and stir in the vanilla. Serve warm or chilled.

Makes 6 servings

Per serving: 334 calories, 23 g protein, 52 g carbohydrates, 3 g fat, 15 mg cholesterol, 1 g dietary fiber, 396 mg sodium

3½ **Carb Choices**

- 1 **can (12 ounces) fat-free evaporated milk**
- 1 **can (8 ounces) sliced peaches packed in water, undrained**
- 1 **tablespoon butter**
- ½ **cup uncooked arborio rice**
- 2 **tablespoons dark rum or ½ teaspoon rum extract**
- ¾ **cup apple juice**
- 1 **tablespoon packed dark brown sugar**
- ¼ **teaspoon ground cinnamon**
- ⅛ **teaspoon salt**
- 1 **teaspoon vanilla extract**

QUICK
SWITCH • Replace the peaches with apricots.

Strawberry-Rhubarb Crisp

[Photograph on page 269]

This rich-tasting, old-fashioned dessert is best served warm. I like to top it with a
dollop of either nondairy whipped topping or fat-free frozen yogurt.

FILLING

1 package (16 ounces) frozen unsweetened strawberries, thawed

1 package (16 ounces) frozen unsweetened rhubarb, thawed

⅔ cup sugar

¼ cup quick-cooking tapioca

½ teaspoon ground cinnamon

¼ teaspoon ground ginger

2 teaspoons vanilla extract

TOPPING

⅔ cup old-fashioned rolled oats

⅔ cup whole wheat flour

⅔ cup packed light brown sugar

½ teaspoon ground cinnamon

¼ teaspoon ground ginger

⅛ teaspoon salt

3 tablespoons cold butter, cut into small pieces

1. Preheat the oven to 375°F. Coat an 8" × 8" baking dish with cooking spray.

2. *To make the filling:* In a large bowl, mix the strawberries, rhubarb, sugar, tapioca, cinnamon, ginger, and vanilla. Spoon into the prepared baking dish.

3. *To make the topping:* In a medium bowl, mix the oats, flour, brown sugar, cinnamon, ginger, and salt. Add the butter and mix, using a pastry blender or fork, until the consistency of gravel. Spoon over the fruit mixture.

4. Bake for 50 minutes, or until golden brown. Serve warm or at room temperature.

Makes 9 servings

Per serving: 273 calories, 4 g protein, 57 g carbohydrates, 5 g fat, 10 mg cholesterol, 3 g dietary fiber, 75 mg sodium

3½ Carb Choices

BAKING SHEET SECRETS

When baking fruit pies, crisps, cobblers, or other desserts that are likely to bubble over in the oven, it's a good idea to place a foil- or parchment-covered baking sheet on the shelf below it to catch any drippings. Ditto for casseroles. This saves you from having to clean the whole oven! And when you're making cookies, yams, oven fries, or anything else that'll leave a cookie sheet plenty dirty, covering your baking sheet with foil or parchment will make cleanup a snap. ∎

Cherry Clafouti

[Photograph on page 273]

A clafouti is an easy and inexpensive peasant dessert that originated in the Limousin region of France. I have also served it as a brunch entrée, and everyone raved about it. The reason I suggest placing the pie plate on a baking sheet is that it is almost impossible to put the clafouti into the oven without spilling a little bit of the batter—and it is easier to wash the baking sheet than the oven!

1. Preheat the oven to 350°F. Coat a quiche dish or 10" pie plate with cooking spray.

2. In a blender or food processor, combine the milk, flour, sugar, egg, egg whites, vanilla, cinnamon, and salt. Blend until smooth. Pour a thin layer of the batter into the prepared dish and bake for 8 minutes.

3. Remove the dish from the oven and place on a baking sheet. Spoon the cherries evenly over the bottom. Pour the remaining batter evenly over the top. Bake for 1 hour, or until the clafouti is puffed up and browned. Cool on a wire rack for 30 minutes. Serve warm, topped with the ice cream or whipped topping (if using).

Makes 8 servings

Per serving: 192 calories, 7 g protein, 40 g carbohydrates, 1 g fat, 28 mg cholesterol, 1 g dietary fiber, 112 mg sodium

2½ **Carb Choices**

1 can (12 ounces) fat-free evaporated milk

¾ cup unbleached all-purpose flour

½ cup sugar

1 egg

3 egg whites

2 teaspoons vanilla extract

1 teaspoon ground cinnamon

⅛ teaspoon salt

1 package (16 ounces) frozen unsweetened pitted Bing cherries, thawed and drained

2 cups low-fat vanilla ice cream or thawed frozen fat-free or reduced-fat whipped topping (optional)

QUICK
SWITCH • Replace the cherries with peaches.

Italian Cheesecake

[Photograph on page 270]

I call this recipe shortcut cheesecake because it is so easy to make.

1 **container (30 ounces) fat-free or reduced-fat ricotta cheese**

¾ **cup granulated sugar**

1¼ **cups fat-free liquid egg substitute**

1 **box (20 ounces) lemon cake mix**

1⅓ **cups water**

3 **tablespoons confectioners' sugar**

1. Preheat the oven to 350°F. Coat a 13" × 9" baking dish with cooking spray.

2. In a medium bowl, combine the ricotta cheese, granulated sugar, and ¾ cup of the egg substitute. Using an electric mixer on medium speed, beat until smooth.

3. In a large bowl, combine the cake mix, water, and the remaining ½ cup egg substitute. Beat on low speed for 30 seconds. Beat on medium speed for 2 minutes. Pour into the prepared baking dish. Spoon the ricotta mixture evenly over the top of the batter.

4. Bake for 60 to 65 minutes, or until the edges are lightly browned and the center is only slightly wiggly. Cool on a wire rack until room temperature and then refrigerate for several hours before cutting. Before serving, put the confectioners' sugar in a small sieve and sprinkle evenly over the top.

Makes 15 servings

Per serving: 278 calories, 13 g protein, 46 g carbohydrates, 5 g fat, 1 mg cholesterol, 0 g dietary fiber, 344 mg sodium

3½ **Carb Choices**

QUICK SWITCH • Replace the lemon cake mix with chocolate cake mix.

Chicken and Broccoli Amandine (page 166)

Sweet-and-Sour Chicken on Jasmine Rice (page 162)

Chicken Linguine with Red Pepper Sauce (page 161)

Greek Chicken with Orzo (page 167)

Beef Barbecue Cups (page 179)

Southwestern Beef and Bean Lasagna (page 183)

Macronade (page 186)

Herbed Scalloped Potatoes (page 218)

Tuscan Potatoes (page 219)

Sweet Potato Dip (page 222) and Artichoke Dip (page 223)

Strawberry-Rhubarb Crisp (page 256)

269

Italian Cheesecake (page 258) with Chocolate Sauce (page 235) (bottom) and Orange Meringue Sauce (page 233)

Frozen Peanut Butter Pie (page 280)

Refrigerator Peach Pie (page 278)

272

Cherry Clafouti (page 257)

Lacy Oatmeal Cookies (page 283) and Café au Lait (page 300)

Chocolate Mocha Cheesecake

Good news, chocoholics! This easy chocolate treat doesn't even have to be baked.

1. In a cup, dissolve the coffee powder in the water.

2. Put the cream cheese in a large bowl. Add the coffee, granulated sugar, cocoa powder, and vanilla. Using an electric mixer, beat until smooth. Fold in the whipped topping.

3. Spoon the mixture into the pie crust. Cover and refrigerate for at least 3 hours. Dust with confectioners' sugar (if using) before serving.

Makes 8 servings

Per serving: 236 calories, 2 g protein, 42 g carbohydrates, 5 g fat, 1 mg cholesterol, 0 g dietary fiber, 133 mg sodium

2½ Carb Choices

2 teaspoons instant coffee powder

1 tablespoon boiling water

1 package (8 ounces) fat-free or reduced-fat cream cheese, softened

⅔ cup granulated sugar

3 tablespoons unsweetened cocoa powder, sifted

2 teaspoons vanilla extract

1 container (8 ounces) frozen fat-free or reduced-fat whipped topping, thawed

1 prepared (9") chocolate pie crust

Confectioners' sugar (optional)

Light Lemon Pie

This pie takes literally minutes to prepare. The hard part is waiting for it to chill!
Serve it plain or with whipped topping and fruit.

1 can (14 ounces) fat-free sweetened condensed milk

⅓ cup lemon juice

1 tablespoon grated lemon peel or 1½ teaspoons lemon extract

¼ teaspoon salt

1 prepared (9") reduced-fat graham cracker pie crust

1. In a large bowl, combine the milk, lemon juice, lemon peel or extract, and salt. Stir until thickened.

2. Pour into the pie crust. Cover and refrigerate for at least 3 hours, or until firm.

Makes 8 servings

Per serving: 250 calories, 5 g protein, 45 g carbohydrates, 5 g fat, 1 mg cholesterol, 0 g dietary fiber, 252 mg sodium

2½ Carb Choices

No-Bake Pumpkin Pie

This easy-as-pie recipe takes literally minutes to throw together. Because it contains neither eggs nor dairy products, it's great for anyone who's cholesterol conscious. And it's the perfect light ending for a big holiday meal.

1. Place the cool water in a cup. Sprinkle with the gelatin and let stand for 5 minutes, or until the gelatin is softened. Add the boiling water and stir until the gelatin is completely dissolved.

2. In a blender or food processor, combine the pumpkin, tofu, brown sugar, cinnamon, allspice, nutmeg, salt, and vanilla. Blend until smooth. Add the gelatin and blend well. Spoon into the pie crust. Cover and refrigerate for at least 3 hours, or until firm. Spread the whipped topping (if using) over the pie or garnish each serving with a spoonful.

Makes 8 servings

Per serving: 216 calories, 14 g protein, 28 g carbohydrates, 6 g fat, 0 mg cholesterol, 2 g dietary fiber, 257 mg sodium

1½ Carb Choices

2 **tablespoons cool water**

1 **envelope unflavored gelatin**

¼ **cup boiling water**

1 **can (16 ounces) solid-pack pumpkin**

1 **package (12.3 ounces) low-fat silken extra-firm tofu, drained**

½ **cup packed light brown sugar**

1 **tablespoon ground cinnamon**

1 **teaspoon ground allspice**

¼ **teaspoon ground nutmeg**

¼ **teaspoon salt**

1½ **tablespoons vanilla extract**

1 **prepared (9") reduced-fat graham cracker pie crust**

Fat-free or reduced-fat frozen whipped topping, thawed (optional)

Refrigerator Peach Pie

[Photograph on page 272]

Easy to assemble, rich tasting, low in fat—
this is everything you'd want in a fun dessert!

½ **cup graham cracker crumbs**

2 **tablespoons cool water**

1 **envelope unflavored gelatin**

¼ **cup boiling water**

¾ **cup fat-free or 1% cottage cheese**

3 **tablespoons packed light brown sugar**

1 **teaspoon vanilla extract**

½ **teaspoon almond extract**

¼ **teaspoon ground cinnamon**

1 **package (16 ounces) frozen unsweetened sliced peaches, thawed**

1. Preheat the oven to 350°F. Coat a 9" pie plate with cooking spray. Add the crumbs and tilt the plate to cover the entire inner surface. Bake for 7 minutes, or until lightly browned. Cool on a wire rack.

2. Place the cool water in a cup. Sprinkle with the gelatin and let stand for 5 minutes, or until the gelatin is softened. Add the boiling water and stir until the gelatin is completely dissolved.

3. In a blender or food processor, combine the cottage cheese, brown sugar, vanilla, almond extract, and cinnamon. Blend until very smooth. With the motor running, pour in the gelatin and blend well. Add ½ cup of the peaches and blend until smooth. Transfer to a medium bowl and stir in the remaining peaches.

4. Pour into the prepared crust. Sprinkle with more cinnamon. Refrigerate for at least 3 hours, or until firm.

Makes 8 servings

Per serving: 112 calories, 13 g protein, 14 g carbohydrates, 1 g fat, 2 mg cholesterol, 1 g dietary fiber, 140 mg sodium

½ **Carb Choice**

QUICK
SWITCH • Replace the cinnamon with cardamom.

Piña Colada Pie

Talk about a taste of the tropics! This simple pie is sure to be a big hit
after any meal—especially so with Asian or Caribbean menus.

1. Place the cool water in a cup. Sprinkle with the gelatin and let stand for 5 minutes, or until the gelatin is softened. Add the boiling water and stir until the gelatin is completely dissolved.

2. In a blender or food processor, combine the pineapple, cottage cheese, cold water, milk powder, sugar, vanilla, and coconut extract. Blend until smooth. With the motor running, pour in the gelatin and blend well. Pour into the pie crust and sprinkle lightly with cinnamon. Refrigerate for at least 3 hours, or until firm.

Makes 8 servings

Per serving: 216 calories, 13 g protein, 29 g carbohydrates, 5 g fat, 1 mg cholesterol, 1 g dietary fiber, 214 mg sodium

1½ Carb Choices

2 **tablespoons cool water**

1 **envelope unflavored gelatin**

¼ **cup boiling water**

1 **can (20 ounces) crushed pineapple packed in juice, drained**

½ **cup fat-free or 1% cottage cheese**

¼ **cup cold water**

3 **tablespoons fat-free milk powder**

1 **tablespoon sugar**

1 **teaspoon vanilla extract**

1 **teaspoon coconut extract**

1 **prepared (9") reduced-fat graham cracker pie crust**

Ground cinnamon

Frozen Peanut Butter Pie

[Photograph on page 271]

The wife of a Georgia peanut farmer gave me a wonderful pie recipe when I was a guest for dinner in their home. It is a quick, easy, and sinfully delicious dessert that you can keep in the freezer for unexpected guests or for those occasions when you just don't have time to make dessert for your family. Plan to serve this pie after a low-fat meal. (Even though this version is lower in fat than the original, it is not quite diet food.)

1 **package (8 ounces) fat-free or reduced-fat cream cheese, at room temperature**

⅔ **cup confectioners' sugar**

½ **cup creamy peanut butter**

¼ **cup water**

2 **tablespoons fat-free milk powder**

6 **ounces thawed frozen fat-free or reduced-fat whipped topping**

1 **prepared (9") chocolate pie crust**

2 **tablespoons crushed peanuts (optional)**

1. Place the cream cheese in a large bowl. Beat with an electric mixer on medium speed until fluffy. Beat in the confectioners' sugar and peanut butter until smooth.

2. In a cup, stir together the water and milk powder until the milk powder is dissolved. Slowly beat into the cream cheese mixture. Fold in the whipped topping until no streaks of white show. Spoon into the pie crust and sprinkle with the peanuts (if using). Cover and freeze for at least 6 hours. Allow to soften at room temperature for 15 minutes before cutting.

Makes 8 servings

Per serving: 290 calories, 6 g protein, 36 g carbohydrates, 13 g fat, 1 mg cholesterol, 1 g dietary fiber, 251 mg sodium

2 Carb Choices

Crustless Shoofly Pie

This inexpensive Southern dessert supposedly got its name because it was so sweet that it was hard to keep the flies away. It is usually made in a very rich pastry shell, which adds enormously to the total fat content and takes more time. I suggest placing the pie plate on a baking sheet because the pie occasionally boils over.

1. Preheat the oven to 400°F. Coat a 10" pie plate with cooking spray.

2. In a small bowl, mix the water and baking soda and stir until the baking soda is completely dissolved. Whisk in the corn syrup and let cool for 1 minute. Then whisk in the egg white.

3. In a medium bowl, mix the flour, brown sugar, cinnamon, nutmeg, salt, ginger, and cloves. Add the butter and mix, using a pastry blender or fork, until the consistency of gravel. Place alternating layers of the liquid mixture and the dry mixture in the prepared pie plate, ending with the dry mixture as the top layer.

4. Place on a baking sheet and bake for 20 minutes. Reduce the temperature to 300°F and bake for 20 minutes, or until firm. Cool on a wire rack.

Makes 8 servings

Per serving: 163 calories, 2 g protein, 34 g carbohydrates, 3 g fat, 8 mg cholesterol, 0 g dietary fiber, 367 mg sodium

2 Carb Choices

¾ **cup boiling water**

1½ **teaspoons baking soda**

½ **cup dark corn syrup**

1 **egg white**

¾ **cup unbleached all-purpose flour**

½ **cup packed dark brown sugar**

½ **teaspoon ground cinnamon**

¼ **teaspoon ground nutmeg**

¼ **teaspoon salt**

⅛ **teaspoon ground ginger**

⅛ **teaspoon ground cloves**

2 **tablespoons cold butter, cut into small pieces**

Fudgy Brownies

This is a dessert I originally developed for the National Milk Producers' Light Milk and Cookie Break program. This very chocolatey brownie is sure to be a hit with your whole family. And it is truly best served with a cold glass of milk!

⅔ cup unbleached all-purpose flour

⅔ cup granulated sugar

⅓ cup unsweetened cocoa powder, sifted

¾ teaspoon baking soda

½ teaspoon baking powder

⅛ teaspoon salt

1 teaspoon instant coffee powder

⅓ cup boiling water

⅓ cup fat-free or 1% milk

1 jar (2½ ounces) baby-food pureed prunes

2 egg whites

1½ teaspoons vanilla extract

Confectioners' sugar (optional)

1. Preheat the oven to 350°F. Coat an 8" × 8" baking dish with cooking spray.

2. In a large bowl, mix the flour, granulated sugar, cocoa, baking soda, baking powder, and salt.

3. In a medium bowl, dissolve the coffee powder in the water. Stir in the milk, prunes, egg whites, and vanilla. Pour over the cocoa mixture and mix well. Pour the batter into the prepared baking dish and bake for 30 minutes, or until a knife inserted in the center comes out clean.

4. Cool on a wire rack for 10 minutes. Invert onto a cutting board and let cool completely before cutting. Dust with confectioners' sugar (if using) before serving.

Makes 16 brownies

Per brownie: 106 calories, 2 g protein, 24 g carbohydrates, 0 g fat, 0 mg cholesterol, 1 g dietary fiber, 103 mg sodium

1½ Carb Choices

THE ICING ON THE CAKE

When you're out of frosting, try a dusting of confectioners' sugar for a quick embellishment right out of the cupboard. Place a little of the sugar in a fine-mesh strainer and tap it over the top of your cake. For a fancy touch, place a paper doily, small cookie cutters, or clean paper cutouts on the cake's surface, shake the sugar over the top, and remove the shapes to reveal a dazzling design. ∎

Lacy Oatmeal Cookies

[Photograph on page 274]

These delicate-looking cookies are so good they may be habit forming.

1. Preheat the oven to 350°F. Coat 2 large baking sheets with cooking spray.

2. In a large bowl, combine the egg, egg white, granulated sugar, brown sugar, baking powder, vanilla, salt, and cinnamon. Beat with an electric mixer on medium speed until smooth and slightly increased in volume. Stir in the oats, flour, and oil.

3. Drop by tablespoonfuls onto the prepared baking sheets, allowing 12 per sheet and leaving space between the mounds. Bake for 10 to 12 minutes, or until golden brown. Using a spatula, immediately remove the cookies from the sheets and allow to cool on wire racks.

Makes 24 cookies

Per cookie: 68 calories, 2 g protein, 12 g carbohydrates, 1 g fat, 9 mg cholesterol, 0 g dietary fiber, 73 mg sodium

½ **Carb Choice**

QUICK
SWITCH • Add chopped nuts or raisins to the batter.

1 **egg**

1 **egg white**

½ **cup granulated sugar**

¼ **cup packed dark brown sugar**

1½ **teaspoons baking powder**

¾ **teaspoon vanilla extract**

½ **teaspoon salt**

½ **teaspoon ground cinnamon**

1⅓ **cups old-fashioned rolled oats**

3 **tablespoons whole wheat flour**

1 **tablespoon canola oil**

Lemon Drop Cookies

These crunchy cookies have a refreshing lemon flavor that is perfect after almost any type of meal. They can turn an ordinary fruit plate into a truly special dessert. I often take them to parties as a hostess gift and always get asked for the recipe.

1 **egg**

½ **cup sugar**

1½ **teaspoons lemon extract**

½ **teaspoon baking powder**

⅔ **cup unbleached all-purpose flour**

1. Preheat the oven to 325°F. Line a baking sheet with foil.

2. Place the egg in a medium bowl and whisk until frothy. Add the sugar and whisk until dissolved. Whisk in the lemon extract and baking powder. Then slowly whisk in the flour until smooth.

3. Drop the dough by tablespoonfuls onto the prepared baking sheet. Bake for 14 minutes, or until the cookies start to color. Cool completely on a wire rack before peeling the cookies off the foil.

Makes 16 cookies

Per cookie: 48 calories, 1 g protein, 10 g carbohydrates, 0 g fat, 13 mg cholesterol, 0 g dietary fiber, 15 mg sodium

½ **Carb Choice**

Granola-Peanut Candy

Nobody will refuse these treats! They couldn't be easier, and they're healthy to boot.

1. Coat a 9" × 5" loaf pan with cooking spray.

2. Bring the honey to a boil in a large saucepan over medium heat. Immediately remove the pan from the heat and stir in the peanut butter. Add the cereal and granola; mix well. Spoon into the prepared pan. Moisten your hands with cold water and press the mixture into an even, firm layer.

3. Refrigerate for several hours or overnight. Turn out onto a cutting board and cut into squares. If the pieces start to crumble, just press them back together again. Store in the refrigerator.

Makes 32 pieces

Per piece: 35 calories, 1 g protein, 5 g carbohydrates, 2 g fat, 0 mg cholesterol, 0 g dietary fiber, 10 mg sodium

0 Carb Choices

¼ **cup honey**

¼ **cup creamy peanut butter**

1 **cup puffed wheat or rice cereal**

¾ **cup reduced-fat granola**

Beverages

Whether it's party time or just time to get out of your standard-drinks rut, these beverages are tailor-made for fun. They're alcohol-free and run the gamut from iced to spicy hot and from breakfast-in-a-glass to evening relaxers. That gives you options for year-round sipping that your tastebuds can get excited about. (Wait till you try the south-of-the-border coffee. It's got a smooth blend of spices that's just as good cold as hot.) You won't need any bartending skills to impress your friends, and all of these drinks come straight from the pantry for impromptu entertaining.

in this chapter . . .

Pilot's Cocktail

This is a refreshing nonalcoholic beverage that both looks
and tastes like a "real" drink. It is aptly named for the one person on
an airplane who cannot drink alcoholic beverages either before or during a flight.
It's also perfect for the designated driver on the ground!

1 cup sparkling water, chilled

Angostura bitters

Lime or lemon juice (optional)

1. Pour the water into a tall glass and add a few drops of bitters to taste. Stir in a few drops of lime or lemon juice (if using).

Makes 1 serving

Per serving: 0 calories, 0 g protein, 0 g carbohydrates, 0 g fat, 0 mg cholesterol, 0 g dietary fiber, 2 mg sodium

0 Carb Choices

Pure-as-Snow Mary

This spicy beverage gives a snappy start to your day and is a big hit at brunches.

1. In a large pitcher, combine the vegetable juice, lemon juice, horseradish, Worcestershire sauce, and pepper. Stir well. Refrigerate until cold.

Makes 7 servings

Per serving: 47 calories, 1 g protein, 12 g carbohydrates, 0 g fat, 0 mg cholesterol, 2 g dietary fiber, 702 mg sodium

½ **Carb Choice**

1 can (46 ounces) V8 vegetable juice

¾ **cup lemon juice**

¼ **cup prepared horseradish**

1½ **teaspoons Worcestershire sauce**

½ **teaspoon ground black pepper**

QUICK
SWITCH • Replace the lemon juice with lime juice.

Fruit Frappé

When you're in a hurry in the morning, this portable breakfast in a glass
can get you on your way fast. Choose whichever fruit you like best.
Leftovers keep well in the fridge.

1 **can (12 ounces) fat-free
evaporated milk**

1 **can (8 ounces) fruit packed in
water, undrained**

1 **teaspoon sugar**

¼ **teaspoon vanilla extract**

3 **ice cubes or ½ cup crushed
ice**

1. In a blender, combine the milk, fruit, sugar, vanilla,
and ice. Blend until the ice is completely pulverized
and the drink is thick and frothy.

Makes 3 servings

Per serving: 118 calories, 9 g protein, 21 g carbohydrates, 0 g
fat, 4 mg cholesterol, 1 g dietary fiber, 133 mg sodium

1 Carb Choice

QUICK
SWITCH • Replace the vanilla with ⅛ teaspoon almond
extract.

Banana Shake

I always keep plastic bags of sliced bananas in my freezer. I put half a banana
(about ½ cup) into each bag, which is the amount I need to make this high-calcium,
high-potassium drink. This drink is also a sensational topping for dry cereal.
In fact, I like it better than the usual combination of sliced bananas
and milk because the banana flavor is more intense.

1. In a blender, combine the water, banana, and milk
powder. Blend until smooth.

Makes 1 serving

Per serving: 320 calories, 23 g protein, 57 g carbohydrates, 1 g
fat, 12 mg cholesterol, 3 g dietary fiber, 327 mg sodium

3½ Carb Choices

⅔ **cup water**

½ **cup frozen banana slices**

½ **cup fat-free milk powder**

**QUICK
SWITCH** • Replace the water with fat-free milk.

Peanut Butter Shake

If you like peanut butter—and who doesn't?—you'll love this drink. It is
a satisfying breakfast beverage, a great snack, and even a unique dessert soup.
For a richer-tasting drink, use fat-free milk in place of the water.

1½ **cups fat-free milk powder**

1 **cup water**

¼ **cup creamy peanut butter**

3 **tablespoons sugar**

1 **teaspoon vanilla extract**

2 **cups crushed ice**

Ground cinnamon (optional)

1. In a blender, combine the milk powder, water, peanut butter, sugar, vanilla, and ice. Blend until smooth.

Makes 4 servings

Per serving: 295 calories, 20 g protein, 36 g carbohydrates, 8 g fat, 9 mg cholesterol, 1 g dietary fiber, 318 mg sodium

2 Carb Choices

Honeyed Strawberry Flip

This pretty pink drink can double as a cold soup or a fruit sauce.
I like it over angel food cake for dessert.

1. In a blender, combine the strawberries, water, milk powder, lemon juice, and honey. Blend until smooth.

Makes 2 servings

Per serving: 267 calories, 7 g protein, 67 g carbohydrates, 0 g fat, 3 mg cholesterol, 4 g dietary fiber, 83 mg sodium

4 Carb Choices

1½ cups frozen unsweetened strawberries

½ cup water

¼ cup fat-free milk powder

2 tablespoons lemon juice

2 tablespoons honey

QUICK
SWITCH • Replace the strawberries with raspberries.

High-Protein Strawberry Smoothie

I created this smoothie for the healthier alternative menu program
aboard Holland America Line cruise ships. It is a wonderful breakfast drink and also
a refreshing pick-me-up anytime during the day.

1 cup frozen strawberries

⅔ cup fat-free or 1% milk

**2½ tablespoons vanilla
high-protein powder**

1. In a blender, combine the strawberries, milk, and protein powder. Blend until smooth and frothy.

Makes 1 serving

Per serving: 152 calories, 18 g protein, 19 g carbohydrates,
1 g fat, 3 mg cholesterol, 3 g dietary fiber, 161 mg sodium

1 Carb Choice

Berry Berry Smoothie

You can use any kind of fruit or fruit juice in this recipe to suit your tastes.
If you like, stir in a teaspoon or two of honey for a little extra sweetness.

1. In a blender, combine the raspberries, strawberries, and pineapple juice. Add the yogurt. Blend until smooth.

Makes 2 servings

Per serving: 195 calories, 7 g protein, 43 g carbohydrates, 1 g fat, 2 mg cholesterol, 3 g dietary fiber, 79 mg sodium

3 Carb Choices

½ **cup frozen unsweetened raspberries**

½ **cup frozen unsweetened strawberries**

¾ **cup unsweetened pineapple juice**

1 **cup fat-free vanilla yogurt**

Peachy Smoothie

This recipe calls for a fresh peach, but you could also use
frozen or canned if you have them on hand.

1 **large ripe peach, sliced**

1 **tablespoon sugar**

1 **cup fat-free vanilla ice cream**

½ **cup orange juice**

   Pinch of ground cinnamon

1. In a blender, combine the peach and sugar. Add the ice cream, orange juice, and cinnamon. Blend until smooth.

Makes 2 servings

Per serving: 236 calories, 4 g protein, 54 g carbohydrates, 0 g fat, 5 mg cholesterol, 2 g dietary fiber, 81 mg sodium

3½ Carb Choices

Spiced Cider

[Photograph on page 116]

This versatile drink is comforting served hot on cold winter nights
and delightfully refreshing served cold on hot summer afternoons.
Try adding a little sparkling water when serving the drink cold.

1. In a medium saucepan, mix the cider or juice, allspice, cloves, and cinnamon. Bring to a boil over medium heat. Reduce the heat to low, cover, and simmer for 10 minutes. Strain out the spices or remove them with a spoon. Serve hot or cool to room temperature and then refrigerate.

Makes 4 servings

Per serving: 117 calories, 0 g protein, 29 g carbohydrates, 0 g fat, 0 mg cholesterol, 0 g dietary fiber, 7 mg sodium

1½ Carb Choices

1 **quart apple cider or apple juice**

10 **allspice berries**

10 **whole cloves**

2 **cinnamon sticks, broken into pieces**

QUICK
SWITCH • Replace the cider with cranberry-apple juice.

Chai Tea Smoothie

Chai is a very popular beverage that originated in India. It's made from a combination of milk, tea, and ground spices, including cinnamon, cardamom, ginger, nutmeg, and cloves. You can find the tea powder in specialty coffee and tea stores.

3 tablespoons spiced chai tea powder

¼ cup boiling water

⅔ cup crushed ice

½ cup cold fat-free milk or soy milk

1. Place the tea in a cup and pour the boiling water over top. Stir to dissolve.

2. In a blender, combine the dissolved tea, ice, and milk. Process until smooth.

Makes 1 serving

Per serving: 153 calories, 6 g protein, 28 g carbohydrates, 2 g fat, 2 mg cholesterol, 0 g dietary fiber, 153 mg sodium

1½ Carb Choices

PANTRY POPCORN

A nice drink and a bowl of popcorn. Now all you need is a good video or DVD. But don't spend good money for flavored popcorn that's loaded with salt and probably high in fat. Just toss plain popped corn with dried seasonings—such as Chinese five-spice powder or Cajun herb blend—and create your own fancy snack.

Start with 6 cups of plain popcorn that you've prepared in an air popper or microwave. Place the popcorn in a large bowl and lightly toss while misting the popcorn with cooking spray. Sprinkle with the selected seasoning and toss to mix. Coat 2 large foil-lined baking sheets with cooking spray, evenly spread the popcorn on them, and mist the top with more spray. Bake at 300°F for 3 to 5 minutes, or until the popcorn looks dry. Create your own flavor combinations or try these.

Harvest: ½ teaspoon **each** ground cinnamon and ground ginger plus ¼ cup **each** dried apples and raisins

Indian: ½ teaspoon **each** ground coriander, ground cumin, curry powder, dry mustard, and turmeric

Italian: ½ teaspoon **each** dried basil and dried oregano plus ¼ cup grated Parmesan cheese and ⅛ teaspoon red-pepper flakes

Jamaican: ½ teaspoon **each** ground allspice, ground cinnamon, jerk seasoning, and onion powder

Mediterranean: ½ teaspoon **each** grated lemon peel, dried marjoram, dried sage, and dried thyme

Mexican: ½ teaspoon **each** ground coriander and ground cumin plus ¼ teaspoon **each** cayenne and chili powder ∎

Café au Lait

[Photograph on page 274]

This beverage couldn't be simpler: Just mix equal amounts of hot coffee
and scalded milk. Here is my favorite version, which pairs fat-free evaporated milk
and vanilla decaf coffee. It's rich and satisfying for breakfast, coffee breaks,
and even dessert. For best results, start with strong coffee made by using
2 heaping tablespoons of ground coffee per cup of water.

1 can (12 ounces) fat-free
  evaporated milk

1½ cups hot strong vanilla
  decaffeinated coffee

  Ground cinnamon or nutmeg
  (optional)

1. Place the milk in a medium saucepan and warm over
   medium heat until very hot but not quite boiling. Stir
   in the coffee. Serve sprinkled with the cinnamon or
   nutmeg (if using).

Makes 3 servings

Per serving: 91 calories, 9 g protein, 13 g carbohydrates, 0 g fat,
4 mg cholesterol, 0 g dietary fiber, 134 mg sodium

½ **Carb Choice**

QUICK
SWITCH • Replace the vanilla coffee with hazelnut coffee.

South-of-the-Border Coffee

This spiced coffee is an ideal beverage with Southwestern dishes of all types. It can be made with regular or decaffeinated coffee and served hot or cold, giving it great versatility for any occasion. I usually double or triple the recipe so that I have leftovers to store in the refrigerator for iced Mexican coffee the next day.

1. In a large saucepan, combine the water, cinnamon, and cloves. Bring to a boil over high heat. Reduce the heat just enough to prevent the liquid from boiling over and simmer for 3 minutes. Add the brown sugar and stir until dissolved. Stir in the coffee grounds and bring back to a full boil. Immediately remove from the heat and allow to stand for 3 minutes.

2. To serve, pour the coffee through a very fine-mesh strainer to remove the spices and all of the coffee grounds.

1 **quart water**

1 **cinnamon stick**

4 **whole cloves**

2 **tablespoons packed brown sugar**

⅓ **cup coffee grounds**

Makes 4 servings

Per serving: 17 calories, 0 g protein, 4 g carbohydrates, 0 g fat, 0 mg cholesterol, 0 g dietary fiber, 2 mg sodium

0 Carb Choices

Pantry Menus with Panache

Cooking from the cupboard is tailor-made for informal meals that have to be on the table fast. But it's also a godsend when company arrives—whether you have advance notice or not. You can pair up scores of the recipes in this book to turn out memorable luncheons, dinner parties, and other festive fare. Here are some sample menus to get you started. They'll make entertaining easy on you and a treat for your guests.

Cocktail Party

Artichoke Dip (page 223)

Sweet Potato Dip
(page 222)

Crab Cakes; form into 16 tiny
patties (page 137)

Holiday Brunch

Honeyed Strawberry Flip
(page 293)

Make-Ahead Florida French Toast
(page 22)

Chicken Sausage
(page 173)

Fiesta Buffet

Gazpacho (page 36)

Taco Salad (page 79)

Chicken Enchilada Casserole
(page 169)

Fiesta Grapefruit (page 249)

South-of-the-Border Coffee
(page 301)

Ladies' Luncheon

Hearts of Palm and Mandarin
Orange Salad (page 64)

Lobster à la Newburg (page 150)

White rice

Refrigerator Peach Pie (page 278)

Latin Seafood Supper

Green Bean Caesar Salad
(page 72)

Garlic Croutons (page 85)

Tuna Veracruzana (page 135)

Brown rice

Cold Spiced Peach Soup
(page 37)

Asian Delight

Tropical Fruit Salad
(page 61)

Teriyaki Salmon and
Vegetables on Brown Rice
(page 142)

Frozen Peanut Butter Pie
(page 280)

Meatless and Marvelous

Mixed green salad

Sun-Dried Tomato Dressing
(page 84)

Fettuccine with Shiitake
Mushrooms (page 93)

Italian Cheesecake
(page 258)

Picnic Feast

Black Bean Salad (page 69)

**Tuna Tailgate Gumbo
(page 114)**

**Southern Bacon Cornbread
(page 32)**

**Crustless Shoofly Pie
(page 281)**

Country French Dinner

**Mixed green salad
with toasted almonds**

Dill Sauce (page 226)

**Chicken Stew Provençal
(page 155)**

Light Aïoli (page 82)

Low-fat vanilla ice cream

Chocolate Sauce (page 235)

Lacy Oatmeal Cookies (page 283)

Russian Surprise

**Jelled Borscht Salad
(page 66)**

**Beef Stroganoff
(page 182)**

Strawberries

Secret Sauce (page 232)

EMERGENCY SUBSTITUTIONS

My pantry-stocking suggestions in the first chapter of this book will go a long way in helping you fill your cupboard, fridge, and freezer with the ingredients you'll use most. But, no matter how hard you try to keep your pantry stocked for all contingencies, you'll run out of something. And as luck would have it, the chances are good it'll happen during a blizzard or on a holiday when all of the stores are closed! Here are replacements you can use in a pinch.

IF YOU DON'T HAVE THIS . . .	USE THIS . . .	ADJUSTMENTS NEEDED
Baking powder, 1 teaspoon	¼ teaspoon baking soda + ½ teaspoon cream of tartar	—
Bread crumbs, dry, 1 cup	¾ cup cracker crumbs OR 1 tablespoon quick-cooking oats	Adjust seasonings to compensate for salt (if any) in the crackers.
Buttermilk, 1 cup	1 cup plain yogurt	For baking, no change needed. In casseroles, you may want to use ¾ cup, because the yogurt is denser.
Chocolate, semisweet, 1 ounce (1 square)	½ ounce unsweetened chocolate + 1 tablespoon sugar OR 3 tablespoons cocoa powder + 1 tablespoon vegetable oil + 3–5 tablespoons sugar	—
Chocolate, unsweetened, 1 ounce (1 square)	3 tablespoons cocoa powder + 1 tablespoon vegetable oil	—
Cornstarch, 1 tablespoon	2 tablespoons all-purpose flour OR 2 teaspoons arrowroot OR 1⅓ tablespoons quick-cooking tapioca	The flour will cause a somewhat duller appearance, so it's best used for gravies, stews, or other mixed combos.
Egg white, 1	1 tablespoon powdered egg white + 2 tablespoons water	—
Egg, whole, 1	2 egg whites OR ¼ cup egg substitute OR 2½ tablespoons powdered whole egg + 2½ tablespoons water	—

(continued)

IF YOU DON'T HAVE THIS . . .	USE THIS . . .	ADJUSTMENTS NEEDED
Garlic, minced, 1 clove	½ teaspoon jarred minced garlic OR ⅛ teaspoon garlic powder	—
Herbs, fresh, chopped, 1 tablespoon	1 teaspoon dried OR ¼ teaspoon powdered or ground	Dried herbs are stronger, so add them earlier in the recipe.
Honey, 1 cup	1¼ cups sugar + ¼ cup liquid called for in recipe	—
Italian herb seasoning, 1 tablespoon	1½ teaspoons dried oregano + ¾ teaspoon dried basil + ¾ teaspoon dried thyme	—
Ketchup or chili sauce, ½ cup	⅓ cup tomato sauce + 2 tablespoons sugar + 1 tablespoon vinegar	—
Lemon juice, 1 tablespoon	1½ teaspoons white wine vinegar	This is not recommended for baked goods.
Lemon peel, grated, 1 teaspoon	½ teaspoon lemon extract	—
Lime peel, grated, 1 teaspoon	½ teaspoon grated lemon peel	—
Milk, fat-free, 1 cup	⅓ cup fat-free dry milk + ¾ cup water	—
Mustard, prepared, 1 teaspoon	1 teaspoon dry mustard + 1 teaspoon water	Powdered mustard is concentrated, so use it sparingly.
Olive oil	Equal amount of any vegetable oil	The consistency will be the same, but the flavor will change.
Rice wine (mirin), ½ cup	½ cup dry sherry	—
Roasted red peppers	Equal amount of pimientos	—
Sherry, 2 tablespoons	2 teaspoons sherry extract or vanilla extract	—
Sour cream, 1 cup	1 cup evaporated milk + 1 tablespoon lemon juice	To speed curdling, microwave on high power for 30 seconds.
Sugar, confectioners', 1 cup	⅞ cup granulated sugar ground in a blender or food processor with 1 tablespoon cornstarch	—
Sugar, granulated, 1 cup	1¾ cups confectioners' sugar OR 1 cup packed light brown sugar OR 1 cup superfine sugar	—
Sugar, light brown, packed, 1 cup	1 cup granulated sugar + 3 tablespoons molasses OR ½ cup dark brown sugar + ½ cup granulated sugar	—

IF YOU DON'T HAVE THIS . . .	USE THIS . . .	ADJUSTMENTS NEEDED
Tomatoes, fresh, chopped, 2 medium	1 cup drained chopped canned tomatoes	—
Tomato juice, 1 cup	½ cup tomato sauce + ½ cup water	Tomato sauce has more added salt, so adjust your seasonings accordingly.
Tomato sauce, 1 cup	⅜ cup tomato paste + ½ cup water OR 1 can (8 ounces) stewed tomatoes, blended in a blender	—
Vinegar, 1 teaspoon	2 teaspoons lemon juice	Adjust seasonings for changed flavor.
Yogurt, 1 cup	1 cup buttermilk OR 1 cup milk + 1 tablespoon lemon juice	—

HERB MATCHUPS

Rosemary goes on chicken, but what complements squash? You like dill on fish, but will it work with dips? There are dozens of common herbs and spices to choose from. The list below will help you make good flavor matches and decide what you'll want to keep on hand. (Be sure to store dried herbs and spices in a cool, dry place.)

HERB/SPICE	CHARACTERISTICS	COMMON USES
Allspice	Round berries with hints of cinnamon, cloves, and nutmeg	Caribbean soups, marinades, savory sauces, chutneys, curries, spice cakes, sweet breads, puddings, fruit desserts
Anise seeds	Tiny seeds with a licorice flavor	Seafood, chowders, sweet breads, cakes, cookies
Basil	Sharp, refreshing green leaf with hints of mint, anise, and pepper	Pesto, red sauces, tomato salads, green salads, Italian soups, vinaigrettes, pasta dishes
Bay leaf	Pale green leaf with a subtle woodsy flavor, and brittle texture	Bouquet garni, poaching liquids, soup, stews, marinades; always remove the bay leaf before serving
Caraway seeds	Small seeds with a licorice scent	Rye bread and biscuits, roasted poultry, Eastern European dishes, root vegetables, cabbage dishes, coleslaw
Cardamom seeds	Hints of citrus and ginger	Curry dishes, rice puddings, pickles, chutneys, Scandinavian desserts
Celery seeds	Subtle celery flavor	Coleslaw, salad dressings, pickles, poultry stuffings, potato salad
Chervil	Delicate green leaf with hints of parsley, anise, and celery; looks like very fine Italian parsley leaves	Sauces for chicken and fish, egg dishes, salads; used in fines herbes
Chives	Tender green shoots with faint onion and scallion flavor	Creamy soups, chowders, dips, egg dishes, vinaigrettes, salads; used in fines herbes

(continued)

HERB/SPICE	CHARACTERISTICS	COMMON USES
Cilantro	Pungent flavor; appearance is similar to Italian parsley	Asian, Mexican, and Indian dishes; salsa, rice, beans, curries, peanut sauces, chicken, fish
Cinnamon	Sweet and fragrant	Poultry rub, pilafs, curries, cakes, muffins, rice puddings, pumpkin soups and pies, mulled drinks
Cloves	Intense, burnt-orange scent and fragrant, pungent flavor	Indian curries and chutneys, rice dishes, sweet breads, muffins, spice cakes, mulled drinks
Coriander seeds	Lemony, musky flavor	Prevalent in Thai and Indian curries, Middle Eastern legume dishes, Mexican dishes, black bean soup, Asian peanut sauces, pickles
Cumin seeds	Earthy, rustic flavor	Salsa, Indian curries, Mexican rice and grain dishes, black bean soup, hummus, Tex-Mex chili, chicken, fish, guacamole, chutney
Dill	Refined feathery green strands with distinctive lemony caraway flavor	Vichyssoise, sauces for fish and chicken, seafood chowders, cucumber salads, chilled bisques, yogurt dips
Dill seeds	Similar to caraway seeds but milder	Gravlax, potato salads, mashed root vegetables, pickles
Fennel seeds	Slightly sweet with a licorice-anise taste	Breads, Mediterranean fish stews, borscht, cabbage dishes
Garlic	Pungent, strongly scented member of the onion family	Virtually all savory dishes, including soups, salads, pesto, garlic bread, stir-fries; roasting makes garlic's flavor milder
Ginger	Slightly sweet, pungent flavor with spicy aroma	Chinese dishes, curries, carrot and sweet potato dishes, chicken, fish, meats, gingerbread, cakes, pumpkin pie, fruit salads; fresh, ground, and candied forms are not interchangeable
Horseradish	Very hot and pungent	Sauces for roast beef, chicken, fish, eggs; salad dressings, cocktail sauce, sandwiches, borscht; available as a whole root or grated
Lemon grass	Sturdy, pale green-to-white tightly furled stalk with mild lemony flavor	Stir-fries, Asian soups, peanut sauces, soy-based sauces and marinades, chicken, fish; sold primarily in Asian markets; available fresh and dried
Mace	Very similar to nutmeg but more pungent and intense	Sauces for vegetables, puddings, cakes, muffins, sweet breads, fruity desserts; mace is the outer covering of the nutmeg seed

HERB/SPICE	CHARACTERISTICS	COMMON USES
Marjoram	Small green petals with oregano-like resinous flavor	Tomato sauce, fish, red meat, poultry, grains, marinades, sauces for pasta, soups, dressings, dips
Mint	Forest-green to dark green leaves with refreshing, palate-cleansing taste and clean nuance	Fruity salads, condiments for lamb and game, tabbouleh, yogurt sauces, desserts, jelly, teas
Mustard seeds	Powerfully pungent	Forms the basis of many condiments, such as pickles and chutney
Nutmeg	Sweet, fragrant flavor with hints of allspice, cinnamon, and mace	Cakes, sweet breads, rice dishes, broccoli, poultry marinades
Oregano	Dark green petals have resinous pine-needle flavor	Italian and Mexican soups, chili, pasta sauces, Greek salad dressing, marinades; prevalent in Italian, Mexican, and Greek cooking
Paprika	A dark red powder made from dried peppers; varies from mildly sweet to hot	Spanish and Hungarian stews, chowders, chicken, broiled fish, roasted or mashed potatoes, Tex-Mex chili
Parsley	Italian flat-leaf parsley has a slightly stronger flavor than curly parsley	Soups, dressings, sauces, dips, marinades, meats, fish, vegetables, chicken, potatoes, grains, pasta
Peppercorns	Black, grayish-white, or green berries with a spicy floral taste	Soups, stews, salads, meat, poultry, fish, vegetables, dressings, egg dishes
Poppy seeds	Tiny blue-gray seeds with a slightly sweet, nutlike flavor	Noodle dishes, salad dressings, coleslaw, breads, rolls, cakes, quick breads, pastries
Rosemary	Narrow needlelike leaves with a fragrant evergreen scent	Lamb, pork, poultry, potato chowders, roasted root vegetables, grilling marinades, focaccia
Saffron	Mild aromatic scent with rich yellow-orange hue	Spanish paella, curries, sweet breads, Spanish and Middle Eastern rice and grain dishes, Milanese risotto
Sage	Pale green to silvery leaves with earthy, musky flavor	Poultry stuffing, stewed white beans, pasta sauce, Italian soups
Savory	Summer savory is mild and grassy; winter savory is spicier	Legume dishes (especially lima beans and lentils), poultry, vegetable entrées
Sesame seeds	Mild, sweet, nutty flavor	Breads, Middle Eastern spreads like hummus, casseroles, salads, cakes; toasting the seeds releases their rich nutlike flavor
Star anise	Star-shaped brown pod containing eight shiny seeds; similar in flavor to anise seeds but more bitter	Chinese dishes, teas, baked goods; an ingredient in Chinese five-spice powder

(continued)

HERB/SPICE	CHARACTERISTICS	COMMON USES
Szechuan pepper	Similar in size to black peppercorns with a mildly hot, pungent flavor	Chinese dishes
Tarragon	Long feathery green leaves with a subtle anise flavor	Sautéed chicken, pasta salad, potato salad, seafood entrées, egg dishes, mustard sauces, vinaigrettes; used in herbes de Provence and fines herbes
Thyme	Tiny greenish-gray petals with a pungent earthy flavor and strong scent	Potato and fish chowders, squash bisque, vinaigrettes, marinades, roasted vegetables, poultry, wild rice; appears in bouquet garni
Turmeric	Mildly pungent flavor with yellowish-orange hue; often substituted for the more expensive saffron for its color	Gives mustard pastes, curries, and rice dishes a brilliant yellow glow
Vanilla	Sweet, mellow, aromatic flavor	Baked goods and other desserts

INDEX

Note: Underscored page references indicate boxed text. **Boldfaced** page references indicate photographs.

Conversion Chart

These equivalents have been slightly rounded to make measuring easier.

Volume Measurements

U.S.	Imperial	Metric
¼ tsp	–	1 ml
½ tsp	–	2 ml
1 tsp	–	5 ml
1 Tbsp	–	15 ml
2 Tbsp (1 oz)	1 fl oz	30 ml
¼ cup (2 oz)	2 fl oz	60 ml
⅓ cup (3 oz)	3 fl oz	80 ml
½ cup (4 oz)	4 fl oz	120 ml
⅔ cup (5 oz)	5 fl oz	160 ml
¾ cup (6 oz)	6 fl oz	180 ml
1 cup (8 oz)	8 fl oz	240 ml

Weight Measurements

U.S.	Metric
1 oz	30 g
2 oz	60 g
4 oz (¼ lb)	115 g
5 oz (⅓ lb)	145 g
6 oz	170 g
7 oz	200 g
8 oz (½ lb)	230 g
10 oz	285 g
12 oz (¾ lb)	340 g
14 oz	400 g
16 oz (1 lb)	455 g
2.2 lb	1 kg

Length Measurements

U.S.	Metric
¼"	0.6 cm
½"	1.25 cm
1"	2.5 cm
2"	5 cm
4"	11 cm
6"	15 cm
8"	20 cm
10"	25 cm
12" (1')	30 cm

Pan Sizes

U.S.	Metric
8" cake pan	20 × 4 cm sandwich or cake tin
9" cake pan	23 × 3.5 cm sandwich or cake tin
11" × 7" baking pan	28 × 18 cm baking tin
13" × 9" baking pan	32.5 × 23 cm baking tin
15" × 10" baking pan	38 × 25.5 cm baking tin (Swiss roll tin)
1½ qt baking dish	1.5 liter baking dish
2 qt baking dish	2 liter baking dish
2 qt rectangular baking dish	30 × 19 cm baking dish
9" pie plate	22 × 4 or 23 × 4 cm pie plate
7" or 8" springform pan	18 or 20 cm springform or loose-bottom cake tin
9" × 5" loaf pan	23 × 13 cm or 2 lb narrow loaf tin or pâté tin

Temperatures

Fahrenheit	Centigrade	Gas
140°	60°	–
160°	70°	–
180°	80°	–
225°	105°	¼
250°	120°	½
275°	135°	1
300°	150°	2
325°	160°	3
350°	180°	4
375°	190°	5
400°	200°	6
425°	220°	7
450°	230°	8
475°	245°	9
500°	260°	–